ANCESTORS

ANCESTORS

WHO WE ARE AND WHERE WE COME FROM

David Hertzel

ROWMAN & LITTLEFIELD
Lanham • Boulder • New York • London

Published by Rowman & Littlefield
An imprint of The Rowman & Littlefield Publishing Group, Inc.
4501 Forbes Boulevard, Suite 200, Lanham, Maryland 20706
www.rowman.com

6 Tinworth Street, London SE11 5AL, United Kingdom

British Library Cataloguing in Publication Information Available

Library of Congress Cataloging-in-Publication Data Available

ISBN 978-1-5381-0436-1 (cloth : alk. paper)
ISBN 978-1-5381-0437-8 (electronic)
ISBN 978-1-5381-6011-4 (pbk. : alk.paper)

∞™ The paper used in this publication meets the minimum requirements of American National Standard for Information Sciences—Permanence of Paper for Printed Library Materials, ANSI/NISO Z39.48-1992.

CONTENTS

ACKNOWLEDGMENTS

I would like to thank first and foremost the thirty-four interviewees who made this project possible, as well as their assistants and contacts. Special thanks to Seonghwan Jack Park, Dr. David Friedman, Mr. Charles Sleeper, Jr., and Esther Oh for their help with translations, interpretations, and follow up edits and explanations. Thanks also to Southwestern Oklahoma State University, for supporting my travel and other activities. I am grateful for advice and reviews from colleagues and friends Phil Holley, John Hayden, Sunu Kodumthara, Howard Kurtz, Jieun Chang, Mark MacDonald, and Laurie Hertzel. Thanks also to transcribers Alicia Chapa and Elizabeth Hertzel. Cynthia Jennings read and offered valuable comments and support. Jakob, Mary, and Elizabeth contributed in many ways patiently, thoughtfully, kindly. The editors at Rowman & Littlefield, Susan McEachern, Rebeccah Shumaker, and Leanne Silverman, gave a rough project definition, clarity, and the presentation these wonderful interviewees deserve.

1

ANCESTORS: WHO WE ARE AND WHERE WE COME FROM

Ancestors are an integral part of our existence. People worldwide and throughout history have incorporated ancestors into their experiences sacred and secular and include ancestors in all types of rituals and practices involving birth, death, and most celebrations in between. People organize kinship groups, aristocracies, and tribes around ancestral identities, and use ancestry to write laws and establish customs that deal with marriage, family names, guardianship, and inheritance. Honoring ancestors in various forms has been a human practice for millennia, and anthropologists describe ancestral remembrances as some of our species' earliest and most widespread forms of religion and ritual.

Scholars in diverse disciplines adopt the terms of ancestry as important to their research and analysis. Medical professionals consider ancestral information significant to the diagnosis of certain patients as well as to the study of disease in general. In the social sciences and humanities, ancestry commonly serves as a determinant of personal, ethnic, and national identities. In psychiatry, information about one's ancestry is useful to an analysis of a patient's mental and physical health, and many psychiatrists consider one's relationship to ancestors critical to understanding the mental and emotional disposition of patients. Ancestors and constructions of ancestry provide material for ideas and practices as diverse and profound as Jungian archetypes, Mormon religious practices, Chinese and Confucian prayers, social organizations such as Hindu caste systems, Shinto, Native American, and various religious traditions occurring across Africa. Christians begin the story of Jesus's worldly life with an account of his lineage and, like religious people from all continents and faiths, instruct followers to respect their ancestors.

Interest in ancestry has not diminished in our modern scientific age and has an established place in popular culture. There are several successful television series on ancestry, and companies that research genealogies or provide personal information on ancestry have enjoyed growing interest and success in the Internet years.

Grand constructions, traditions, and practices of ancestry are ubiquitous in public forums of all kinds. At the same time, the significance of ancestry remains very personal. Even with all its larger philosophical, medical, and psychological implications, one fascinating aspect of ancestry is how passionately many people hold to their own ancestors and identify intimately—even jealously—with their own ancestries.

When ancestors were among the living, they were like the rest of us, members of families and tribes, with ordinary personalities and abilities. But from the perspectives of those who survive them, once relatives pass into death, they acquire special significance. Through living, ancestors perpetuate life, communities, and culture, for better or for worse. Through dying, ancestors move into other worlds, becoming for their descendants links to greater universes, in both material and spiritual senses. On the one hand, ancestors link the material present to the material past, including language, culture, and earthly identities. On the other hand, ancestors represent to their descendants promises of mystical things to come and connect the living to the world of the dead.

Thirty-one interviews with thirty-four elders, practitioners, participants, and scholars of ancestral activities represent the primary sources of this book. The interviews share perspectives and beliefs that can be summarized into five general themes. Although not every interviewee would agree with all five, all would endorse some, and the themes reflect the most widely shared ideas on ancestry.

1. *People intuitively sanctify their ancestors.* All interviewees, whether religious or not religious, sanctify their ancestors through rituals, remembrances, prayers, or other traditions.
2. *People make ancestors in much the same way that people make family.* While all interviewees describe their genetic predecessors such as mother, grandmother, great-grandmother, and so on, as ancestors they also describe more fluid and flexible definitions of ancestry—sometimes in unusual, even surprising, ways.
3. *All people are both ancestors and descendants.* This widespread belief arises from the unanimous belief of interviewees that a person need not have children in order to be named an ancestor.

4. *Ancestral practices—including rituals, stories, and other remembrances—create a living narrative.*

5. *The experiences of suffering and love are shared across generations, transcending death.* This is already obvious in one direction: people continue to love and care for their ancestors, even after ancestors have passed on. But the reverse also emerges as a core idea in many interviewees' views on life, death, and family: the dead also continue to care for and love the living.

These primary conclusions emerge from the personal testimonies of elders and people of prominence from a diversity of cultural and intellectual communities.

There are many important and enduring ancestral practices from around the world that are not addressed in this book. But even in their limited scope, perhaps the interviews and analysis presented here will contribute to larger efforts to consider seriously the meaning of ancestry and of personal and public ancestral ideas, particularly in the modern age. At the same time, these fascinating accounts of belief and experience offer compelling insights into the significance of ancestry.

A NOTE ABOUT THE INTERVIEWS

Interviewees were selected by recommendation from third parties, usually members of a community or organization to which the interviewee also belonged. Most interviewees are elders, or people of prominence within a particular social or intellectual community. Interviewees are accomplished in an area related to ancestry and include genealogists, geneticists, tribal chiefs and elders, researchers, family elders, and experienced practitioners or supervisors of particular ancestral rituals. Elders have done and seen more than have those "less elder," and conversations with elders can be especially reflective. Elders have much to teach about the human condition, in all its variables. When people are younger, their outlooks tend to be less nuanced, less confident, and sometimes more doctrinaire than those of their elders. As interviewee Darold Treffert said, "I scoffed at [certain ideas] when I was in training and said, 'Oh that's just soft science.' But now, I'm open to those possibilities."

Interviewees were selected from a variety of cultural backgrounds, for the purposes of contrast, comparison, and interest. But these individuals are not spokespeople and were not asked to "represent" particular belief systems, doctrines, or people; instead they were asked to describe their own, personal experiences and beliefs involving ancestors. Interviews were freely flowing, with the interviewer following interviewees down whatever strange and wonderful paths their narratives led.

One goal of interviews was to establish how each interviewee used the word *ancestor* and exactly who an interviewee included in or excluded from his or her "ancestry." Interviews opened with the question, "Who are your ancestors?" The conversations that followed were dynamic and flexible, and, given opportunity to more richly develop their answers, interviewees typically broadened their definitions of "ancestors" over the course of conversations. Initially, most participants described their ancestries as including specific, limited groups and individuals, such as those in the descendant's direct genealogical line. But upon further discussion, it became clear that such narrow scopes were not sufficient to encompass the broad, sometimes expansive groups most interviewees ultimately think of as their ancestors.

After establishing each interviewee's personal definition and parameters of "ancestors" and "ancestry," the interviewer asked, "What is your relationship to your ancestors?" This second key question and the conversations it generated delivered the most remarkable responses, including descriptions of interviewees' ongoing relationships to ancestors, the formation of ancestral narratives, myth-making, and stories of personal experiences, both during ancestors' lives and after their deaths. The interviews describe therefore, a broad spectrum of transgenerational experiences and relationships between ancestors and descendants and between the living and the dead.

Interviews were open to the principle that the ideas defining ancestry are generated in part by subjective experience, including what William James might have called "the mystical experience" that lies at the origins of much religious belief. Narratives of subjective experience and belief are the principal paths along which this book builds arguments on the idea and meaning of ancestry. The subject of the external "social constructions" of ethnic, national, and kinship identities appears in the interviews but takes a back seat to personal experiences and interpretations in explaining the nature and meaning of ancestry and ancestral belief.

INTERVIEW WITH DR. HENRIETTA MANN

"People Hearted Alike"

DH: Can you tell me who are your ancestors?

HM: How far back? I can go back. I know my ancestry up to a certain point because I'm Cheyenne. My ancestors are going to be Cheyenne Indian.

Henrietta Mann Explains *Cheyenne Indian*

I am a direct descendant of a survivor *Homa'oestaa'e*, called White Buffalo Woman. She is my great-grandmother, the grandmother of my father *Mo'ehno'hamemeo'o* Horse Road, the mother of his father *Vovo'hase'hame'e*, Spotted Horse. I am one of the "Hearted-Alike People," who are known most commonly as Cheyenne. Based upon geography, I am a member of the southern group, known as the *Heevahetane'eo'o*, the Hair Rope People.

HM: I know my father and my mother. I know my father's father and I knew my grandfather. I knew both grandfathers, my mother's grandfather, and my father's. I knew my mother's father and my father's father. But I never knew my grandmothers, they were both gone. . . . I know my great-grandmother, who's that woman holding the cradleboard, I mean in that cradleboard! Her name is White Buffalo Woman. [She points to a framed photograph in her office.]

Henrietta Mann Explains *Cradleboard*

A cradleboard is a traditional kind of Native American baby carrier. The baby is swaddled and strapped to a specially designed flat board, usually made of a wood plank. The cradleboard can then be carried in the mother's arms, worn on her back like a backpack for travel, or propped up on the ground like a baby chair. The swaddling wrap provides the same warmth and safety as in the mother's womb. The child when carried or propped in the board has the ability to view the earth and sky offering comfort.

Dr. Henrietta Mann.
Courtesy of Phil Shockey.

DH: So you knew this woman? You met this woman, but you didn't meet your grandmothers.

HM: But I would know my great-grandmother.

DH: And would you consider people . . . you've mentioned people in your direct line . . .

HM: Two grandfathers I knew, of course my parents, and then two grandfathers. Never the grandmothers. But a great-grandmother.

DH: Funny how it skipped like that.

HM: Mmhmm [agreeing]. But she has had more impact upon my sense of ancestry and where I believe I belong than anybody else that I know.

DH: Your great-grandmother.

Henrietta Mann Explains *Sand Creek*

In 1864 [Colorado Territorial Governor John] Evans issued two proclamations. The first in June 1864 was to the "friendly Indians of the plains" in which they were promised sanctuary at specified forts where they also would be given food. The Arapaho and Cheyenne were to report at Fort Lyon. He followed this with a second proclamation in August 1864 in which he authorized the territorial citizens to "kill and destroy . . . hostile Indians."

Initially, some women thought the sound was an approaching herd of buffalo. However, it was Colonel Chivington, the "fighting parson," who had "damned" any man or men in sympathy with Indians. He rode at the front of his army of seven hundred men, including the 3rd Colorado Volunteer Cavalry Regiment, who were being referred to as the "bloodless third." Chivington brought with him four mountain howitzers—short cannons. Except for a few women, everyone else was still peacefully sleeping.

As the firing commenced, Black Kettle called his people to him as he stood holding a tall lodge pole from which fluttered a United States flag and a small white flag of peace. He was confident the soldiers would not fire upon *their* flag or they would cease-fire. When the shooting did not stop, those huddled around him fled, and he was the last to leave his position.

The mind-numbing slaughter and savage mutilation of the dead and dying that day is difficult and horrible to describe. This testimony is but an example of the bloodthirstiness that occurred that bitterly cold November day.

HM: Mmhmm [Yes]. . . . And I knew her only as a child.

DH: And what did she convey to you?

HM: A lot of it, I'm sure, had to just be through contact. I was born in 1934 and I was, as she told my father on her deathbed, the child that she waited for. She wanted to see his child and that child was me. So, I don't know what it is that I can tell you explicitly in the four years that we had together and what she taught me but what she taught me is . . . is . . . what she prayed for me, I'm sure, and what my life was going to be like. When she was on her deathbed she told my father, "You know I have seen harsh times, I have seen good times." This, from a woman who was at the massacre at Sand Creek.

This, from a woman that was at the Battle of the Washita.

She was never jaded by life. She said, "But I lived long enough to see my grandchild," and that grandchild was me. "I've seen hard and good times in my life, but the only thing that is really hard is death, because memories linger on." But what she told me is . . . what she instilled in me what, I'm sure directly by talking to me, but what must've been her prayers, her thoughts for me, her teachings that she passed on to her son and her grandson, because I can remember my grandfather saying, "This is what my mother used to tell me about our values system, about who we are."

Henrietta Mann Explains *Battle of the Washita*
(also known as the *Massacre of Washita*)

Black Kettle and five other chiefs signed the Fort Wise Treaty of 1861, relinquishing the bulk of Fort Laramie treaty lands for a small reservation in southeastern Colorado.

Little Raven and two others signed for the Arapahos. The treaty caused much dissension within the tribe, with the Dog Soldiers and Northern Cheyenne exceptionally dissatisfied. They consequently joined the Sioux in raids along the Platte River.

The new citizens of the territory wished to see Indian title to Colorado extinguished, and anti-Indian sentiment was rampant. The stage was set for the Massacre at Sand Creek, which was a precursor to the Washita Massacre. They are two halves of separate tragic events in history that must be viewed together inasmuch as they affect the same people.

A member of Black Kettle's band, White Buffalo Woman, was but a child of eleven years on that fateful morning of November 29, 1864. Black Kettle and his people had reported to Fort Lyon as "friendly," in response to Governor Evans's proclamation, whereupon they were ordered by the military to camp along Sand Creek. They were sleeping when Colonel John Milton Chivington, a Methodist minister and commanding officer of the District of Colorado, led his seven hundred troops in a surprise attack upon their camps at dawn on November 29, 1864.

DH: Are there more direct ways that she continues to instruct you or to teach you or to convey these ideas to you, rather than through memories?

HM: My father would say, "My grandmother told me this, these are my grandmother's words," and when he went on he said, "I don't have anything to leave you except my words," and that's what my dad told me when he passed away. "I have nothing to leave you," is what his mother told him so those words have been handed down through the generations and I believe that that is how she continues to instruct me this day in terms of what it is to have a view of the world as a Cheyenne woman. Influence, like my ancestry, that's who I am.

DH: And, so, are you thinking of your ancestry as a community of people? Or as individual people with names, or . . . both?

HM: A community. I just, I'm going to have to define *community* in a very different way than you've . . . than we might think of community. . . . It is really a larger, a very large, tribal context because the community of people that instruct me are just not Southern Cheyenne, as we're called here in Oklahoma. I lived for [many] years in the north and I have relatives up there too. And so they are my—they are my community by virtue of being, how do I put this . . . one of the Ceremonial Women of the tribe, a Prayer Woman, I have a whole other community, a spiritual community so to speak. . . . The values are

---

Henrietta Mann Explains *Prayer Woman*

I hope to live as long as White Buffalo Woman, our family matriarch from the buffalo days, who walked this earth for some eighty-five years. She was a brave-hearted woman who survived the 1864 Sand Creek Massacre in Colorado Territory and the 1868 Massacre of the Washita, here in Indian Territory. She has played a critical role in giving me an identity and defining who I am. As she prepared to leave, she told the grandson she had reared that her prayers had been answered in living long enough to see his first child. Then she sang her death song: "I have seen good and harsh times, but the only thing that is hard is death because memories linger on." That grandson was my father, and I was that first child. My father often reminded me that I was the answer to his grandmother's prayers, and to remember that. Being a "living prayer," so to speak, carries certain obligations and responsibilities. It essentially mandated a *life of service*. Even before I entered school at the age of five, I decided that I was going to become a teacher and teach Indian children.

---

the same for the community at large as they are for me individually in terms of my family and what has been passed down to me through time.

DH: When you define that word *community*, are you extending it outside of the physically living? Are you extending it to include the past and future?

HM: Yes.

DH: Would you say that you've helped write what this community is? Helped build this narrative of people that are your ancestors?

HM: In what we're doing here even through the tribal college and through the courses we teach and specifically what I do, like for example this afternoon we're talking about our languages which have come down orally . . . how we save it or how we preserve it and pass it on to the future. Because language is our way of expressing our culture and our teachings and our ways of life. And so it is critical that we keep these languages, the way we express our relationship to the world and everything . . . how I define myself as a person? I would say *Natsista*, meaning "I am a Cheyenne," but we never call ourselves . . . *Natsista*. [We would just say] "I'm a Cheyenne," *Tsitsistas*, [which means] "I am one of the people hearted alike." We have the same kind of heart, we have the same vision, we have the same view of the world.

DH: Would you include as ancestors people who might not think of themselves as Cheyenne, a third cousin who entered into the community from someplace else or somebody who genealogically wasn't related to that community?

HM: Because we adopt, we make relatives.

DH: And are those people part of your ancestry?

8

HM: [Pause] I'm trying to think. . . . I'm trying to think whether or not my great-grandmother . . . I'm sure that they must have made relatives with some of the Lakota people. I'm trying to think if my grandfather had forged a relationship with anybody that would have welcomed them into the community that was not Cheyenne. He was a member of the Peyote church and it's quite likely that there was someone from another tribe that followed the Peyote way. My father . . . yes, yes. My mother, yes.

Henrietta Mann Explains *Peyote Church*

Peyote church, also called the Native American Church (NAC), is a Native American religion characterized by the use of peyote.

DH: So genealogy isn't the defining feature?

HM: No, because it's more pronounced. Just one generation older than me, my parents, my mother has a daughter. Several daughters. They're not related by blood but still her daughters and I call them "sister." There's one that lives here. My father too has non-Indians who call him "Dad."

DH: You mentioned earlier a spiritual relationship . . . are the ancestors who aren't here anymore, are they still alive in the sense that they have souls or they have spirits that are alive? Do you have a relationship with those people in that sense?

HM: [Pause] How do I say something without sounding crazy?

DH: I think maybe the question is badly worded.

HM: Let me put it this way: I have been around this one man who's no longer here but I was at a conference and I was speaking and I went to set down and he was so excited—Jan was his name, I can't remember his last name. And Jan says, "Oh Henrietta I've got to talk to you, I've got to talk to you." "Okay. You were up there," he said, "and you had two grandmothers standing to the side of you," and he said, "I saw the . . ."—this is curious—"I saw you but they were there with you." But I thought, two grandmothers, who would they be? Were these the grandmothers I never knew? Or are these the great-grandmothers—

DH: —who you did know.

HM: Yeah, better, than—my mother's grandmother too was at Sand Creek who too was at the Washita I never knew. Her name was Vister, V-I-S-T-E-R. So I think that there are . . . I don't necessarily pray to them but I acknowledge them in all that I do, that I acknowledge the fact that the past talks to me. The culture, the way of seeing, a way of being.

DH: But not just metaphorically or symbolically.

HM: Yes. . . . That there's a continuing influence of people from where you came, on a daily basis. You have the same thoughts, or people say that you might . . . but you're thinking of it also as something extra-physical. That they're there, that if I need help there's someone there that helps me. Just like keeping my father in my journeys for the first time last week and my father has been dead and gone since 1990. He's been gone for a long time. And I had this dream, and I was going to be giving a speech at this very important venue in my dream. And he was there and even in my dream, in my dreams I dream of someone I know that they're dead in my dream. But with my dad, I didn't and he was just sitting there. And I looked at him and I smiled and it was a matter of how I get to the podium. And I was being rushed away, and I had this one speech and all of a sudden I realized my speech was gone. I had left it on the little railing and I went to get it and there were three men. Three men! And one of them had his hand on my speech, and so I went back and I said, "Oh," I said, "thank you! Here, I'll take my speech." And I got there and he just ground it and took it and wadded it up. He said, "It's all still there," and I [thought] "you just, in my mind, contaminated it! I'm not going to take it." Even though they weren't, you know, hazardous materials kind of thing. So I turned around and I said, "I can give a speech without my notes. I'm going to have to." And I looked at my father again and he was still sitting there just waiting for me to do . . . so I wound around up and down stairs even though I couldn't walk stairs and I told Gail, "You ought to find me a way to get to the podium so I don't do these stairs." It was like a castle, she took me up stairs. . . . And in my dream, and we ended back up where my father was. From then, I had a ramp-like thing to the podium. Then I ended up looking out to the audience and the room was just packed, and I was introduced and I thought, "I've got to get up there. I don't have a speech." I was just horrified. And I thought, "I can speak, but what's my topic? What did they ask me to speak about?" And I was trying to say, what, what was my title and the whole time my father was sitting there, just patiently waiting for me to speak, very confident. And so I think in that dream, I learned that my dad is around to help me. That he's there, and that he still communicates with me. I had not known, not been as conscious of it.

DH: And he's teaching you things?

HM: Yeah. He's still teaching me the ways. My grandmother used to tell me this, my dad said his mom said this.

DH: Do you think that you needed to have known that person in life in order for that person to do that? Or could there be ancestors from more generations back who do something . . . maybe it's more subtle or you don't recognize them.

HM: Because we . . . in terms of ancestors physically, I can only go back to my great-grandmother. I do know that her father's name was Eagleman and that's as far as I go. Five generations, I guess.

DH: Would you only include people in your understanding of ancestry?

HM: No, it includes that kinship to everything in this world. Those are our teachings.

DH: Can you explain . . . what is your relationship to that large body of ancestry?

HM: [Laughing] Okay, talking about kinship. If you stop and look at the four basic elements of which all life is made. Water, earth, air, fire, it's everything. Different, I mean compositionally different . . . making us related to the plants. . . . And without them, where would we get our oxygen? The *tree people*! So there is that aspect of mutuality and reciprocity. But that makes us related; I guess they're made of the same things that you and I are made of. We're [Mann and Hertzel] even related. You would be a part of my ancestry. . . . Whenever you stop and look at the fact that everything is made up of those four basic elements, that takes everything in universally, I mean everything out there down to even the smallest of ants, kinfolk.

DH: Is there something religious in your understanding of ancestors and ancestry?

HM: I would say spiritually.

DH: Spiritual. Yes. Is there a god in there? I mean, is God recognized in your relationship with your father and with your grandmother and with the people who are with you on the stage?

HM: But we have this view of, in our language, *Ma'heo'o*, the Great One, the Creator who made this world and placed us in it. There was a great deal of influence in this particular creation story from the Catholics of the Northern Cheyenne reservation, but in this world the difference being that the humans resemble the spirit being. *Ma'heo'o* made everything else and finally, almost like an afterthought, made human beings. And made them—and I hate to use the biblical term *in his image*—but made us physically like him-her, androgynous!

DH: Is a spiritual relationship culturally [influenced]?

HM: She raised more questions than she answers. [Laughing]

DH: What about bad ancestors? People who behaved poorly, people who contributed—

HM: You're still related but you don't behave like them. You take lessons from them and say, "Oh, that's how not to be."

DH: So are ancestors models for behavior? Are they models for social behavior?

HM: You can see me shaking my head yes. I'm shaking my head yes. [Laughing]

DH: Do you see specific lessons you can name?

HM: Yeah. That men are protectors and the providers and they really are to respect women. Ceremonially, women have very high places in our ceremonies. Our Sundance, you can't have a Sundance without a woman. And so there is much more of an egalitarian view of the roles of men and women and as people.

Henrietta Mann Explains *Sundance*

The Sundance is a deep traditional spiritual ceremony representing life and rebirth. The ceremony is also a New Year's ceremony celebrated in the summer. During the three days of Sundance, dancers relinquish food and drink until the ceremony is over. A cottonwood tree, chosen for its extraordinarily sacred ability to represent the Great Spirit, stands in the center of the Sundance circle and lodge. The woman *Sundancer* has a deep spiritual role in which she prays to the Sun for the Tribe and individual people. The three days are spent in dance, prayer, and meditation. Due to the deep spiritual commitment of dancers, some aspects of the Sundance are not open to the general public.

DH: And are these eternal in the sense that these are abiding rules or lessons for all people of all times?

HM: Yes, yes.

DH: The way you think of your father in your dream and the grandmothers Jan saw with you and the others, who you might not be able to identify but might be there also, do you feel the same is happening in the direction of the future? So your descendants would have the same relationship with you that you have with the people who came before you?

HM: Yes, I would hope so.

DH: You wouldn't be one of the bad ones, right?

HM: I try not to be, but I probably do, I probably would. Don't be like her, she talks too much, she laughs too loudly!

DH: Aren't talking and laughing good things though? [Laughing] Your descendants would know that.

Would a person who has no genealogical descendants also have those same opportunities? Those same relationships with descendants? In other words, you include cousins and uncles and so on. . . .

HM: I don't have cousins; they are all my brothers and sisters.

DH: Okay.

HM: What did you get out of it Dr. Hertzel? It was a lot of shaking heads yes, no. You really had to pull that out of me. It's just there, it is a way of being, it's a way of thinking, and I never think about it. It just is.

DH: So many people take ancestors so much for granted. But if you ask, it's very important to people. Ancestry, ancestors, both.

HM: When I begin a speech, I don't begin until I acknowledge them and the fact that they gave me life, they gave me identity. They have also given me my purpose in life.

DH: How is that?

HM: Who I am is one of the hearted-alike people, but the purpose is to maintain our ways, to care for others, to teach, to teach our younger people.

DH: Is grandfather specifically sacred? Symbolically sacred?

HM: It's specific in the way that my father expected me to be that way, my grandfather, my grandfather's mother who taught him, who taught my grandson. My father was raised by his grandmother.

DH: You make selections about that too don't you? Make selections about which person you want to learn from, which actions you want to model?

HM: Well, we have what you call freedom of choice. And there is good here. And every-thing about us is Cheyenne; supposedly it's up to the good in everything. Even in worst situations, find the good there, because we also believe that we are here one time. But I don't have a second chance to come back and correct anything that I may not have done right. Neither do they, but it's still a choice that we make individually. But I think that the Cheyenne way is strong enough that you emphasize the good, you look to the good, you look at the good usefulness that sustained us over time. You live that way. You look at our ceremonies that continue to help us maintain our identity and responsibility to earth. It's our way of giving back to the earth to renew her.

DH: It's a complex relationship you are describing and it raises some big questions, but everybody seems to be interested in it. Can you say why people are so interested in their own ancestors?

HM: Because they provide the blueprint for how we are to live today. . . . I'm choosing to think that they were very courageous. That they were very brave to have walked through the trauma they did and the conflict and still come out at the other end and be hopeful about life. I don't know that I have that courage sometimes. And I sit here and I look to the east to that place that is supposed to be funding the tribal college. They want us to be patient. I am supposed to be patient and understanding. My father says to, my grandma used to tell me that understanding is a wonderful thing. I am still working on that.

2

SACRED IS AS
SACRED DOES

S *acred* is a provocative word and concept, suggestive and sometimes controversial; its uses and meanings are relative to people and circumstances. The Latin *sacer*, from which the English word *sacred* is borrowed, referred in ancient times to deities both good and evil, mirroring the capricious character of Roman gods. In modern times, the most common usage of *sacred* comes from Emile Durkheim, the turn-of-the-nineteenth-century French sociologist who defined *sacred* in distinction to *profane*. Durkheim's definition is used in popular and academic discourse and defines *sacred* not as necessarily divine but as something special, set aside for extraordinary consideration. *Profane*, in contrast, refers to everyday, mundane things. The *Blackwell Dictionary of Sociology* describes profane as ultimately knowable, while sacred is "ultimately unknowable."[1]

Nothing is inherently sacred—sanctity must be assigned by people or institutions. The *Oxford Dictionary* describes *sacred* as something "regarded with great respect and reverence."[2] It is in the authority of a group or individual to "regard" that which is and is not sacred. Sacred may be, but it is not necessarily religious or even ritualistic.

The widely cited and influential nineteenth-century *Pulpit Commentaries* notes that the Fifth Commandment of Moses, to "Honor thy father and mother," is a universal mandate, practiced by not only Christians, Jews, and Muslims. The *Commentaries* reports, "The obligation of filial respect, love, and reverence is so instinctively felt by all, that the duty has naturally found a place in every moral code."[3] Indeed, Confucian, Hindu, traditional African, and even modern secular practices and laws grant special privileges and terms of respect to ancestors, beginning with parents and grandparents, and reaching beyond, to parents of grandparents and grandparents before them.

Even if filial reverence is universal, as the *Commentaries* and others suggest, there is widespread belief among many Christians and Muslims in particular, and to a lesser extent religious Jews, that God alone deserves worship and therefore sanctifying ancestors should be approached very cautiously or even avoided altogether, as sanctifying anything or anyone other than God the Creator might lead to idolatry. Yet, there is widespread revering, and ritually "setting aside" of ancestors throughout the traditions of the three related religions. Muslim and Christian believers hold funerals, arrange marriages, pursue adoptions, have personal namings, establish inheritance laws, and follow many other ordinary customs that grant special status to ancestors, ancestral symbols, and ancestral identities. Sanctifying ancestors, in these ways whether or not as part of a sanctioned religious practice, is as common among the Christians, Jews, and Muslims of this study's thirty-four interviewees as it is among the Hindus and Buddhists.

Interviewee Simon Jacobson, scholar of Jewish civilization and *Chabad Chasid** author, says ancestry is "absolutely sacred. The Talmud talks about . . . when the Messiah will come, Elijah the Prophet will clarify people's ancestry; who belongs to which tree, which has become confused over the years." Sanctifying ancestors not only does not violate the will of God, in Jacobson's understanding, sanctifying ancestors fulfills the will of God. Following Jacobson's interpretation, a search for one's ancestry is both a sacred and a religious act.

Interviewee Yaakov Kleiman is an Orthodox rabbi and kohen living in the Old City of Jerusalem.[†] "The whole Jewish tradition," says Kleiman, "is based on ancestry; not only culture and religion, but of genetics to a large degree." Kleiman describes Jewish ancestors as carrying spiritual value, and one's lineage as part of God's divine order. Kleiman says that when new members are welcomed into a Jewish family (usually through marriage), their "soul changes and becomes an [new] identity." He believes his personal, ancestral association with his kohen lineage carries a sacred significance, ordained by God. Ancestry is "significant to God because we have lists within the Torah . . . the whole Book of Chronicles is a list of 'A begat B and B begat C.'"[‡]

Interviewee Loubert Trahan is a family genealogist and faithful Roman Catholic who has recorded the names of more than 120,000 ancestors and

---

Chasid refers to the Hasidic movement, that is, the wing of Judaism and of the Jewish world that was begun by the Baal Shem Tov (Rabbi Yisrael ben Eliezer, d. 1760).

[†]*Kohen* is a Jewish ancestral line of priests.

[‡]The Torah is the basic sacred text of Judaism and includes the five books that come from Moses. The Book of Chronicles is a book of the Old Testament.

relatives in his family's database, coming from his Acadian and Cajun families.* Trahan visits the graves of ancestors on All Soul's Day, Easter, the birthdays of ancestors, and other special days to honor "deceased parents, grandparents, et cetera." He sanctifies his ancestors through ordinary rituals and, while he says those particular practices are "in a way" religious, Trahan clarifies that they are more "personal rite[s] of remembering . . . and honoring" than they are officially sanctioned practices. Trahan's remembrances are less institutional than personal. He honors his ancestors more intuitively than doctrinally.

Trahan is careful to point out that he does not believe the spirits of his ancestors "are still with us" and he does not pray directly to living spirits. He says a sense of the ancestors' ongoing "presence" comes instead from the acts of honoring and revering. "Naturally," he adds, "when I'm attending Catholic Mass through the sermons et cetera it can't help but come to mind those that preceded me and hoping that they are wherever they wish to be and I wish I am there too, eventually." Trahan's family research codifies his and his ancestors' shared identities and carefully follows the accepted practices and methods of genealogists. But his "personal rites" are more reserved, intimate, and private. Both types of work, however, establish his ancestors as "special" and "set aside" for extraordinary consideration.

Interviewee Sheryl Siddiqui is a longtime convert to Islam and at the time of her interview was spokesperson for the Oklahoma Islamic Council in Tulsa, Oklahoma. Siddiqui relates that after her father's death some years ago, she performed holy obligations for him, including the hajj, required of all Muslims.† If a man is unable to perform hajj in his lifetime, Islamic teaching allows one of his children to perform the obligation on his behalf.

> There are three things that can continue to bless us after our deaths: one . . . one of our own children who blesses us . . . [the hajj] is one of the things that I can do with his soul that he sacrificed for me; this is my opportunity to give back to him, spiritually now. I certainly appreciated his provisions and he can appreciate mine.

When asked, "Why does God acknowledge your holy work on his behalf? Could you do the hajj for a person who is not a parent?" Saddiqui replied, "No. It's family." God acknowledges her ancestral family and its relationship to the living.

Sheryl Siddiqui does not describe her father as personally sacred; nor has her father through death become divine. But the suggestion of the holy substitution

---

*Acadian and Cajun are, principally, the French-speaking regions and people of Louisiana, Nova Scotia, and New Brunswick.

†Hajj is a holy obligation of pilgrimage to Mecca.

is that God acknowledges special significance of a father-daughter (parent-child) relationship. These and other practices apply Durkheim's and the others' definitions of *sacred* to the father and his legacy while still not contradicting Islamic prohibitions on idolatry.

The interview with Henrietta Mann (as well as interviews with an Arapaho chief and a Choctaw archivist and family historian) shows that within the languages and practices of selected Native American traditions there are also rich opportunities to sanctify ancestors. Within those modern communities, educated, professional people live their lives in daily communion with ancestors. Henrietta Mann, Chief Charles Sleeper, and Jason Felihkatubbe practice and believe in many religious and cultural respects differently from Siddiqui, Trahan, Kleiman, and Jacobson and describe the relationships between ancestors and their living descendants differently one from the other. But the construction of ancestors—the broad teaching that ancestors have special, unknowable, and sacred natures—is as prevalent in the lives of Mann, Sleeper, and Felihkatubbe as it is in the lives of the other four.

Dr. Henrietta Mann lives closely to her ancestors in body and soul, joining the living and the dead into a single, organic community. Dr. Mann surrounds herself with images, artwork, and everyday items of her ancestors as she sustains her Cheyenne identity from personal stories and lessons handed down from her ancestors. "I have nothing to leave you but my words," Dr. Mann's father related from her grandmother, and Dr. Mann adds, "I believe that that is how she [Grandmother] continues to instruct me to this day in terms of what it is to have a view of the world as a Cheyenne woman. . . . Ancestry . . . it is who I am."

Charles Sleeper is a traditional chief of the Arapaho Tribe of Oklahoma and college instructor of the Arapaho language. Sleeper describes a universe composed of diverse and sacred elements, including ancestors. The spirits of Chief Sleeper's ancestors connect him to a spiritual world, to truth, and to creation. He says he begins each day with prayers of thanks, recited together with ancestors and relatives of many kinds.

Recent research published in the *Journal of Analytical Psychology* suggests that people who are disassociated from their personal ancestries can suffer psychological trauma and a loss of identity.[4] Several interviewees, including Chief Sleeper, express similar ideas, describing what they see as the psychological and spiritual importance of connecting to ancestors. Chief Sleeper contends that without understanding from where and what a person originates, his identity is diminished and his sense of place in a spiritual universe is corrupted. On the other hand, a strong understanding of one's origins makes people better adjusted and better grounded. Sleeper adds that those who become disconnected from their ancestors "are psychotic." To be healthy, people must remember their ancestors and join them in prayer.

Chief Sleeper looks to the spirits of his ancestors for advice and reassurance. "They come in many forms," he says, ". . . usually they tell you why they're here and what you need to do." In particular, during times of great stress, people might have nightmares, "to release the stress and pressure, and sometimes they dream about them [ancestors] and the spirits come and comfort them."

Jason Felihkatubbe describes ancestors expressing an ongoing spiritual presence and cultural influence that parallel Chief Sleeper's description of his own ancestors' visits. Felihkatubbe says that ancestors visit the dreams of their descendants bearing messages, comfort, and advice. Ancestors' spirits also bless with their presence important social events and activities, such as graduations, weddings, and religious services of tribal members. Referring to his father, who passed away before Felihkatubbe graduated from college, he says, "When I walked down the aisle [to receive my] bachelor's degree, you know, he was there with us. . . . For me and my family, when we do those things, those passed can see them and they are there to celebrate with us."

Interviewee Sri Acharya Srinivasa Vedala, Sanskrit* scholar and temple priest, says he and other Hindus "remember all of them [ancestors] but we celebrate daily the First Man, the *Kutastha*, the *Rootman*. . . . We remember because we are descendants to First Man." Vedala describes "Rootman" as the original ancestor of his culture and his people. Ritualistically, Rootman represents the whole body of ancestors.

PV: We are respecting him.

DH: Why?

PV: That's because we are descendants to him. . . . He created some kinds of purpose and cause for us.

DH: But it's not only him. There are so many along the way.

PV: So many. So many on the way down. All of them that believe . . . like the First Man. Like Buddha was the First Man for Buddhists. Like that. . . . He is the root man. A man of the root. We say *Kutastha*. *Kutastha* means "a man at the root."

No one knows *Kutastha* by name or family line; instead he is known by reputation and title. Rootman was the first one, the original, the beginning, at

---

*Sanskrit is the ancient language of Hindu and the language of many sacred texts, including the *Mahabharata*.

the origin of all things Hindu, including Hindu people. He is a true progenitor, though not personally divine. Every society and every civilization has such an individual, says Dr. Vedala, to whom cultural and genealogical descendants can look for an archetypal beginning. The original person is not necessarily worshipped, but he or she is sacred and represents sacred things.

Rootman's precise identity and story are lost in the distant shadows of the past. But his being is manifest in the body of Hindu people and Hindu ways. Rootman is knowable but he is also not knowable. He is a mystery who connects people of the present to their origins. Rootman's enlightenment is embodied in traditions that surround the Hindu of the present day, but his personal nature is mysterious. He is a bridge connecting the culture of the present to protocultural causes and beyond. Honoring and knowing Rootman is a path to the meaning of the Hindu Self.

The several interviewees who identify as Buddhists offer a variety of ways of honoring and sanctifying ancestors. While some dismiss belief in an afterlife, others embrace a life after this one. Some Buddhist interviewees hold that there is no God, while others believe in God. All these interviewees, however, honor ancestors and, at a minimum, celebrate ancestors' memories through funerals and other rituals, stories, dance, music, and feasting.

Interviewee Irene Goto is a minister's assistant at the Seattle Buddhist Church. She is an enthusiastic supporter of and longtime participant in Seattle's largest Bon Odori, or Obon, an annual celebration dedicated to the honor of ancestors. Celebrants of the festival gather in Japanese communities around the world to remember ancestors and to celebrate their ancestors' lives with dance and music. Ms. Goto does not challenge that the "original reason" for the festival involved souls of ancestors and that many participants still understand the festival in that way. But concerning interaction between the living and ancestral spirits, Ms. Goto says, "I don't believe that." She does not profess specific beliefs in an afterlife or in God. Still, Goto dances at the Obon,

> In their [ancestor's] honor, yes. . . . It's in the honor of their memory but not really in the honor of an existing soul that will somehow benefit, exactly. It's in my mind. It's to help my—it's to help me remember them and to be grateful for them. Because I cannot remember them every second if they're not on my mind constantly. And it's kind of nice to be in a collection of people who are also remembering.

Ms. Goto's initiative to honor ancestors at the festival comes in part from her feelings of responsibility towards ancestors, in particular the two most recent generations.

I feel I need to live a good life because they gave me a good life. And I feel a responsibility to my children to show them what my parents showed me. So . . . I do feel responsibility to my parents.

Goto's personal belief to celebrate ancestors blends institutional to personal practices, for while the public dancing at the Obon is ritualized, Ms. Goto's emotional participation is personal—a natural voice, a sacred expression of joy. When Goto dances to the memories of her ancestors, she is not praying but she is doing what might instead be described as a form of "calling," in the sense of summoning the ways of her ancestors, resurrected in the joy of the dance, the music, the incense, the colorful outfits, and the gathering of descendants who share, remember, and show gratitude. Irene Goto's performance expresses the fullness of her appreciation of those who made her life possible.

Interviewee Kiyoko Messenger offers a perspective that contrasts with the more secularized Buddhist practices of Irene Goto. Messenger, who identifies as Buddhist and Christian, believes the spirits of the dead—ancestors and other loved ones—continue to interact with her in many ways, including by bringing her advice and comfort. Her most frequent and important spiritual visitor is her late husband, though he is only one of many, mostly unnamed ancestors and spirits in her life. Ms. Messenger honors all her ancestors because "without them there would be no Kiyoko."

The four interviewees from Korea have backgrounds of mixed Buddhist and local religious practices. Including three members from two generations of the Park family, and "Grandmother Kim," all four Koreans regularly honor and sanctify their ancestors by tending ancestral graves, praying to and for ancestors, and celebrating in ancestors' honor. But Mr. Park (Park Sin Joo) says that even during "ordinary day[s]" on which he does no particular ritual, he and his family still, "in my heart appreciate the help of ancestors." His mother, Lee Guem Ok (Park), describes the presence of ancestors in ways that are both ordinary and extraordinary. She says ancestors' spirits are aware of the world and the ways of the living and are concerned even about the mundane activities of her daily routine, such as shopping, conversing with friends, and driving her car around town. Asked if ancestors were present for our interview, for example, Lee Guem Ok responded casually, "Yes, of course. They are buzzing around the room like flies."

Interviewee Janna Thompson is a scholar and for the most part a secular thinker. Regarding her ancestors, Janna Thompson takes an approach similar to that of Irene Goto. Thompson visits graves and remembers ancestors in stories and through a "family ethos." Thompson says she "thinks of what my mother or father would have said . . . you have a recollection of them saying something. So in that sense they are kind of present." But by "present" Janna Thompson means the ancestors are memories and constructions produced by the living, not spirits. Still, the pull of ancestral identity and remembrance is strong. "It has to do not just with intellectual but with emotional, and attitudes towards the world and the way you place yourselves with other people." For this and other reasons, Thompson interprets "the truth about your ancestry" as being closely related to "the truth of your identity."

At the time of his interview, Jeff Livingston lived in an extended family "colony" in southern Iowa. Though a Christian and personally religious, the way Livingston honors ancestors is not well integrated into his religious belief. Instead, Livingston expresses his respect and honor for his ancestral family through work—particularly farming—cooperation with family, telling stories, and respect for elders. "I live in a community where . . . we basically have four generations living together," he explains. A sense of ancestral history gives "a child some feeling of belonging to something. Family history keeps that coming to you." Maintaining family traditions and telling stories about the people of the past ideally also lead to better futures for the children. "I hope that my children and grandchildren tell stories about me. I hope I can live the kind of life that produces stories."

Like Livingston and others, interviewee Daniel Essim sanctifies his ancestors through rituals, remembrances, and stories. Essim is Christian, and his sanctification of ancestors is interwoven closely with his faith, religious ritual, and belief in God.

> We go to the church and give thanks and offer a church service for them [ancestors]. We want to keep her [Mother's] memories alive so we honor [the] life she had lived . . . for all the children. And . . . to remind her that we're still thinking about her.

Dr. Essim consciously interacts with the living spirits of ancestors and, paralleling the beliefs of Henrietta Mann, members of the Park family, and other interviewees, Daniel Essim believes the living and the dead dynamically exchange and communicate.

> Because we have this belief that the dead still listen to us. So there are times when you are having hardship, you pray to the Lord and also you pray to your late mom to guide you through the hardship.

There is an element of trust in Essim's universe that reaches beyond the initiatives of the living and their ancestors. There is a trust that the universe behaves in such a way that spirits comfort the living and that love can cross that great divide. Essim adds, "Whether she is listening or not, whether she is actually guiding you or not, you believe in it."

Interviewees from across a broad spectrum of beliefs, backgrounds, and environments sanctify their ancestors. Religious practices influence the forms sanctifications adopt, but even within specific religious traditions there is a great variety of sacred expression. Even those interviewees who are not religious have their forms of honoring and sanctifying those who came before them. And even where religious instruction proscribes the "worship" of ancestors, predecessors are honored, remembered, prayed for, danced for, danced with, sung for, prayed to, talked to, or listened to. The suggestion from the sum of interviewees' testimonies is that these practices and beliefs do not occur simply because interviewees have been instructed by custom or by religious authorities to do so. Instead, interviewees widely insist that honoring ancestors arises from innate impulses to honor those who brought them here. As the *Commentaries* suggest, ancestral reverence is "instinctively felt."

INTERVIEW WITH FATHER CHRISTOPHER TRAN

"It Gave Me Hope, That Light"

DH: Can you tell me your name and title?

CT: I am Father Christopher Tran. I'm the Pastor here at Saint Eugene's.

DH: Is English your first language?

CT: No, Vietnamese is my first language.

DH: Who are your ancestors?

CT: Vietnamese people. [Laughs]

DH: So do you think of your ancestors as a nationality?

CT: I guess so.

DH: And do you think of the whole group [of Vietnamese] as your community of ancestors?

CT: Yes . . . we have a long history over there. Like four thousand years of history over there. So it's not like America only two hundred years ago. . . . So that means, in America . . . they keep all the records . . . and you can go back and look for your last name, but in Vietnam or in China I don't think anybody is doing that. So it's hard for us to go back

Father Christopher Tran. Courtesy of Christopher Tran.

for the beginning, for the root. But original Vietnamese [were] invaded by Chinese for one thousand years ago. So, maybe my ancestor is Chinese.

DH: And before Chinese would be something else and before that something else?

CT: That's right.

DH: When you think of ancestors, are you thinking of people? Are you thinking of culture? Are you thinking of groups? In what shape are you thinking of ancestry?

CT: I think of the group of people. . . .

DH: More than individuals?

CT: Right. More than individuals.

DH: Do you also think of individuals? Grandfather, great-grandfather, great-great-grandfather?

CT: Yeah. You know, I don't even know my grandmother. She died as a martyr . . . when my dad was fourteen. And now he's eighty-six. So even my grandmother I didn't see her, I only know her. She was killed as a martyr, they buried her alive. And I don't know much about her. And then, and on my mom's side, my grandfather died but when I was little, I knew him but when I grew up we moved. Because for Vietnamese, there was a lot of war going on; my father [was] a commander from the south so wherever he [would] go, I [would] go. So my family moved a lot. On my dad's side I don't even know who is my grandmother. . . .My last name is Tran. In Chinese they have some Trans too. So maybe I'm kind of Chinese . . . it's all connected. We're all connected. I talked about my grandmother. She was a martyr. Sometimes I felt like that she's still here with us though. You know, she still prays for us because I know she's in heaven right now . . . . The communists killed her because she wanted to keep her faith. And I only have the connection with that. . . . But I always remember [ancestors] and pray with them just like they're still here.

DH: What do you mean to pray with them?

Father Tran Explains *Pray with Them*

We look at the Church as being in three states: the Church here on earth, the Souls in Purgatory, and the Saints in heaven. We believe that we are all united—the living, the Souls in Purgatory, and the Saints in heaven—around the Cross and Resurrection of Jesus. This is the communion of saints that we profess our faith during the Creed of the Apostle: "I believe in the Holy Spirit the Holy Catholic Church the communion of Saints the forgiveness of sins the Resurrection of the Body and life everlasting." Believing in the communion of saints means believing that the saints in heaven are praying for us; including our own relatives who we hope now share fully in the happiness of the Kingdom of God.

As Christians, we believe that death is not an end. It is a change. It is not a break in existence. It is a transformation. We believe that when the hour of our death arrives, when our existence on this earth reaches its end, we do not find ourselves facing nothingness. We end up facing the merciful hands of the living God who welcomes us and converts our death in to the beginning of our resurrection. Christians believe that death is not final. We will be raised from the dead. We do not give up our lives in vain; we return them to the Creator. In death we attain the fullness of our being and we reach true life, which we call eternal life. Death is not the end. We can still be united with our loved ones. We are all, living and dead, united around the Cross of Jesus and His Resurrection.

CT: Because . . . being in the Catholic way means that we're all united. If you know that your grandfather, your great-great-grandfather has done something bad or whatever, they cannot get to heaven but in Catholic way we always pray for the dead, no matter what. Even my grandfather died forty years ago and each day, every time I have a chance to say Mass, I pray for him. We always pray for the dead and then one day they become a saint and they pray for us. So one day, we die and then that means it's a connection like that. Not just like you died, that's it the end.

DH: And is this more true or is this especially true for you and your grandfather because he is your grandfather?

CT: Mmhmm. [Affirmative nod]

DH: Why? Why is it more true because he's your grandfather than somebody else's grandfather?

CT: Because I know my mom told me . . . [she] loved that person and then . . . Just like you love that person and then you had the connection with them, you don't even know them.

DH: And how is the connection different from a connection to anybody else?

CT: Spiritual, I don't know. But like it's something that's in your blood.

DH: What does that mean?

CT: That means you know when something is really closer to you, is personal.

DH: Is that recognized by God? The closeness?

CT: No, not even recognized by God. But you pray for them, you pray for them. But you pray for everybody, you know. You pray for everybody that's brothers and sisters. Even as I say Mass I pray for everybody. You know we're connected by God. We are children of God.

DH: All people?

CT: Yeah, yeah. But that's why I pray for everybody. When we say Mass we pray for the general. For everybody, we are all brothers and sisters.

DH: Is there something particular about your grandfather, your grandmother?

CT: That [is] more personal to me. That means they are closer to me, because my mom, my aunt, all that they told me.

DH: What if they hadn't told you? Then . . .

CT: Somehow, something is still there.

DH: If you had never heard of your grandmother before, you didn't know anything of that, would she still be here with you in the same way?

CT: See, I told you my grandmother that she died before my mom and my dad get married. And I have a very special connection with her through whatever my dad told me . . . I feel very close to her. . . . If my grandfather died and he commits some sin, in the teaching of the church I can pray for him [grandfather].

DH: Can I also pray for him?

CT: You can pray for him.

DH: Is it different for you to pray for him than for me to pray for him?

CT: No, no you remember them more than other people. Just like in our culture that people pray for the dead. And that's the only best gift that you can give to the dead right now . . . We pray for our ancestors. Even if we don't know them. We pray in general.

And that's how I look at it. We can pray specifically for our own ancestors. And even if they committed sins, we can pray for them.

DH: Does God have some special recognition of you doing something special for your ancestors?

CT: How would I know? We don't know that. After you die, just like the Gospel of the Bible says that a woman had seven husbands. And after she died, which one would be her husband? The woman married his brother. Then his brother died but he had a child with her. And then they feel sorry for her and take over and then take care of that child and [another brother] marries her. And then after that he died and then the little brother want to take care of her children and marries her. Seven of them. And then after that, which one of the seven of them is going to be her husband in heaven? The only answer is, after you die, no husband, no wife, nothing—you are children of God. Everybody the same.

Father Tran Explains *Family in Heaven*

The Sadducees' question to Jesus was that, if there is life after death, which of the seven men would be her real husband in the next life? Jesus answers them on two fronts. First, he says that in the next life marriage will no longer exist. People will all be related equally in a common relationship with God. Second, Jesus reminds them that God spoke to Moses from out of the burning bush and said, "I am the God of Abraham, the God of Isaac, the God of Jacob" (Exodus 3:6). So Jesus adds: "He is God, not of the dead but of the living." God did not say to Moses: "I was the God of Abraham," or "I used to be the God of Abraham" but "I AM here and now the God of Abraham."

I believe that my prayer here can help my [ancestors] where they are now. I know that prayer is powerful and I believe that we can help the departed by praying for them. The best gift we can now give to our loved one is to pray for them. There is nothing that you could now do that would be more helpful for them than praying for them, if you say just one "Hail Mary" for our departed [ancestors], it will last into eternity. Prayer has lasting value.

DH: So it sounds like here in your lifetime, there is a matter of consciousness. You're aware of some people; you have a connection to them. You know their story and this makes them more personal to you. You were talking about your grandmother and that your grandmother is here sometimes with you. . . . When your grandmother is present, is it your idea of your grandmother or is it really your grandmother?

CT: I know it's true, she's here, she's present. When I was in the seminary if I study or I struggle with anything, I would pray with her, say, "Grandmother you have to help me go through this. I know you." You know why I keep saying "my grandmother"? Because she was martyred. You know in Catholic way if you are martyred, you are a saint. So that's why I keep praying with her. Why do I keep mentioning that? I keep mentioning my grandmother even though I didn't know her; but it's because I have that connection with her. And you know it's just not a superstition in our culture. In a way the faith told me that she's with me and she prays with me.

And then sometimes I [was] studying in the chapel, [when I was] in the seminary. And if I struggled with the study, I left everything there and went to the chapel, the chapel in the dark. And you see the tabernacle, you don't see God. But you see the little light, that lamp, the tabernacle lamp that you see, a red light. But that only tells you that something's there. You know He's present . . . for me that's from the beginning; when I was young, my mom and my pastor they give me that faith. . . . Faith is a gift not just like you want to own that, you want to have that. So just for me I look at that tabernacle, [and] I thought, "Where's God?" Nothing there. How do you see God there? But when I entered that chapel in the seminary everything was very dark; I only see that light, the red light right there. It just reminded me that I'm on a boat, that we are on the boat. I remember exactly the night I left. The sky was a full moon, and my family lost me, and it broke my heart. The first day I was lost in love. I was in the sad refugee camp. What would become of my two hands? I could die and be unknown. A total of seventy-six people were forced to endure indescribable conditions. A tempest was raging in my mind. And I had no idea where I was going. I spent that night in terrible anguish.

We spent six days on the sea without food or without water on the boat. The nights were dark and the small boat was pitched about on the heavy seas. We escaped from Vietnam, we traveled for seven days, seven nights without food and water. And then on the last day, on last day of the journey, I see, I see a light in the far away distance, but it takes all night long to get to that light. It was a lighthouse. But one thing I know . . . that if we get to that light, there are islands or something that can save us. You know what I'm saying? It gave me hope, that light on that night when I traveled, escaping from Vietnam to Indonesia. So that light reminded me when I come to the chapel, even in the dark, you know there's nothing there. I see that light again. Why is that light there? Just like the lighthouse that shone on the ocean . . . something is there if you hope God is present. I came in to that chapel, I prayed with God, but I ask for intercession of my grandmother to pray with me, pray for me, for right now, "I need your help". . . but only God knows, we don't know. I see that light, I pray with God, but through the intercession of my grandmother. "Help me to pass this test," or, "Calm me." Even with anxiety, worry, and studying you came back and you study. And it looks like everything becomes calm.

DH: Does your grandmother have special affection for you because you're her grandson?

CT: True, that's true.

DH: Might ancestors visit their descendants?

CT: That's possible, yes. It's good to remember that the Mass is the greatest prayer for the dead. I know of a priest who is now known as St. Malachy who did not get along

> **Father Tran later added:**
>
> Our faith is strong when everything is going well, but when the crisis hits we pray like Habakkuk, we say, "How long, O LORD, must I cry for help and you do not listen? You do not intervene" (Habakkuk 1:2) and we have questions about God and we wonder if God exists.
>
> The following was found written on a cellar wall in Cologne (Köln) after World War II:
>
> I believe in the sun even when it is not shining.
> I believe in love even when I feel it not.
> I believe in God even when he is silent.

with his sister who died. But she came to him wearing a black garment and he was standing outside the church in his dream and she said, "I'm hungry. I'm thirsty." She visited again and then he realized that in thirty days he had not said any Mass for her. And then after that dream he came up and said Mass for her. And after thirty days she came back dressed in a white garment. And in his vision he showed that his sister could go to heaven. From that day, that tradition in the Catholic church is that we say the Mass for that person that's very close to you. If your son or grandson or daughter or whatever, you want to pray for them, offer them a Mass. It's true, you know.

SANCTIFYING ANCESTORS IS INTUITIVE

Psychologists use the term *intuition* to refer to an understanding that arises from combinations of experience, reason, and instinct. Intuition is a process that gives people an ability to know something "directly," bridging conscious to nonconscious, without instruction from analytical reasoning. Intuitions are "presumptions and perceptions and beliefs that are more or less instantaneous, rather than derived and reasoned."[5] Sanctifying ancestors is intuitive. If the interviewees' own descriptions are to be believed, the sanctification of ancestors is presumptuous, bridging conscious and nonconscious, and its spontaneous nature is consistent with these definitions.

The Swiss psychiatrist Carl Jung wrote that he "very strongly" felt he was "under the influence of things or questions which were left incomplete and unanswered by my parents and grandparents and more distant ancestors. It often seems as if there is a personal karma within a family which is passed on."[6] Not surprisingly, Jung counted ancestors among the archetypes, which are themselves constructed as instinctual phenomena.

Perhaps humans have an innate desire to comprehend their origins and this desire is linked to sanctifying ancestors. The kabbalist* mystic and twentieth-century activist Rabbi Benjamin Kook universalized as he spiritualized human desire to connect to their origins when he wrote,

> All beings long for the very source of their origin. Every plant, every grain of sand, every lump of earth, small creatures and big ones, the heavens above and the angels, every substance together with its particles—all of them are longing, yearning, panting to attain the state of holy perfection.[7]

Connecting to ancestors takes an individual one step closer to his origins. If a path to origins is sacred, ancestors also, by the very virtue of their cosmological position, from the perspective of a descendant, are linked to the unknowable, and possibly to the divine.

Not only human beings, but all biological life, in fact all *things* have genealogies and descend from like things. When an individual connects to her origins, she enters an eternal succession of descent and relations. An individual may be but a minuscule cell in a vast universe, but when she joins a culture of reproduction, descent, and lineage, she shares in the greatness of the process and composition of that universal whole, from which and into which all things descend. By engaging the ancestral enterprise, the tiny individual becomes meaningful, finding a place in the natural cycles of creation and re-creation, not only through biological procreation, but through spiritual and cultural reproduction at the same time.

Several interviewees assert that the community of their ancestors is the same as that of their families, past and present. Family situates the individual in something larger yet still accessible; the individual ties her own personal meaning to the meaning of the family. Family and tribe carry a descendant along paths of ancestral names, identities, and stories, back through time, recently to parents and grandparents, further back to a more broadly defined community, and perhaps still further back to origins.

A family identity carries a person into the past but it also pulls an individual's identity forward, into the family's future. In the views of many interviewees, ancestry appears like a mandala traveling a road of kinship past, present, and future, as it sacredly perpetuates life. Interviewee Glenda Mattoon says, "When God put man and woman on the Earth, He told them, 'You will live as a family.'" The creation of family was a sacred act of God at the scale of life and

---

*The kabbalah is an ancient Jewish method of interpreting sacred texts, widely studied by Jewish mystics.

Glenda Mattoon honors her place in the order through her research and the documentation of her ancestral family.

The practices interviewees perform regarding funerals, prayer, naming, and so forth are generally consistent with the traditions and teaching of their religious affiliations. David Dollahite, Irene Goto, and Simon Jacobson, for example, cite religious doctrine and texts as the basis for many of their particular personal beliefs. Others, including Daniel Essim, Kiyoko Messenger, and Darold Treffert, tend to believe and practice in ways that push the boundaries of the doctrines of their religions. In other words, their religion accommodates their personal, intuitive interpretations of their own experiences. And some go further than that.

Several interviewees describe their ancestral beliefs developing through their lives independent of the explanations of their religious educations. These interviewees do not claim their religious instruction is wrong about the nature of ancestry or ancestral-descendant relations but claim to trust their own intuition as the final arbiter and interpreter of their ancestral beliefs, even when their intuitive understanding appears to contradict the practice of their religions. It is clear that some interviewees consider existing institutional definitions insufficient to comprehend the perceptual realities of their ancestral experiences. An intellectual autonomy of ancestral experiences suggests that the ancestral experience might arise as much from nature as it does from nurture.

Contrasts between teaching and experience might develop because of the apparent inadequacies of language to describe the depth and breadth of the ancestral universe. Glenda Mattoon describes the supernatural basis of ancestry and along with that, she hints at the incomprehensible magnitude of the ancestral cosmology.

> Well, the basis, we believe that the basis for society, the very basic—boil it all down, is the family. And a nuclear family—father, mother, children—and then you go back from there and you add in the grandparents and back from there and the great-grandparents and so forth but . . . we do have a spiritual connection, you know, in what we're doing . . . a spiritual, well connection . . . a spiritual . . . aspect to what we do.

Mattoon's ancestral belief and practice is consistent with the doctrines of her Mormon belief. Yet she hesitates in the interview, searching for words to contain the enormous significance she feels ancestry carries. And she insists that doctrine is subordinate to her own experience.

Surely teaching, language, and culture exert enormous influence on personal interpretations of experience of all kinds. But there are also compelling arguments that support interviewees' claims of autonomy. The ancestral beliefs and practices of many interviewees evolved from early to later life from more doctrinal in the direction of more intuitive. Interviewees describe their early beliefs inflexibly molded by the instructions of their religious institutions, while belief and practice later in life aligned more closely to their subjective experiences. Interviewees assert they revised the instructions of their youths to accommodate the ancestral experiences of their more mature selves. When experience clashes with doctrine, the elder interviewees say they subordinate doctrine. As ninety-two-year-old Kiyoko Messenger says of her own ancestral beliefs, "I know these things because of my experience. . . . People are very flexible. . . . Maybe I am not a good Christian. Something happen[s], and [people] will change one-hundred percent. Like Mount Fuji, people are trying to climb up, you say this is the best way or that is the best way; people will climb the best way."

Grandmother Kim explains that when she was a young woman, she frequented her local temple and saw how the (Buddhist) priests and elders performed ancestral rituals. She learned from them and adopted some of their ways. But as she grew in years and wisdom, she conducted ancestral rituals to better conform to her subjective experience. "I watched the monks, and I learned from them how to do those things. That was my own experience. Then I made the rituals my own." As she gained self-confidence, Grandmother Kim used the religious vocabulary of the monks' teaching to help her interpret for herself her relationships to her ancestors, which eventually included visits from ancestral spirits. She sees her desire to cling to, care for, and honor ancestors as arising from neither monks nor Buddhism. Instead, these impulses originate from her own natural desire, similar to her "natural" desire to care for her children and other descendants, intuitive impulses that doctrine and instruction must serve. A method of child rearing might, for example, be learned, while the ultimate drive to care for one's dependents is natural and instinctive. Kim claims the same regarding caring for ancestors.

When he was young, interviewee Rama Swami Mohan did "whatever we were expected to do, daily rituals . . . we did it to make our family happy. [But] when my parents passed away, my father passed away . . . belief followed." Mohan's growing trust in his own perceptions, guided by his love for his parents, shaped his evolving ancestral belief. Mohan sees Hindu doctrine as the "cultural aid" to his natural experience. Mohan says, "Initially you do it by rote but as you do it, you are forced to think about it . . . you are forced to remember . . . in a particular, organized way." After years of meditation on ancestors, love, doctrine, and experience, Mohan came to "a fraction of a second . . . a spark" of happiness and a single moment of true connection to his spiritual and ancestral identity. That moment came about outside of doctrine and might have been achieved, according to Mohan, with or without formal religious associations. His "moment of connection" was principally natural and innate, spontaneous, and uniquely personal.

Interviewees describe several factors that trigger shifts from early life's mechanical practice to later life's organic, intuitive comprehension of their relationships to deceased ancestors. Some interviewees, like Rama Mohan, say belief became deeply sincere only after the deaths of loved ones. Others relate the visits of the spirits of ancestors, arriving unsummoned, offering comfort or information to their descendants as transformative events. Visits might not have been part of interviewees' belief systems prior to an event, but once interviewees accepted visits as "real," their religious beliefs conformed accordingly.

Interviewees also attribute the evolutions of their ancestral beliefs simply to becoming adult, being married, having children, and meditating. "Compared to my past," explains Grandmother Kim, "my thoughts are a lot deeper. . . . I gain my ideas [from personal experience] and put them into action." Most interviewees also identify love either towards the ancestors or from the ancestors as a liberating force allowing intuition to blossom and confidence to grow, ultimately transcending doctrine.

In some few cases, religious doctrine is explicitly confirmed by ancestral experience, perhaps as a sort of revelation. David Dollahite describes his grandfather coming to him in a dream, to address his grandson's religious belief.

"So, I saw my grandfather and I came up to him and he said to me, 'I love you, I'm still alive. What you've been taught about the life after death is true. I am still who I am and we will see each other again, and I'll be fine.'"

In an unusual twist, Dollahite's mystical experience confirmed his doctrinal belief.

Interviewees describe the sanctification of ancestors as occurring both consciously and unconsciously. Institutionalized instruction might codify what a descendant feels he or she already "knew" subconsciously. As Rama Swami Mohan says, the written (Hindu) scriptures are available "to help the process but the main is the remembrance and the feeling of the *gothra*."*

Other interviewees also offer the idea that reverence for ancestors is natural, only given form by doctrine and religion. The innate impulse might occur with or without "the formal process" of religion. Interviewee Lee Guem Ok describes the development of her ancestral belief.

Gothra is a Sanskrit word meaning family or race.

DH: Do you have responsibility and obligation to [your ancestors]?

LGO: Yes, the obligation is the ancestral ritual. After I die, my son has to do it. After he dies, my grandson has to do it. It's like after marriage, we have a responsibility to our children as well as to our ancestors.

DH: Where did you learn how to do this?

LGO: I just thought and spoke. I didn't learn anything from others. I am illiterate. All of these are from my own head.

DH: Do you have a specific event, which led you to know your obligations?

LGO: I didn't learn anything, so I just told you what I know from myself. . . . I establish my own thoughts about them during my lifetime.

Lee Guem Ok answers to relatives in two directions, the past and the future. Her ancestral responsibilities embrace her grandparents and her grandchildren, as well as the people of her own generation. She assumes that loving and honoring all three groups is stirred by instinct, automatic, subconscious, innate, and essentially preceding doctrine. Caring for children as well as grandparents alive and dead is an obvious natural drive, she says, which requires no explanation, despite cultural variations. Lee Guem Ok assumes those of future generations will serve her as naturally as she has served those from previous generations.

Many of the interviewees say that ancestors' lives play a role in the health of future generations and that this is also intuitive, in both directions: descendants are aware of their psychological and spiritual dependence on ancestors, and ancestors are aware of their influence on descendants. But even more than that, in an ironic twist of time, ancestors have during their lives already begun shaping the conditions of not only their immediate descendants, but the conditions of the descendants of their descendants and possibly further than that. Because rather than standing as the silent fossils of previous communities, now dead and disassociated, the people of the past set the stage and wrote the scripts for the performances of the generations to follow; their ways flourish in the lives of those who follow them. For good or bad, the identities the ancestors established find fruition in the ways of their descendants.

Interviewee Darold Treffert believes there is hard evidence that ancestors influence descendants physically, two and three generations after them. Treffert maintains that not only genetic traits but also the lifestyles of ancestors affect the health and well-being of descendants.

DT: When we're looking at family history, of the savants, looking for any earlier persons, we have to think in terms of aunts, uncles, cousins, and much more than just mom and dad.

DH: And how far would you extend that?

DT: Well, I think we've gone as far as . . . first or second cousins. In some cases, it will be an aunt or an uncle and in some cases it may be several generations back; we're not talking about dad's brother but people several generations back. . . . One of the things that also has broadened my view of genetics is epigenetics.* There is a fair amount of research now in epigenetics which shows for example . . . looking at a very closed population in northern [Europe], they simply kept impeccable records of the weather and of the seasons, and of the crops. . . . And going back and looking at these records, [researchers] have discovered that the results of a famine, for example, several generations back may show up in shortened longevity two or three generations later. In other words, our genes are modified by our experience and those modified genes can be transmitted by what's happened to us. . . . And so . . . not just the prior generation but it can go back a long ways. And that is not just a matter of learning, or handing down stories; it actually is handing down the genes. So I am a product not just of what my mother ate, but what my grandfather and my grandmother and my great-grandfather and my great-great-grandmother ate, in terms of my constitution and the way I handle glucose and other kinds of things.

The influence of ancestors reaches into cultural, genetic, and biological areas beyond our current scientific understanding.

Dr. Darold Treffert. Courtesy of Darold Treffert.

Interviewee Lee Guem Ok's ancestral practices contradict neither the tone nor the intent of religious practices in the society around her, but she adds her own unique elements to her belief and to her ritual. Both Korean grandmothers interviewed, Kim and Lee Guem Ok, describe their personal ancestral practices evolving out of blends of experience, intuition, and example. Both women describe the spirits of ancestors visiting them, and the two agree that spirits of ancestors visit during times of stress. However, Lee Guem Ok says she is visited only by spirits she knew during her lifetime, while Grandmother Kim reports that she is sometimes visited by spirits of ancestors she does not recognize, and those ancestors appear to her initially not as people but as cows. To identify ancestors who visit in the form of cows, Grandmother Kim solicits help from a family member who might have known the person in life and can

---

*Epigenetics is the study of effects on genes that occur outside the influences of DNA, such as environment.

recognize a visitor from his or her "messages." Alternatively, she says she might ask a local medium, who "lives with the gods" and might be better informed about distant spiritual realities.

The spirits of Grandmother Kim's ancestors first visited her when she was twelve years old. She did not perform ceremonies for her ancestors until several years later. Kim describes both intuitive and institutional sources contributing to her interpretation of ancestral visits.

DH: Where did you learn to do these things?

GK: Because I have watched *Jesa*, I know.* And all I know becomes my own experience.

Grandmother Kim's understanding of the nature of ancestors contrasts in specific ways to those of the people around her on topics such as the spiritual relationship between ancestors and descendants, the prescience of ancestral spirits, and ancestors' spirits' relationships to God. One point, however, on which the Park family's grandmother, father, and mother, Grandmother Kim, and their prevailing, respective religious cultures all agree is that ancestors and descendants alike naturally and inherently deserve equal honor and sacrifice.

Biologist and interviewee Dr. Peter Grant offers his own scientific explanation for why honoring ancestors might be a natural inclination. Dr. Grant speculates that in prehistoric times,

> there was only a tiny group of people that kept everybody alive, protected each other from predators, brought in food, cared for the sick, and that group was important. They had an identity so strangers were probably killed or chased away . . . and I'm wondering if those genes are engrained in us.

Professor Grant sets aside the spiritual nature of ancestral sanctifications others raise and looks instead for evolutionary explanations. He constructs ancestors as the guardians of community and culture and argues that for this they need to be remembered and their identities sustained.

Loubert Trahan's view of his Cajun-Acadian heritage intersects neatly with Professor Grant's theory and might even be applied as a case study. Trahan argues that his own ancestors represent a collective identity that serves as a cultural defense against outsiders. The rituals he performs at cemeteries, during Mass, and at reunions are the substance of the defense, built out of the ancestral names, personalities, and stories. "We were not a cloistered order you know," Trahan says, but he and his ancestors view problems of the world outside Cajun-Acadian society as

---

Jesa is a Korean ancestral ceremony.

problems of outsiders, "fools . . . in big cities in America" who suffer with rampant crime and drug abuse. Trahan's own Cajun-Acadian people perpetuate a separate identity, endorsed by ancestral traditions, nurturing and defending "God's Oasis." Following the example of ancestors, Trahan's people do not

> look favorably on the practices of some other cultures and they did not want to be part of or associated with it. . . . If you come in here and you're a rogue . . . you know, you'll be frowned on. I don't mind saying that. You're not going to be an outcast but I don't think you'll be as welcomed.

It seems natural and intuitive to Peter Grant and Loubert Trahan for a community to defend itself by maintaining a cultural-ancestral bulwark. Ancestors represent an exclusive *We*, united against an external *They*.

The Buddhists among the interviewees provide a wide range of ancestral practices and beliefs. While the Korean Buddhist interviewees share some ceremonies, such as tending to graves and so forth, the six Japanese and Japanese-American Buddhists share the celebration of the Bon Odori. Also called the Obon, the occasion is based on a story of Maudgalyana, a disciple of Buddha who dreamt he saw his deceased mother suffering in hell. Upon waking and filled with terror, Maudgalyana ran to Buddha to beg his counsel on how to relieve his mother's suffering. The Master told him to give food to monks and perform charitable deeds. When he did as he was advised, Maudgalyana saw in a vision or dream his mother released from hell and he was filled with joy. Japanese people the world over celebrate their ancestors through the auspices of this story.

Irene Goto dances the Bon Odori every year. She finds the meaning of the celebration less spiritual than emotional, psychological, and social, though she is aware of prevailing spiritual interpretations. Irene Goto says,

> As I understand it at this point in my journey, it is not a concern whether or not Maudgalyana's experiences really happened. It can be taken as a metaphor for the power of doing good deeds or as a tale to convey the release a person can feel for atoning for another's misdeeds.

Ms. Goto celebrates Bon Odori because she enjoys sharing the event with other dancers and performers. Her sense of gratitude to her ancestors rises from her natural affection for her mother and her own children. Doctrine and tradition define the festival practices: the dance, the dress, the music, the order of events; but Irene Goto's personal memories of her mother animate the doctrine with meaning. Her affection is natural and intuitive; the festival is doctrinal and institutionalized. Dancing unites the two.

For many celebrants, the joy of the Obon lies in honoring life's fullness and gifts; ancestors are part of life's fullness. The Obon is a celebration of thanks but also of responsibility—beginning with recognizing the work of those who came before, furthered by the introduction of new generations to the circle of life and into the circle of dancers. Some celebrants believe ancestors are indeed spiritually present, following the smoke from festival fires to discover the party and its celebrants, their descendants. Other Bon Odori participants say ancestors are present only in the minds of dancers. But the external order is the same—a loving, working, sacred order, dancing and performing the past into the present and the present into the future. Whichever way of thinking a participant follows, the celebration naturally contains all the qualities of intuitively making the ancestors sacred: gratitude, special remembrance, mystery, and love.

INTERVIEW WITH KIYOKO MESSENGER, WITH THE VENERABLE SOZUI SENSEI

"Friendly Ghosts"

DH: Can you tell me your name?

KM: My name is Kiyoko Messenger.

DH: What is your first language?

KM: Japanese of course!

. . .

DH: Can you tell me who are your ancestors?

KM: My father, and my Mama, mother, wonderful people. I am very proud of them! I tell you my father died by cancer, because smoke, smoke, smoke. . . . So anyway, [my mother] died. . . . I was at her bedside and she said, "Kiyoko, some day you are going to get married." I just looked at her like, "What is she trying to tell me?" But you wouldn't interrupt your mama. My father later told me that Mama was beautiful and great and wonderful lady in the world. I was so stunned, my father bragging or telling me how your mother is this wonderful to tell your own daughter, so I respected him. Because I saw their arguments, their crisis, I saw it, but now he told me like this. . . . I didn't say anything, just I was, "Wonderful father, I respect you," that's what I thought. But when I came to America, I didn't have a chance to tell it to my mother. . . . When I came over here I told my husband about it. "Kiyoko," [he said,] "your mother knows it." Oh good! I didn't have to tell her. She knew it, she smart lady. She met my husband when he went back to Japan, so [my husband] always said, "Your mother beautiful, very smart, wise lady." I know, so I just say "So you know [too]?" But now, when I'm getting older, if God said, "Kiyoko, you've been so good so that I'm going to give you some reward. Who would you like to see in the world? Only one person." I would like to see my father or Mama. . . . Now being a married woman, I understand my father. My mother, she was a grandmama, but I don't have children. She's very patient, she's very patient. And a Japanese man is very dogmatic. . . .

DH: You say your father is your ancestor, your mother is your ancestor, who else?

KM: My father side, my mother side, grandparent, I know, that's all. But not very many. Because they lived in the countryside.

DH: What about their brothers and sisters?

KM: I didn't have much experience with them. But cousins.

DH: Cousins?

KM: Mmm hmm. [Yes.]

DH: Are cousins also your ancestors?

KM: Of course, it's a family.

DH: Do you think of ancestors as part of a family?

KM: I think so. I think [but] during the war time, they separate all the family.

Kiyoko Messenger with Ven. Sozui Sensei. Courtesy of Sozui Sensei.

DH: And, when you married, then your husband had ancestors also.

KM: Oh yes.

DH: Are they also your ancestors?

KM: By law yes, but um . . .

DH: Not so much by law, but by you. Do you think of them as your ancestors?

KM: I have never seen my husband's father. . . . My husband said, he was very strict, very—music and dance, everything. But when I got married and came to America I got a letter from his father, beautiful, so sweet.

DH: To you?

KM: Yes!

DH: Personally?

KM: So sweet. "I like your father," I say. "He's not mean he's very nice to do that." I like to see him, but I didn't have a chance. One day, sheriff came to knock at the door, why do sheriffs come? What did I do? What might happen? He says, "Give this to Mr. Messenger." "Ah yes, just a moment, he taking shower." So then, "Somebody, like a policeman, uniform, he want to give this to you, you have to talk to them." It was his father died. You see I didn't have a chance to meet.

DH: Do you think of ancestors only as the people you knew? Or, might you also think of your great-great-grandfathers as your ancestors?

KM: Of course! I don't see them, but of course. Because, if they are not there, no grand-parent, if there are no grandparent, no my parent, if they are not, Kiyoko is not existing here this moment. I respect them. I don't know who they are, I never saw them, I never spoke to them, but if they are not there, Kiyoko is not here.

DH: Why do you respect them?

KM: Because, because, ancestor!

DH: And, do you think of their brothers and sisters and cousins, as your ancestors?

KM: I never thought about it. I never extended that many.

DH: Not that direction?

KM: No, no I didn't.

DH: So, do you think of ancestors more as your direct line, not the larger family?

KM: No. I . . . my uncle and auntie and that's it.

DH: Even though they're not your direct line?

KM: Yes.

DH: So, then, do you think of it as a family group, or a cultural group? And a genealogical group?

KM: It's different. It's different.

DH: The two groups are different, genealogy and culture?

KM: Mmm hmm. [Yes.]

DH: Do you think of yourself as a descendant of a cultural group?

KM: Oh yes, oh yes. Of course.

DH: How?

KM: How? Because without Japanese, I don't have Japanese culture. So many foreigner come to Japan to stay—like, Japanese, then speak like Japanese, on outside, wonderful, "You speak so fluent Japanese, where did you learn?" they tell them—and do what we do but somehow, nuance or something is different. Because I am here, I just become American citizen, many years ago. I've been here fifty years, in America, but when, after few years, I just became American citizen . . . not perfect English, but I like American way of life. It's different. I like both. But, even if I speak fluent English, Americanized, but I am not very American.

DH: So you don't think of American culture as part of your ancestry? Only Japanese culture?

KM: Well, let me see. I have two country. I like both. I'm very happy and very greedy. [Laughs]

Ven. Sozui Sensei: Kiyoko, you have the whole world!

KM: I think so yes, I like people. . . . Doesn't matter. Black or white, no matter.

DH: Some people I've talked with say that all people are their ancestors. African people, European people, Native American, they're all ancestors because they all come from the same people. Do you ever think that way?

KM: No, I'm still small world.

DH: Only two countries.

KM: But well, I don't want make a fence, I want to be free. Because, I happened to be, born in Japan, in a Buddhist family. So then I just grow up, they don't tell me what is Buddhism. "What you have to do, Kiyoko, [what] you don't have to do." Don't do that. Never told me. I grow up watching my parents what they're doing daily, every day. In the morning, they go to bed, the next day, I just doing how they do. Watching.

VS: Did you have a family altar?

KM: Oh yes. In Japan. Mmmm hmm.

DH: How far back would you say your family, or your ancestors go? Do you think they go back to a first person, or a first culture?

KM: I don't know. I don't know. But I hate war. They have a family, they have a parent, they have children, we don't know. But why do they have to kill each other? It's awful!

DH: Do you think of animals as part of your ancestors?

KM: I don't think so. Animals are animals. . . .

VS: How about monkeys?

KM: Oh, I like monkey, but I don't think they are my ancestor. I don't know. I like animal, and monkey.

DH: But all life is related.

KM: Because we have life, we have blood, when you cut, blood came out. Even a small bug. We have life, life somebody gave to us. That's all the same. All same.

DH: And all related.

KM: Oh yeah, that's the reason.

DH: Do you think in any way your ancestors go back to God?

KM: How do I know?

DH: Is God your ancestor?

KM: God is more mighty.

DH: Can you tell me what is your relationship to your ancestors today? Do you have a relationship to your ancestors?

KM: Mentally or physically or . . . ? Well, we're related. We're related somehow.

DH: Do you have an active relationship, like a living relationship with your ancestors in any way? Do you think about them, do you talk to them, do you hear from them?

KM: I didn't understand your question.

DH: Mmmm, I know.

VS: You talk to your husband, no?

KM: Yes, I don't know. My husband is somehow related, and we don't know, but somehow, why I came over here to America, why I married American. He was wonderful, you see. [For many] years we [Japan and the United States] fought, killing each other. No reason to killing. Person to person, we have nothing to—no reason to killing, but so many people lost away, to wasting, but after that I came over here, I married. So then . . . America . . . and another country. Two countries.

DH: Did you know your grandparents?

KM: Ahhh yes, when I was a little girl.

DH: Do you have any kind of relationship with your grandparents today?

KM: Of course!

DH: How?

KM: By blood.

DH: By blood, but anything more active? For example, do you have conversations with people?

KM: No I don't have any conversation, they lived country, I lived city.

. . . [Discussion about general ancestral belief.]

VS: [Explains to Kiyoko in Japanese that we are asking about connections with ancestors who have passed on.]

KM: I think [there is] something, I don't know what is it.

VS: She thinks there is some communication going on.

KM: I think so.

VS: On some level.

DH: Why do you think that?

KM: Because, only from my experience. I don't know other people's. Maybe some people wrote a book or are professional. I was born in Japan, and . . . I was Buddhist, but when I came over here, then I just was baptized, but I still like Buddhist. Maybe I am not good Christian, but I like Buddha . . . people are very flexible. Some people said I am a so and so. But you never know. Something happened, they will change one hundred percent! That they will! Like, mountain, Fuji or, Everest mountain, people trying to climb up, this is the best way, or this is the best way, or no that is the best way. But they are going to climb to the top. So they believe this is a good—I don't like kind of a thing. I like more flexible. We are all the same. I don't know what I'm talking about. Such a big subject!

DH: It's a big subject, yes, but you know about your own experience better than anybody.

KM: I'm very thankful to the God . . . I'm very happy.

DH: Did you ever participate in the Bon Odori?

KM: Bon Odori? I enjoyed it to go there. I like it. I like dance! I don't care, and . . . dancing, I don't care. I like it.

DH: This is a festival to remember ancestors, right?

KM: Yes . . . and we always wear the *yukata*,* including summer and the rest. Also, noodles. Noodles are for especially, December 31st the New Year, carnival. . . . Obon . . . ancestors coming back from where they are after they died, coming back to visit us, so then they are welcomed. Then we just burn—after sun goes down, burn this wood. It burned. So then, people just watching, the smoke goes to here, so then, heavenly, or ancestors, deceased people, coming back to us with the smoke.

DH: They find you with the smoke?

KM: Mmm hmm. [Yes.]

DH: Is the wood burned for the ancestors?

KM: Mmm hmm. [Yes.]

DH: Why do they care? Why do the ancestors care to return?

KM: Because, we are living here, they give us our lives, so then we are still alive, they maybe sick, maybe angels, but still they give us life.

DH: The ancestors give you life?

KM: The husband and wife both. When we are born. Born the same way, like animals.

DH: Can ancestors who don't have children also come back?

KM: I don't know. Ancestor means ancestor.

DH: Means everybody?

KM: Mmm hmm. [Affirmative.]

DH: So, if a family adopts a child?

KM: Of course ancestor!

DH: Then that child is also part of their ancestry?

KM: Ohhh of course.

DH: And when that child grows up and dies, that child will also come back?

KM: Yes.

DH: Everybody is an ancestor?

Yukata is a summer kimono commonly worn at the Obon.

KM: Of course, of course.

DH: And everybody is a descendant.

KM: We cannot just be born in between the worlds, no.

DH: What is the reason why the ancestors follow the smoke and come back to . . .

KM: Well, that is maybe a story or something, about the smoke, we can have holy smoke, when we go to Japan, big temple, the big . . . circle . . . the incense burned, the smoke, burning, kind of if you think it's a superstitious, it's ok, but the smoke, something has to believe it. So then, how many days, I don't remember. A Obon festival, and food too, and altar of the ancestor's place. So then we can eat.

DH: Does that help the ancestors in any way?

KM: A feeling.

DH: Their feeling or your feeling?

KM: I think our feeling. Its thank you, thank you very much for the food, and we are still alive, so then please, over watching us, thank you, because without you we are not here on Earth. Thank you.

Kiyoko Messenger. Courtesy of Sozui Sensei and Kiyoko Messenger.

DH: I see, without you we wouldn't be here. Do the ancestors benefit in any way you know?

KM: They are acknowledged?

VS: Is it good for them?

DH: Yes, is it good for the ancestors that the living remember them?

KM: Oh of course, thank you or something, thank you.

DH: How is it good for them?

KM: Because, when we are happy, must be good. If we are good or happy . . .

DH: They're happy if we're happy?

KM: Yeah!

DH: Why?

KM: Because we try to make them happy, or thank you.

DH: When people perform funerals, or other celebrations after somebody dies, they often have those services for the dead, to help the dead move on, for example. But then after the funeral people have other celebrations, a wake for example, which is performed more for the living. So there is kind of one thing for the dead and one . . .

KM: In other cultures.

DH: Yes exactly, and in some cultures they do things for the dead, to help the dead.

KM: Oh yes. Of course!

DH: What do you think of that?

KM: I like it.

DH: Do you believe that you can do things to help the dead?

KM: I hope so. Because we are trying to from spiritual way, to—some American people ask me, "Kiyoko, why do you take flowers to the place? They don't need it." I don't remember what I answered . . . oh yes. "Why take the flowers to the place . . . the grave-yard? They cannot smell, they cannot see."

DH: And what is your answer?

KM: You know, sometimes my English will not come up.

[Kiyoko describes arriving in the United States and the language difficulties she had. She concludes with a story describing how spiritual things are "higher" than other things.]

DH: Why are spiritual things higher?

KM: Oh yes! Of course, always!

DH: But why? Or in what way?

KM: Material sometimes it comes and it goes. Spiritual all inside. No one can take it, even the fire, earthquakes, nothing. It is just in you.

DH: Does that not go when your body goes?

KM: I don't know [gasps].

DH: Can you tell from other people who have died, if that's true?

KM: In my experience again. When my husband died. All this . . . we didn't have children. When he goes to barber shop, he takes me with him. When I go to beauty shop, he comes with me . . . so, my mother told me, "Kiyoko, when you are in Japan—you were born in Tokyo, you know everything but when you go to another country, you know nothing. You don't know nothing. When you are by your husband, you have to do it, ok? So, jealousy is your number one enemy." That is what she told me. I said "Oh, ok." When my husband comes home, sometimes he likes meat, sometimes he likes fish. So I had the two of them. If he doesn't like meat, we have the fish, I bought it all together . . . then when he died I'm really . . . I feel like I don't know what to do. I don't have to have breakfast. When a bill comes, I say "Oh, how to do it?"

DH: And when you say "How to do it?" are you talking to him?

KM: [Emphatically] I always talk to him! His spirit! Help!

DH: And are you talking to him or to a memory of him?

KM: Not memory. Talking.

DH: How can you tell the difference?

KM: I just told him. "But what to do?" Even this morning when I woke up, I thought, "I'm going to do this one, okay? If I make a mistake I'm sorry, but I'm going to do this one. Okay? I'm going to go to Peace Church."

. . .

DH: Do you talk to anybody else? Or only your husband?

KM: Only him.

DH: Why only him?

KM: Because I lived with him. This was the daily life. Like the check was the real thing. That's why I'm going to ask him. I want to keep whatever he was doing so then I think to transfer to me doing things.

DH: Do you ever dream about . . .

KM: Oh yes!

DH: Your husband or father or grandfather?

KM: Not very much father but mother and husband. I had this dream not too long ago after he died. You know the Dead Sea? I have a dream, there was salt so I was floating like this and all the sky and the water were all the same I was nobody but Kiyoko by herself, I don't sink, I just hold like a pedestal, like an umbrella, I hold like this, so enjoying, nice, sky blue, water blue, nobody, I just me. So then suddenly I saw it and the water was clear and a big concrete slab and so I just stand up, I stand up touched my concrete slab somehow thought that's a funny dream so when I stand up I saw it way far away kind of water coming this way like its HATCHA! [Kiyoko makes a frightened yell] like dark sky and storm is coming and I thought, "Oh no I was right there enjoying it but now oh my goodness, oh that is too dark too strong!" I said. I heard it in my ear then I saw right beside big tall man, white, so white so like bear, so he was watching me. "Too dark! Too strong for me!" I just repeated twice then I saw just the profile, calm, breathe. So suddenly I woke up I remember my voice screamed so to wake up the next room. Rocked my bookshelf. . . . Yea, that is the dream. I don't know why I had the dream, I don't know who was standing in front of me.

DH: It was after your husband died? So do you feel like it was your husband?

KM: It was connected with my husband. I believe. I don't know what. People say after you die, everything goes, but I think something . . . something . . . I believe it.

DH: Was the dream different from other dreams?

KM: Yes . . . sometimes I am laying and watching TV . . . I don't watch TV often, but laying and sipping tea and knitting and feel sleepy. It is dozy time, dozing, not sleeping. I feel like this and then always suddenly somebody is sitting next to me, or moving around. I can feel them moving around. Sometimes they are standing. Sometimes I wake up and think, "What Kiyoko, are you going crazy?" No, but I saw it, I heard something, people are laughing. Me too! I'm enjoying! People think Kiyoko is crazy. No. But then I just try to close eyes . . . to see them around, but I cannot come back. Then I told, "I join you one day!" Then again the next day and the next day. I thought just participating with them, laughing with them, sometimes moving around, I can see. I love them, I heard my voice. So then dozing, dozing, I can see them moving around.

DH: And you feel like they care about you?

KM: I like it! That's why I close my eyes. It happened. I told my minister! "Kiyoko," [he] told me, "Kiyoko, that is like a friendly ghost."

DH: Friendly ghosts?

KM: "Are you scared?" "No! I would like to see them come back tonight again," I said!

DH: Did you ask your minister? Or did you tell him about this?

KM: No, not ask, just tell him.

DH: Did you ever see them?

KM: No, just to—not color, just the same color, white, moving around, something moving.

DH: Do they know you?

KM: I don't know! Sometimes around, usually this side . . . yea. I like it. I like them around. Thank you! I enjoy talking with you. And this is the perfect place [Buddhist Temple].

VS: . . . to talk about ghosts! [All three laughing]

KM: Yea, you see, you are complete stranger but I'm talking about my spiritual things. But inside things.

VS: Not many people are interested.

KM: Thank you. Thank you. I don't know. I like it. Because the inside things. You just got . . . I don't know. You are always thinking. . . . [changes the subject to thank the priest for the lunch she has prepared]

DH: Do you know the story of the origins of the Bon Odori? The disciple of Buddha dreamed his mother was in hell?

KM: Yes, yes.

DH: What do you think of that story? Do you think that story truly happened?

KM: I don't care. Like Pandora's Box.

DH: Please tell me.

KM: Like the *Urashima Taro* story in Japan, is like Aesop's story. Like Pandora, gift of a box, somebody gave like a gift. There was a fisherman one day at the beach. So then children were beating a big turtle. So then he went to the kids and said, "Don't you do that. Don't you do that!" So the same turtle came out and he talked to the fisherman and he [turtle] said, "Thank you very much, you saved my life." So he tossed it back into the water and he told his Queen of the Turtles so she said, "We'll give him a very nice present." So the turtle talked to him and said "I'm going to take you to a beautiful place," so he rode on the turtle then he enjoyed it every day, he enjoyed it dancing and everything. So the same turtle brought him back to the beach. So then he had gotten a beautiful gift. "You see it is a beautiful gift. But don't open up. If open it up you will be a hundred . . . you will die from getting old." Then he was so curious. So one day he opened up and then smoke came out and he suddenly getting old man. That like Pandora story. Yea. So I don't know my life but I don't care. I don't think about it . . . I am ninety-two! [Kiyoko laughs and passes her driver's license around the table.] So, life is marvelous. Life is marvelous. Beautiful.

NOTES

1. Allan G. Johnson, *The Blackwell Dictionary of Sociology: A User's Guide to Sociological Language* (Oxford: Wiley, 2000). Also, Émile Durkheim, *The Elementary Forms of the Religious Life, a Study in Religious Sociology* (London: George Allen & Unwin, 1915).

2. "Sacred," *Oxford Dictionary*, https://en.oxforddictionaries.com/definition/us/sacred, accessed May 20, 2016.

3. Exodus 20:12, *BibleHub, The Pulpit Commentary, Electronic Database*, http://biblehub.com/exodus/20-12.htm, accessed January 2015.

4. Angela Connolly, "Healing the Wounds of Our Fathers: Intergenerational Trauma, Memory, Symbolization and Narrative," *Journal of Analytical Psychology* 56 (2011): 607–26. Also, Judith Pickering, "Bearing the Unbearable: Ancestral Transmission through Dreams and Moving Metaphors in the Analytic Field," *Journal of Analytical Psychology* 57 (2012): 576–96.

5. Daniel Kahneman calls intuition "a position . . . between the automatic operations of perception and the deliberate operations of reasoning." Daniel Kahneman, "Maps of Bounded Rationality: A Perspective on Intuitive Judgment and Choice," Prize Lecture, December 8, 2002, Princeton University.

6. Carl Jung, *Memories, Dreams, Reflections* (New York, Pantheon Press, 1963). On the "recurring" archetype of family, see Carl Jung, "The Structure and Dynamic of the Psyche," in *The Collected Works of Carl Jung*, Volume 8 (Princeton, NJ: Princeton University Press, 1996), 156–57.

7. Rabbi Benjamin Kook, cited in *Modern Jewish Thought: A Source Reader*, ed. Nahum N. Glatzer (New York: Schocken Books, 1977), 71.

3

WHO ARE YOUR ANCESTORS?

Culturally defined and personally refined, the term *ancestors* is remarkably flexible, relatively constructed to adapt to circumstances, experiences, and traditions. There is no single, complete definition of *ancestry* shared by all or even by a majority of interviewees, as there is a great variety of ways interviewees explain both the forms and functions of their ancestors. Interviewees describe "ancestors" and "ancestry" in diverse genetic, cultural, spiritual, local, national, and universal compositions. Most interviewees describe ancestry as beginning with genealogy—parents and grandparents—but in nearly every conversation, interviewees go on to expand definitions to incorporate cultural, intellectual, and familial groups, with some advancing ancestry to include all humanity, the universe, and spiritual realms.

Some interviewees identify their ancestors by tribal communities, such as "Cheyenne" or "Choctaw," others national or cultural groups, such as "Acadian," "German," or "Vietnamese." Some claim for their ancestors all those people from the past sharing a family name, such as the name Park, and still others describe as ancestors mentors and political predecessors as much as genetic grandparents. Several interviewees name animals, plants, and other forms of life as ancestors, while other interviewees insist that could not be possible.

How far back in time and how laterally distant to cousins interviewees shape their ancestries is also variable and contingent on multiple factors. Many interviewees construct ancestries such that they might be divided into two sets, *cultural ancestors* and *genetic ancestors*, which unavoidably overlap. A close relationship in life might foretell a close relationship to ancestors after life, though some interviewees offer no concessions to an afterlife. Despite these many differences, there are important elements to the descriptions of ancestry shared by all or nearly all interviewees.

Interviewees generally use "ancestors" and "ancestries" as both collective and personal. Ancestries are fluid, flexible, and contingent on culture, environment, and other circumstances. Every interviewee includes as part of his or her ancestry people who married into, were adopted into, or who assumed the family or tribal name of the ancestral community, regardless of lineage. All interviewees count among ancestors uncles, aunts, and cousins, including those who did not have children. All interviewees think of ancestors as essential to their identities, and most interviewees describe ongoing, progressive relationships with their ancestors, sustained along spiritual, ritualistic, or cultural pathways.

In discussing his ancestors, interviewee Peter Grant distinguishes between "relatedness" and "ancestry." Though he is ultimately related biologically to all living things, Dr. Grant's personal culture of ancestry embraces only the two or three most recent generations of descent. Dr. Grant uses *ancestry* to refer to his recent genetic genealogy and *relatedness* to refer to all those other relations, including cultural. He says, "Phylogeny goes back to the first living organism . . . but . . . talking now about ancestry I think just a couple generations back. Because that's all I know about."* Grant does not precisely define *relatedness* and *ancestry* and leaves those categories open to include subjective factors, such as definitions of *family*, which are variable.

Many interviewees describe ancestries that might be grouped into categories of genealogy, genetics, and culture, broadly paralleling Peter Grant's relatedness and ancestry. Such groupings are, however, seldom neatly discrete, as there is considerable overlap between them. But interviewees resolve discrepancies gracefully and honestly by including elements of free choice in their definitions of ancestors.

Henrietta Mann recognizes many various components to her ancestry. In her description, relatedness and ancestry are indistinguishable aspects of a universal organization of life. Dr. Mann identifies with her Cheyenne ancestry both culturally and genetically because she is genealogically descended from Cheyenne people and, at the same time, "I am one of the people hearted-alike. We have the same kind of heart, we have the same vision, we have the same view of the world." While her identity begins with being Cheyenne, Dr. Mann explains that she is in fact related not only to Cheyenne people but "to everything in this world." Her understanding expands her genealogy even beyond the sum

---

*Phylogeny is the tree of life on which all living organisms share ancestral lineages, if traced far enough.

of Professor Grant's relatedness and phylogeny. Henrietta Mann describes her relations and her ancestry like this.

> If you look at the basic elements of which all life is made: water, earth, air, fire . . . compositionally different, making us related to the planet . . . without them, where would we get our oxygen? The *tree people!* So there it is, an aspect of mutuality and reciprocity. I guess they're made of the same things you and I are made of!

The diverse parts of Dr. Mann's ancestry sustain one another towards a perpetual whole, cycles of life, creation, and ancestry united. Mann includes in her ancestry things Dr. Grant does not include, such as earth, water, fire, and air. Yet her reasoning is similar to his: all life is related, therefore all living things are relatives.

Henrietta Mann expands the concept of "related" to include natural interdependencies. Since all life depends on earth, water, fire, and air to exist, living things absorb those elements and incorporate them into their own compositions. Those elements share substance and sustain each other, and are therefore related. It is a small philosophical step to then extend ancestry to those related elements, water, fire, earth, and air. Henrietta Mann's Cheyenne ancestors' roots reach to all corners and aspects of the universe, beyond human beings, even beyond life, and it must all be honored. Cheyenne people, other people, animals, plants, air, water, and fire; they must all be respected as progenitor.

Interviewee Alexandra Senfft builds her ancestry more from her personal experience than from grand cosmologies. Favoring the cultural over the genetic, Senfft includes in her ancestry, for example, animals who she has personally known and loved. She considers those individual creatures members of her family, and therefore of her ancestry as well.

DH: Would you include animals as part of your ancestral identity?

AS: Yes . . . not on the same level [as humans] but yes animals certainly and nature you know definitely. . . . I include animals in my family concept because I've lived with them for so many years.

Not all interviewees define ancestry as inclusively as do Henrietta Mann and Alexandra Senfft. Jean Neal denies ancestral connections to animals, plants, or anything not human. "My great ancestor is God, Jesus Christ. You know, I was made in the image and likeness of God, not a pear, not an apple, not a fruit!" she emphasizes. Jean Neal might be connected to the whole of the universe through a single, divine Creator but her relationship to those nongenealogical elements is neither ancestral nor related. She could speak for other genealogically inclined interviewees when she explains,

> I don't care where you go, it's all a part of you because it [ancestry] makes up who you are. It makes up your stature, it makes up the way you're built, it makes up the way you look . . . you know, it makes a difference how your eyes are colored. But it all comes together to make who you are . . . I can look in the mirror and I can see her [Grandmother]! You know, I can see her in me because . . . I'm the only one of her children that has her birthmark. And my grandchild is the only one who has it. Do I walk around and talk to my grandmother? No, I do not. That's not the way it works . . . for me.

Though she believes her ancestors survive in a spiritual afterlife, Neal does not suppose they are in contact with her. Still, she is visually, sensually, and politically aware of her ancestors' influence. She finds her ancestors in the social spaces around her, in her body and in her mind, and she honors their lives by remembering their hard work and sacrifices. Ancestors serve her as models of good ethics and social behavior.

Interviewee David Dollahite also excludes nonhuman beings from his ancestry, even while he enthusiastically embraces humanity into a single spiritual community.

Jean Neal. Courtesy of Jean Neal.

> I would see every human being that's ever lived, no matter what tribe or race or language or whatever, as a literal spiritual brother and sister. So my family is very big in terms of that. But in terms of ancestry, yeah I'm talking about a little bit of the more literalist kind of direct line ancestors. . . . In terms of back to animals? No, I don't.

Interviewee Thomas Benjamin Hertzel says his ancestors include cultural as well as genetic predecessors. Hertzel believes his genealogical research is important because "the genealogy is important," but he also researches the lives of cultural ancestors.

> The people that matter [are] not only direct line [but also] their brothers and sisters and spouses, also their children and sometimes their grandchildren . . . there are people who are more important who impacted the family.

The "importance" of a particular ancestor to Hertzel might be measured by that ancestor's influence on the identity of the descendants or on the notoriety of the ancestor.

While all interviewees consider genetics to be an important element of ancestry, many find it awkward to explain the significance of genetic ancestry, apart from medical issues. Any deeper meaning to genealogy separated from culture seems evasive. Jean Neal includes among her ancestors adopted family members, as well as uncles and aunts, none of whom are in her direct genealogical line. Much of her devotion to and respect for her ancestors emanates from cultural legacies as much as from genetic legacies.

All interviewees, including Jean Neal, David Dollahite, and those others who construct ancestry according to strict genealogical methods, concede considerable fluidity and overlap in the definitions and compositions of genetic and cultural ancestors. Some genetic ancestors are not well remembered, many others are not remembered at all. Some cultural ancestors, on the other hand, who have no direct genetic connection to interviewees, are held in high esteem, as part of the ancestral community. Of all the interviewees, Rabbi Yaakov Kleiman is probably the strongest advocate of a strict genetic definition of ancestry, one built from DNA and historical records. But even Rabbi Kleiman, in describing the significance of genetics, drifts towards using culture to justify honoring genetic ancestors.

DH: You are also connected to a lot of other families, wouldn't you agree?

YK: Well everybody is. . . . We're all related to Alexander the Great!

DH: Sure. So how do you choose this one line to identify with, sort of in preference to the others?

YK: It's a direct parental line. Father to son from one hundred generations. The DNA, which was interested in this whole kohen thing, is so significant [to] all the things that come up, your questions about ancestry. So, one of my reactions was a very personal one, because knowing one's ancestry, especially how you define it through history, almost all the world history from the ancient Hebrews . . . three thousand years ago has become the number of years for the receiving of the Torah at Mount Sinai. We're about to celebrate, actually, tomorrow night the holiday of Shavuot . . . the holiday of the receiving of the Torah. All of the religious Jewish people will treat the day like Shavuot in no work and special prayers.

Ultimately, Kleiman argues the significance of both cultural and genetic ancestors but he builds the importance of genetics by explaining the cultural.

DH: So on the one hand you have genealogy and genetics, and on the other you have the spirituality and culture. . . . How are those groups related?

YK: Each reinforces the other, that's the beauty of it. You know, looking for holism or unity . . . the concept [that] God is one.

Culture and genetics are evidence for and fulfillment of the significance and worth of the other. Ancestral records cannot ever be "complete" and only rarely can they be completely accurate, as there will always be in family histories and documents uncertain and false testimonies and interpretations. People keep secrets, hide parents' identities or places of birth, have illicit affairs (sometimes with "outsiders") that are neither publicized nor recorded. Record-keepers and storytellers tell less than they know, and sometimes they tell more than they know. Confusion and misinformation about ancestral people come from the reality that people migrate and intermingle, and names and spellings of names change, so this results, over time, in great social and genetic fluidity and heterogeneity. A general commotion of family activity that cannot be reduced to names and dates was as prevalent in the past as it is in the present. With every passing generation, there is much information lost, changed, or forgotten.

Family has always been a complex and fluid construct. Today's perceptions of the composition of families past reflect all the complexity, secrecy, and fluidity of kinships past. Large designations of "my people" naturally exclude many, many individual ancestors who have disappeared from written records and thousands of years of evolving memories. Over time and circumstances, entire genetic lines are forgotten or expunged from family and ancestral narratives. This has always been true. There is an ongoing attrition to ancestry.

At the same time, an ancestry grows and changes through multiplication, invitation, and discovery. An ancestry also evolves through the choices of its descendants, as groups invite in members by family or by individual, through marriage, friendship, adoption, and cultural engagement. An ancestry is therefore fluid and dynamic, like any living community. It seems self-evident that ancestry commonly begins with parents and grandparents—where that knowledge is available—but as generations pass, ancestral narratives advance beyond simple direct lines. Ancestral communities are complex, and descendants choose to include individuals sometimes far removed from a group's own genealogy.

Only the broadest definitions can therefore encompass the ancestral constructions of all interviewees. Even classifying ancestral groups as "cultural" and "genetic" leaves open many questions and interpretations. "Cultural" might describe a tribal group (itself fluid and dynamic), a family name, or "fictive kin." The "genetic" ancestries of many interviewees also intersect and overlap many nongenetic predecessors, including cultural ancestors, and can even extend to all humans, prehumans, and early life forms, or rocks, the wind, the oceans, the universe, and God. But it is safe to conclude from the great variety of responses to the question, "Who are your ancestors?" that for all interviewees, "ancestors" are *predecessors with whom a descendant identifies and forms personal belief and community.* And all people are becoming ancestors.

INTERVIEW WITH SIMON JACOBSON

"Let's Start with Being Human"

SJ: My name is Simon Jacobson and I am the author of *Toward a Meaningful Life* and other popular books.* I am the dean and director of the Meaningful Life Center and the publisher of the *Algemeiner Journal,* the largest Yiddish-English newspaper.

DH: What is your first language?

SJ: Yiddish and English.†

[Discussion about languages, Yiddish and Hebrew.]

DH: Who are your ancestors?

SJ: This has a lot to do with how we see the origin of our species. You know the story about young Lucy who is beginning to study biology and she is confused. You know that one?

DH: No.

SJ: So, coming home from school one day confused by her class on biology, she asks her mother what is the origins of our species, where do we come from? With her face beaming with pride her mother tells Lucy, "Oh, your grandmother came from Poland, your grandfather from Russia; a few generations back we had a great-grandfather that was a great scholar, wrote important books on Torah law. The farther back in history we go, the better our pedigree gets, we're direct descendants all the way back to Abraham, Isaac, and Jacob, all the way to Adam and Eve in the Garden of Eden."

When Lucy's father comes home, she asks him the same question, "Where do we originate from?" In stark contrast to his wife, Lucy's father gets all serious. "I always rued this difficult day. Brace yourself Lucy, sit down and I will tell you. First we originated from apes and before that, from amphibians and prior to that bacteria, and

---

*Simon Jacobson and Menachem Mendel Schneerson, *Toward a Meaningful Life: The Wisdom of the Rebbe* (New York: William Morrow, 1995).

†Yiddish is an Eastern European Jewish language, based on German, with some Hebrew and local vernacular words. It is written in both Hebrew and Roman lettering. In modern times, it is diminishing as a living language.

Simon Jacobson. Courtesy of Simon Jacobson.

as far back as we can go, a few billion years ago, we evolved from a ball of gas!" Lucy, of course, is now more confused than ever, so she runs back to her mother and asks her, "You told me one thing, Dad told me something altogether different!" Her mother calmly replied: "We both told you the truth: Your father told you about his side of the family and I told you about my side of the family."

This is a Jewish joke, one that perhaps resolves the debate once and for all between creationism and evolution.

When you asked me who are my ancestors, this joke came to mind. But on a serious note, from a Jewish-Torah perspective, we all trace our roots in a direct line to Adam and Eve.* The Bible documents the names of fathers, sons, mothers, daughters, who are our direct ancestors. Obviously, not that everyone can retrace their complete lineage generation by generation, but nevertheless in general terms we all trace our direct ancestry to the humans that lived before us.

Jewish priests, kohanim, trace their lineage to Aaron and to the tribe of Levi. Every Jew originates from one of the twelve different tribes. Most Jews today originate either from the tribe of Judah or the tribe of Benjamin.† Now, some individuals actually have a documented pedigree (called a *shtar yichus*‡), which traces their lineage from generation

---

*The Torah is the law God revealed to Moses.

†Aaron was the first high priest of the Jewish people, and his descendants are known as cohens (kohen, plural is kohanim), or priests. Both Aaron and Moses were from the tribe of Levi; Levites are members of this tribe, and had the role of assisting the priests in their duties. Priests and Levites continue to hold an honored status in the Jewish world.

‡*Shtar yichus* is an official document that functions as a genealogy chart, showing one's descent from a particular tribe or ancestry, that is, documentation to prove a part of their ancestry.

to generation, from parent to child, going back to the beginning of time. But most of us do not have that distinct family tree. Nevertheless we all can trace our general lineage to the original tribes, with a general sense of the generations that have passed from then till now. For instance, we know that we are around ninety generations from the time of Moses. And Moses back to Adam and Eve are another twenty-six generations. So basically according to Jewish biblical history, the span of human history is around one hundred and twenty generations.

DH: Who then in your mind are your ancestors?

SJ: It's not just in my mind; it's based on universally accepted criteria on how we determine our ancestry, which includes a combination of observation, testimony, family, friends, data, and historical documents, among other factors.

I obviously have my biological parents, Gershon and Sylvia Jacobson, who in turn are children of their respective parents, going back generation to generation. I am Jewish by birth, born to a Jewish mother and father, who in turn were born to their Jewish parents. Judaism traces its lineage, as we discussed earlier, back to the twelve tribes, and to the biblical patriarchs and matriarchs. These are the facts about my ancestry based on commonly accepted empirical evidence.

Lineage and ancestry is a crucial component in Judaism. Indeed, many wonder what is the secret to Jewish continuity—how did Jews continue to survive, while far greater populations, civilizations, empires, and cultures disappeared, without leaving descendants and family lines that can trace their lineage to their ancestors? One of the obvious explanations for this is Judaism's very strict laws around the sanctity, fidelity, and integrity of marriage and parenting, with tremendous focus on "family purity" (the laws surrounding the sanctity of sexuality within the sacred union called marriage). These meticulous laws, coupled with the extraordinary emphasis on family in all Jewish traditions and holidays, which were rigorously followed by Jews throughout the ages, helped preserve strong family lines and helped assure that the lineage remain intact. It's also interesting to note that one's Jewishness is determined by one's mother being Jewish. Because since a child is carried and borne by its mother, a mother's lineage is almost impossible to deny.

Obviously, there are aberrations due to infidelity and other causes, which can cast doubts on one's lineage, but these are exceptions. Generally speaking, lineage can be trusted in Judaism. And unless proven otherwise, I have to trust that my parents gave birth to me.

So my perspective is that, yes we have a pretty clear picture of generations. There may be some gaps here and there but I can more or less trace it to the tribe of probably Judah, in biblical times. This is based on grandparents' testimonies, documentation, and other things.

DH: Just staying with the question about parameters and definitions, would you consider great-uncles and great-aunts part of your ancestry?

SJ: Yes. In truth, every family ancestry tree broadens out the further back we go generationally. At the end of the day, the entire human race can trace its ancestry to one common father and mother, Adam and Eve. We're all part of the same family. I'm probably related to you somewhere back a few centuries. So, the question is how far back do you want to go?

Are you asking me about my uncles and aunts on a personal level?

DH: Yes, yes.

SJ: It's a subjective question. I have quite a large extended family. My mother is the oldest of nine children. My father was the oldest of three children. So I have a number of uncles and aunts, and great-uncles and -aunts. I have many cousins—probably close to two hundred first cousins, and of course, many more second cousins. Naturally, I know the older ones (closer to my age) better than I do the younger ones. That's a circumstantial factor. So you're asking me who I know? They're all my relatives. They're all my blood relatives. What are you trying to ask me? Depending how you define family would determine who is included in my extended family. Do you consider your uncles part of your family? What would you say?

DH: My answer would be yes, but now there are two groups in your ancestry.

SJ: I saw it all as one to be honest. It's a family tree. It's a tree. A tree goes like this. You have father and mother, siblings, and then your extended family. You go back a generation and you have grandparents, you have four grandparents. So as you go back in generations, the tree widens. Thus my answer: of course all branches are all part of one expansive tree. A complete picture of one's ancestry would require building out the family tree. GENI is a popular online site where you can build out your family tree, and connect it with many other family trees. We actually built one for our family, and it includes literally thousands of different scions. I was involved in building it originally. It's a pretty big family tree, and I was able to successfully trace many of our family lines, and many of my cousins added stuff. So, it's like a tree. Exactly like a tree. And it all comes back to one trunk. So in the broadest possible sense, my answer I would say is that the whole flow of the human race is ultimately connected. I—and you, and all people—have the collective genes of thousands of people.

DH: And do you think of all those people as your ancestors? Or just the ones you could trace back to the tribe?

SJ: Obviously we would need to distinguish between immediate family, and extended family and extended extended family. First come my immediate parents and my siblings, with whom I share and can identify common features and personality. These are my closest family. My cousins and second cousins, uncles and aunts are one step away. That's how I think about in qualified terms. The farther away you go from your immediate ancestry, the less you really can identify patterns. But overall I feel I'm a citizen of the human race, and I'm a citizen of the Jewish people. And I'm a citizen of a certain tribe and of a certain family line, until I get to my immediate family line. I think of all that as my ancestry. It's all part of the picture. I can't say I see one and not the other.

DH: Do you have a philosophical concept of ancestry?

SJ: I have a philosophical and psychological interpretation of ancestry. Let's start with the human. First of all, I am a human being. I see myself as distinctly human as opposed to being, say, from the "animal" or "vegetable" species. I see a psychological and philosophical distinction between being human and being from other living species, including animal, plants, and mineral.

DH: Some interviewees say animals are their ancestors; in that we share DNA with animals. Others say God created animals as part of the same community. It sounds like you want to be clear from that.

SJ: I go with the biblical approach. The Bible explicitly states that the human was created distinct and uniquely different than the animals of the earth. The Bible describes the human being as being created in the divine image.

Now, common science today—and most people will say—that humans just evolved from animals. All life is seen as stemming from one common ancestor. Humans first originated from apes, they evolved from other species, and so on. I've chosen to not go by that theory; I'm not getting into my scientific reasons for that but suffice it to say, as you're asking my opinion: I see human beings as unique. Unique in having free will and in their capacity to make moral choices. Unique in their spiritual and transcendent dimension. Unique as well in their ability to control the world around them. For example, animals don't subdue humans; humans subdue animals. Even though they may be more powerful than us, we have the power to subjugate them and even, sadly, to hunt them down and make them extinct. We've developed through our intelligence all sorts of ways to tame the elements and create habitable homes for ourselves in what was once a hostile wilderness. Some people argue that intelligence is a quirk and some say it's fundamental to the human being. Being that I chose to believe that the human is uniquely created with superior intelligence, I clearly take the latter position. And this is a choice I made long ago, though I understand both arguments—I made a choice! It's a moral choice, a spiritual choice, if you wish. And it goes like this: I expect from myself and others the highest expectations. We're not just egocentric beasts, as in Freud's id, that have evolved and therefore our ruling force is only survival of the fittest, and we just follow our own whims and temptations, et cetera, et cetera, but since we need to coexist we have superimposed rules, red lights and green lights, to keep us in line. Rather, I've chosen to embrace a different approach: that human beings are fundamentally divine creatures. Thus, [they] have a very particular responsibility and role in this world. And as such, we have, yes, a unique lineage.

DH: Is there anything particularly divine or more divine about the people who preceded you? Do you think of them in that way?

SJ: I think there is something common in us all. All human beings have the ability to refine themselves and refine the world around them and in that sense there is a divine element in all of us. A spiritual element. . . . Being I didn't live back then, I can't tell you what life was like then. But I can answer based on what is written. The Talmud and other sources tell us that earlier generations were on a higher spiritual plane than us, as well as more innocent.* On the other hand, in some ways we have more spirituality today than they did, because spiritual strength is accumulative and we are like midgets that stand on the soldiers of the giants before us. We also have the power to both build and destroy in unprecedented ways. Technology can turn you into a monster or into an angel; things our ancestors were not able to do. In the past, no one was able to press a button and destroy the world, or press a button and transform the world. Based on this, I can say we have more opportunities and more challenges. That's how I would define it.

DH: Rabbi Kook wrote that all things, all creatures long for the origins of their being. He refers to people who pursue God as their origin.

SJ: And what do animals pursue?

DH: I don't know. But I wonder if people's interest in ancestry is part of that longing for origin?

SJ: I know no studies that show that animals, vegetables, and minerals pursue their origins as we do. Many creatures certainly return to their place of birth, as spawning salmon do. But none seek out their ancestors, their grandparents! I don't think you're going to find much evidence that elephants in the wild, for example, are looking for their great-grandparents. However, I will say the following: They do pursue the genetic behavior passed on to them. Which means they will perpetuate the nature and "legacy" of their great-grandparents. Maybe as humans we need to seek it out because we can waver for our roots. Animals will never waver from their role. So in a way, this "seeking out of our roots" is almost like a checks and balances, so we don't wander away too much from our calling!

DH: How would seeking out our roots do that?

SJ: When I was in high school we always used to ask our history teacher, "Why do we study history?" And he never had an adequate answer. And therefore it was a pretty boring study. But then later in life I realized we study history because we want to understand ourselves and when you see yourself in different contexts, you see the march of human progress, you see that man invented the wheel, the numbers, the sciences. So our roots allow us to understand ourselves and our future better. Studying that which came before us helps us be more objective about ourselves. Most people live their lives with a myopic perspective which only relates to the here and now. "What do I need right now? I'm hungry, I'm thirsty, I need to satisfy my immediate needs." But when you look at history, you look back at your roots and ancestry, your perspectives broaden and you

---

*Talmud is the body of Jewish law.

realize that, "Okay, my grandparents, they had similar aspirations to me, but they didn't have the same opportunities." I think wisdom is based on a cumulative knowledge. Ancestry helps you connect and continue that which came before you. Using the expression I mentioned earlier—Newton coined it but it originates in Jewish books earlier—"A midget that stands on the shoulders of giants." And that's an expression in Jewish books that we're like links in a chain. That's lineage. That's ancestry.

DH: What is at the end of that chain?

SJ: The beginning or the end?

DH: The beginning.

SJ: The biblical beginning is Adam and Eve in the Garden of Eden.

DH: Would the beginning be Adam and Eve or the Creator who . . .

SJ: Yes, the beginning would be the Creator who put all things in place, the architect so to speak.

DH: So in a sense the searching for ancestry could be or maybe is a religious experience.

SJ: It could be phrased that way. Looking for our real selves. Who is the real you? I would say that's a good way to put it. But it doesn't have to be. Personally, I look to my ancestry for two reasons: Firstly, on a basic personal level—to see my true self in the true context of things. Looking at my ancestors makes me wonder, "What would I look like if I lived then? And what would they look like if they lived now?" Ancestry is about connection: how did I get here? Stepping back in history is like suddenly finding yourself somewhere new, you have no idea where you are, what would be your first step? And how did I get here? Ancestry is almost like existential coordinates that help us find our bearings. In a sense, a spiritual GPS. Trying to find, "Where am I?" I'm here in New York. When I look at where my father came from, okay that's where I came from. Where did his father come from? Where did his mother come from?

Additionally, there is definitely a spiritual/religious side to ancestry, which begs the question: Where does it all come from? How did we get here? And who are we really, what is my true identity?

Looking back at my ancestry today has taken on another dimension. I see it also very much like a reflection of my own life. I am playing out what has been played out before me. A link in a chain. I have little grandchildren today. And I look at them as I say "I was once a baby like that" . . . but I don't remember myself. . . . Past generations? I can't even figure out my own history! We have an entire history of our first two or three years, which we have no memory of at all! And those formative years have shaped you completely. That is you! That's in a way the purest you, before you became jaded, before you became polluted, before you assumed attitudes of your parents and of your society. So I sometimes see, this search in history for the first humans so to speak, as being a search for my own childhood, my own lifetime, my own innocence. That's how I see it.

DH: This would possibly also be a religious or mystical experience.

SJ: For me it is mystical because I am a spiritual person. So for me, I'm not satisfied with an existential perspective on life, which is just surviving. And doing the best with what I have. I do see myself as a spiritual creature, as they say, "a spiritual creature on a physical journey, not a physical creature on a spiritual journey." You know, a soul that has entered this existence. I relate more to the soul than to the world of the body. So to me, when you ask, "Where does the soul go upon death?" my answer would be like a refrigerator asking electricity, "Where do you go when they pull the plug?" A little box called the material world can't really understand electricity and its unconfined space. So to me, reality is the soul reality. And in this material world we have a little glimpse through our eyes of one little part of the journey. We only have a limited view of the time and space we presently occupy in our lifetimes. We're on a certain section of a long spiral plane called "time," with the past behind us, the future ahead of us, and we occupy this little space in time that we travel through our lives, but there's a whole bigger picture that we really can't see.

That's my take on history. So therefore, the souls that were here before, the lives that were here before for me it's a very spiritual experience; it's all about understanding ourselves in the scheme of the big picture. It's like the pieces of a puzzle.

DH: Have you or your soul lived before in other bodies?

SJ: I don't feel it but I am sure of it. It makes sense to me.

DH: If it had, do you think it likely to have been in the bodies of ancestors?

SJ: We can't surmise this with pure logic. But I have some Jewish books on reincarnation and they describe different scenarios: some of our ancestors reincarnate in us and some do not. There's no rule. Reincarnation does not have to be a soul from your own previous family. Sometimes it is. I carry the name of my father's father who I never knew. I would love to have met him. But Jewish mysticism teaches that a name carries power. Maybe I have some of his genes, his soul.

DH: Did that influence the naming of you or did the naming of you influence that?

SJ: As his oldest child my father honored his father by naming me after his father.

DH: Is there power in the utterance of the name?

SJ: Rabbi Isaac Luria, the great mystic of the sixteenth century, says that the naming of a child is like a mini-prophecy which the parents receive, like a mini-revelation of knowing what name to give your child. It's a spiritual connection. Jewish mysticism elaborates on the spiritual power of a name.

DH: Some people misname their children too I think!

SJ: Yes, you could misname. Take "A Boy named Sue"!*

---

*"A Boy Named Sue" is a Johnny Cash song that tells the story of a father who gave his son the girl's name "Sue" in order to force the boy to defend himself in a tough world.

DH: If the soul survives the body, are the souls of your ancestors still around even after their passing?

SJ: Yes, they're hovering around.

DH: Do you have any relationship today to those people in that sense?

SJ: Yes, but not in a mumbo-jumbo way. Our souls are connected with the souls of our ancestors. They pray and empower us. Our holy books tell us that during wedding ceremonies, the souls of your grandparents and great-grandparents are present. When we are in a soulful place, we can maybe sense the souls of our ancestors. I'm not going to say I sense souls wherever I go. But I believe that though my father passed away seven years ago from time to time I feel like his soul has entered into me in some ways. I feel like he's part of me. But it's not as tangible as a séance where people claim they can speak to a soul that enters their living room.

DH: Some have said [such things].

SJ: Yes, but you're asking me . . . [laughter].

DH: But are you discounting these things? A woman has a dream and her father comes to her . . .

SJ: No, but sometimes people are delusional; they want to believe things. Let's take for example our conversation right now. Who am I speaking to, your body or your soul? If you and I were dead corpses, we wouldn't be speaking to each other. So even in a simple conversation between two living people the matter is not so simple. I like to believe that I talk to people's souls, not just their bodies. However, we do live in a materialistic world, and many interactions between people are body to body, not soul to soul. Take business as an example. When you're doing business with someone, the interaction is about each party feeling that they are gaining something from the relationship. People want something from you. They don't really care about your soul, they want something from you. But we also can speak soulfully with one another. People love each other and care about each other. They have soulful conversations. So you and I could have a conversation that would be purely transactional. You want a loaf of bread, give me a dollar I'll give you bread, goodbye. Nothing soulful about that. But then we could have a conversation that's very personal. So then our souls are communicating, not just our bodies. Now, with people who are physically not here, obviously you can't communicate with conventional words because they don't speak like we do. Yet there are other soulful ways to connect with them. I know they're on the other side of the curtain, they can hear me but I can't hear them.

DH: Did you ever have a dream where [an ancestor] comes to speak to you?

SJ: It's never happened to me. And if it did, I would probably dismiss it. Because a dream can be interpreted in both ways. It can be nonsense or it can mean something. Even when you study mysticism, life is mysterious enough in our conscious lives and waking hours, let alone in our dreams. So I don't probe places that I'm not sure I can figure out. Now, if it was a dream I had consistently, I would not discount that. But if I had one random dream? No. I have dreams, all kinds of dreams, we have all kinds of dreams. I don't really dwell on interpreting dreams, people come to me to interpret dreams sometimes. I try to help them be responsible in their waking hours. And usually dreams follow along. I'm skeptical of people who turn to their dreams when they don't have their lives figured out; it appears to me like a little escapism.

DH: People do have stories about visits from the other side and it is almost always an ancestor who visits. Would you say that is important?

SJ: There's a Talmudic statement that says people dream about by night what they think about by day. Even when we may be dreaming about something unrelated, often things you dwelled upon that day will pop up in the dream. If you thought about somebody, often they'll appear in a dream. So one could argue scientifically that the reason genealogical people appear in our dreams is because that's the people we're aware of and familiar with. I don't think about your grandfather and you don't think about mine, so it's more likely that my grandfather will appear in my dream than in yours.

The Kabbalistic works discuss dreams and one of the criteria in determining the seriousness of the dream is a repetitive dream, as in the biblical dreams of Pharaoh that were repeated twice. If a dream happens once, you can't really know if it's significant or not. The Talmud also says every dream has nonsense and every dream has some revelation. The problem is, that it's all snowballed into one and you can't tell what's what. When it comes to dreams about ancestors, it's hard to determine if the dream is significant. I don't recall seeing in any mystical sources that the people appearing in your dreams are more likely to be blood relatives or ancestors. If it's a particularly weird dream, say where a particular ancestor comes to you saying, "I'm your great-great-grandfather," telling you something unique and specific, I would look at that closer. If that dream was repeated, it may contain a relevant message. In all such mysterious matters we always have to be particularly careful and humble, because the mind can play all kinds of tricks on us in the areas that are beyond our consciousness. We must also avoid the sensationalism that is often associated with exotica. Though Judaism contains many mystical teachings, we're also prudent and cautious not trying to overstep our boundaries.

DH: Is there anything particularly sacred about an ancestral relationship?

SJ: Absolutely! . . . First, let's begin with the Bible. A common staple in the Bible is its repeated references to people's lineage and pedigree: "This one is the son of this one." Establishing ancestral roots is a blessing. When the Bible refers to someone with his parental name (this is the son of Levi, this is the son of Jacob), it is emphasizing that this person has good pedigree, which is a virtue.

Now there are no guarantees. Just because you're the grandson of a distinguished person doesn't mean that you too will be distinguished. Korah, for example, foresaw that one of his descendants would achieve something great.* So he thought he was the one that has to earn the right. Ancestry plays a positive role in many stories. And it can also be misinterpreted as well.

Ancestry also plays a role in identifying an appropriate mate—people want to marry someone who has good pedigree. And some will see it as an insult if you suggest to them somebody who does not have good lineage. . . .

One more point: The Talmud says that one of the hallmarks of Messianic times is that Elijah the Prophet will clarify people's ancestry, who belongs to which tree, something that has become confused over the years.

DH: Is ancestry a reflection of the nature of God?

SJ: In a way losing your ancestry is almost like losing your bearings. Not completely, but close. One of the great historical travesties perpetrated by anti-Semites against the Jewish people was to desecrate their gravesites. They didn't want to just kill Jews. They wanted to obliterate their memories, their roots, their ancestry. Look at what the Nazis did—they tried to destroy not just Jewish lives but even the Jewish bodies, cremating them to leave no remains. Six million Jews murdered who don't even have a marker to remember them. And for Jews—the *Yizkor* is one of the biggest prayers in Judaism. *Yizkor* means "to remember." It's about remembering and declaring the names of our parents.†

DH: Is desecrating graves of another people a cultural insult, or an authentic spiritual insult?

SJ: Both. But above all, a real, spiritual insult. It would be like someone taking away your name. I'm going to destroy your past, I don't even want you to know who your father and mother were.

DH: You might be angry for generations.

SJ: That's one of the most abusive things you can do to a person. You can conquer another country but why would you want to destroy their memories? Memory is sacred. That is why we have Jewish rituals that are all about memory. We remember the exodus from Egypt. We're constantly remembering that which came before us. Memory is considered to be holy and forgetting is considered to be a desecration.

DH: How much of ancestral memory comes from myth?

SJ: For Jews none of it is myth. We feel closely connected to personalities that lived thousands of years ago, and we call them our fathers and mothers. We read, study, and

---

Korach is the story of Korah, who was a relative of Moses. Korah tried to seize the high priesthood and was killed by God in a supernatural event. The story is found in Numbers 16.

†*Yizkor* is a prayer to remember and honor loved ones who have died. It is recited four times a year, once during Passover, once during the holiday of Weeks, once on the last day of the Sukkot holiday, and then on Yom Kippur (the Day of Atonement). The Yizkor can be recited on behalf of any deceased relatives or friends.

discuss their lives and the lessons they offer us today. We know where they lived, where they walked, and we can follow their footsteps. And we remember them—we celebrate and commemorate their lives and legacies.

My father died seven years ago. Following his passing, one of the things I did was—in a sense to immortalize him—I continued the newspaper he founded and published; I did things in his honor. Every year we organize a lecture and event in his honor. You find a disproportionate amount of hospitals with Jewish names because one of the ways Jews traditionally immortalize a soul that has passed on is by building something in the name of the deceased. That concept spawned the idea of building a university or a library in the name and honor of a loved one.

DH: Does it benefit the soul of the person?

SJ: Yes, it benefits them. The cause or building honoring a departed soul is a living memorial; it's a way of giving that soul arms and legs of a different sort. When you and I do something in honor of our parents we become their arms and legs and continue their legacy. I don't know if your parents are alive or not . . . but my father, I loved him dearly—obviously if one had a difficult childhood and difficult parents, it may be a different story—[but] if your father has done something beautiful, one of the greatest ways you can honor him is to continue some of his efforts, his legacy. That's considered a great blessing for the soul. That's why we say kaddish for the departed parent.* Jews have many ways to remember and immortalize the soul of someone who's passed on.

DH: Can it benefit that soul?

SJ: Absolutely! That soul is elevated in the process.

DH: In what time is that soul elevated? In the present?

SJ: It's a good question. The mystics and the Talmudists agree on this: a soul continues to grow, even after death. Some of us have a custom to actually say a chapter of Psalms that corresponds to the age of a soul even after it dies. My father would have now been seventy-seven, so I would say Psalm seventy-eight. Basically, birthdays and other significant dates of the soul in its lifetime continue to have impact even after its lifetime.

DH: Is there any particular goal . . .

SJ: Connecting more to God, connecting with its source, connecting to the truth.

DH: Could you do that for a person who is not an ancestor?

SJ: Yes, but a child has a greater obligation to do it for his or her parent or grandparent. There are people for example who hire someone to say kaddish for their parents.

Kaddish is an Aramaic recitation that is included in the daily prayer book and read/recited during daily prayers. The most famous version is the "Mourners Kaddish"; a variation of this recitation is uttered by mourners in honor of deceased parents, siblings, or children.

Because they don't have time, or they don't know how to do it. But it's better to do it yourself, obviously.

DH: But it can have the same benefit?

SJ: Yes, but the healthiest approach is for the child to honor a parent. Would you hire someone to honor your parents instead of doing it yourself? [Laughing] Some people do! They send somebody to the nursing home to see their father on Father's Day because they don't have time to go themselves.

DH: How is your understanding of ancestry formed? Where does it come from?

SJ: The problem as you know when it comes to this, is that even the answer is arbitrary. It depends on how much real information we have. I'm always intrigued about stories about my grandfather, my namesake. I didn't know him. What do I really know? I know a little from my father, a little from my uncle. There's always a subjective element because of lack of information. Now, if I had a grandfather who was the most famous man in the world, I still may not know him, because I would only know what was published. So, we're dealing with subjectivity, what we call circumstantial subjectivity . . . circumstances we know very little about. We have a picture based on a very limited amount of information. What do I know about my great-grandfather? Almost nothing. I have one great-grandfather who was well known, so I have some stories about him. But they're stories, not a life! Now what do we know about George Washington? Or Hitler? Or Stalin? There are books with contradictory theories about the same guy. Because someone knew him and someone else knew him a different way!

DH: They might all be true.

SJ: Right? And some might have met him and may have a different perspective. So I'm just demonstrating that even if we're talking about people who are world famous, we still have limited knowledge about them! Ask me how much I know about myself. I don't even know that much about myself! So when we talk about "knowing" someone, I don't see how one can have an objective answer to this. There's no way that one can be objective about anything, really. Even a scientist who we can agree is objective may still have limited information. In other words, subjectivity is not only about one's prejudices, but sometimes also about one's scope of knowledge. We are objective as our perspectives and experiences allow us. An objective scientist can say, based on a specific set of data available, here are my conclusions. And if it works, it means the theory has worked!

But I see exactly what you mean. There are some people that thrive on the fantasy of their ancestors. I like to not be a fantasizer; I don't base our ancestry on fairy tales; I want my ancestral story to be based on facts. I turn to the Torah to know about our biblical ancestors. And yes, as a result, I am proud of them. I am proud of Abraham and Moses, and the other great men and women of our ancestry. I revere them. I glorify them. But obviously, this is based on what I read and study. Not my personal experience, since I didn't live in those times.

This is the basis of Jewish ancestry going back to the times of the Bible. But I understand what you are saying that we find people creating a mythological ancestry based on their imagination. Without any factual basis, one can create a fairy tale ancestry. And the farther back you go the more difficult it is to paint a complete picture.

There's a witty expression regarding the fantastic stories told about the Baal Shem Tov, the founder of the Chassidic movement: "Someone who believes all the stories about him is a fool. Someone who doesn't is an apostate, a heretic." So, there's a lot of stories told about great people that are not necessarily true. We try to sift through them to distinguish the ones with reliable sources and the ones without. But this is not the case with biblical stories, which have been passed on from parent to child by millions of people in an unbroken chain. At the same time, I recognize that over time certain stories about some greats may not have sources. In my work and life I have established my reliable sources, people I rely on, teachers who share something that's authenticated. But I know there's a whole bunch of folklore about everything, even about my own parents!

DH: Can the ancestors speak to you, whether through DNA or through ways of communicating?

SJ: I can't tell you because they haven't communicated with me. Regarding DNA—I relate to that. The DNA of those before us is passed on to us and "speaks to us" through our lives. The part about the soul speaking to us, I don't really have direct experience with that.

I mean, for example, I'm studying and teaching a text, every morning. This is from a great rebbe and mystic who lived a hundred years ago.* He is known as the Rebbe Rashab (acronym for Rabbi Sholom Dovber). I never met him. I only know him through his writings and through the students of his students. But I admire his teachings. When I read them, I feel like his soul is speaking to me. But it's through his writings. And yes I would say because I'm so immersed in these writings, one could say that he is communicating with me in some way. I may be walking down the street engrossed in thought about these teachings, and then an epiphany comes to me—that may be a way of him speaking with me. But that's because it's coming through his book. There's an expression that may interest you. The word *Anochi* is the first word of the Ten Commandments. *Anochi* is an acronym of four words that mean, "I have engraved my soul into these words." So, in Jewish thought, we believe the words of a righteous person— the words they have spoken or written, are their soul. That's how they speak to us. As opposed, say, to a dream.

DH: What about other forms of art . . .

SJ: Yes! It's the same thing, anything one creates—a book, art, music—manifests the composer's soul.

DH: So, a culture is also . . .

---

*Rebbe is a title most often used for a Hasidic rabbi, akin to "rabbi" in the larger Jewish world.

SJ: Yes, their soul is like—my soul is engraved in the product . . . any form of language, any form of art . . .

DH: Is that the most prevalent way you interact with your ancestry?

SJ: Yes, that is also the most solid way. You know it's real. I know they wrote it.

DH: You also write it. So you contribute to the . . .

SJ: I'm a writer, so yes when I really connect, I hopefully can capture the soul of the source in a language that connects . . . I'm like a bridge . . .

DH: Between what and what?

SJ: A bridge between the Rebbe Rashab—the author of these works (composed one hundred years ago)—and today's readers. In truth, it's really a bridge between generations before the Rebbe Rashab, because he distilled and bridged the teachings before him and made them available to us. In a broader sense, we are also building a bridge between the divine and the human. When we transmit these teachings to others, something I am dedicated to doing, we become a bridge between these teachings and the people we know. I see myself as a bridge between the spiritual and the secular, through my writings and teachings directed toward secular people who don't have a lot of opportunity to access many of these teachings.

DH: I take it he is not a direct ancestor of yours?

SJ: No, he's a teacher. More of a mentor. A rebbe of my rebbes.

DH: But is there a greater opportunity to perpetuate the teachings of a direct ancestor more than with a writer who is not related to you?

SJ: That's an interesting question. I don't have a grandfather who wrote anything comparable to the treatises of the Rebbe Rashab. If he was my lineage? Of course it would be closer to my heart because it also would be part of my DNA, but we also see our spiritual mentors as "parents." In one place the Bible refers to the children of Aaron as the children of Aaron and Moses. Though they were not the biological children of Moses, yet a teacher who taught someone is considered as if they gave birth to that person. So, you can have ancestry that's spiritual without biological. Biological without spiritual, or both!

DH: And this is your belief?

SJ: Absolutely! That's for sure!

DH: And the brother of the adopted "parent" also believes that?

SJ: Yes. It's Aaron's honor to know that his children were the student-children of Moses. If not, there may be jealousies [laughs] . . . but sometimes students are known to be closer to a teacher than the children of that teacher. I'm not saying that is a virtue, by the way. I'm just saying that it happens. I would like to believe that a father or a mother would put their children first. But sometimes a child has a connection to a teacher in a way that he might not have with a parent.

DH: Is there a lot of responsibility on the living to not lie about traditions, to not make up stories?

SJ: Yes. The Jews throughout history left thousands and thousands of books. We're the People of the Book. We have hundreds of thousands of volumes. You can't imagine how much was been written over the generations. Constant writing, writing, writing. So, we have tremendous amounts of information; we don't need to rely on hearsay and spooky events for documentation.

DH: Is that a documentation of the spiritual relationship between people?

SJ: Some of it is directly spiritual, some of it is just to convey what mattered to them, what they were involved with. Look, any person can write a book reflecting his life. I'm not suggesting that just looking at a book can tell the whole personality of its author, but I definitely get a nice picture of it, because this is what he spent hundreds of hours doing. You can get a picture of his mind. And what is the connection anyway? If I had a great-grandfather who sold ice cream, I'd rather know about his personality than what business he was in—what do I care what business he's in? It's superficial. I'd want to know what he was made of, what made him tick. The bonding, the connection, you want to know everything.

ADOPTION, MARRIAGE, AND ANCESTORS NEVER KNOWN

Interviewees uniformly include among their ancestors people adopted into their families. In real and in hypothetical examples, interviewees say when a person takes a family name and identity, he or she also inherits the ancestry of that family. Some interviewees think of ancestry as a spiritual group, and say that when a person goes through particularly prescribed methods of entry into a family group, he or she also undergoes a transformation and inherits a new spiritual identity, including a new ancestry. Hwang Jeong Soon (Park) says, "As long as the person gets involved in Park's genealogy, he or she is considered one of Park's members . . . the ancestors care about the person who was adopted into [a] family." Overall, there is a remarkable absence of discrimination between genetic and adopted ancestral identities.

Nineteenth-century ancestors of interviewee Stanley Fuke on occasion adopted boys in to their family when there was no male heir to continue the Fuke line. These adopted sons came from different bloodlines but carried on the Fuke name, culture, and identity. "So," Fuke points out, "the lines get a little blurry."

Interviewee Jeff Livingston agrees that adopted children share ancestry with their adopted families. Livingston says he has seen how in his own family adopted children not only become part of families, they begin to think and act like their adopted families. "I have a brother who . . . was raised by my parents and he has some of the same characteristics and family traits. Yet he has his own [genetic family]." And, while culture and environment are important in shaping any person's identity, Livingston adds, "I don't think it's all environmental."

David Dollahite reports he personally knows parents who have adopted children and have come to believe the "spiritual connection between them and their adopted child" is equal to or stronger than connections with genetic children. Dollahite advances this principle further when he asserts that people without biological children of their own nevertheless have descendants. "For me as a person, blood ancestry is obviously very important but there is a spiritual idea of being adopted into Abraham's family," a spiritual community.

People who marry into a family to become aunts and uncles to an interviewee were also universally described as ancestors. Genealogist Glenda Mattoon considers as ancestors all those who married into her family, including the second or third wives of ancestral grandfathers. Mattoon welcomes the married-in grandmothers along with her genetic grandmothers. The family's historical composition is reflected in the modern composition of the ancestry. "[An] ancestor," says Mattoon, "is anyone who is connected to anyone who is connected to me." Unusually succinct and direct though it is, Mattoon's definition is also flexible enough to incorporate the many ways in which people are "connected."

No descended group can identify specifically every one of its ancestors. But even when names are lost, individuals are remembered under broad headings like tribal or family names. When Henrietta Mann says "my ancestors are the Cheyenne people," she includes in her ancestry large numbers of people whose names and faces are long forgotten but who share in a communal identity of "Cheyenne." In this way, a forgotten individual is never forgotten; he and she are honored as collective ancestors, and as contributors to a tribal identity.

Interviewee Muatasem Ubeidat relates that his ancestry reportedly began with three brothers who came out of the desert of Arabia (currently Saudi Arabia) ten or more generations ago. Between the emergence of the three brothers and Muatasem's generation, there are multitudes who are included in the family narrative without being personally identified. And though their names are lost, they live on in the family consciousness and narrative as

Dr. Muatasem Ubeidat. Courtesy of Muatasem Ubeidat.

part of a greater Ubeidat identity. An association with a broad family group ensures that all from those ten generations hold identities within the ancestry and a place in the continuing ancestral story.

Yaakov Kleiman explains that in his own narrative, ancestors whose names are forgotten are incorporated in the ancestral community through groupings such as "Jew," "child of Abraham," or a family name. "The whole Jewish tradition," says Kleiman, "is based on ancestry and the continuation of an unbroken chain," which incorporates large numbers of ancestors through cultural, religious, and genetic lines of descent.

> People convert in and marry in, but the concept is that we are children of Abraham, Isaac, and Jacob and somehow the Twelve Tribes and so that's ancestry. It doesn't mean every Jew necessarily goes all the way back, because once someone converts in, and their children and their descendants, it's all a part of the nation, and in general called the *children of Israel* whether it's necessarily genealogically or whether it's considered conversion. Once they are let in, they are part of the children.

No individual is lost in such an inclusive, collectively formed identity. Those who were part of the group of the past are still implied today. Differences and political identities that might have divided communities of the past become largely forgotten, blending ancestors into inclusive integrated communities.

INTERVIEW WITH YAAKOV KLEIMAN

"Past Is Prologue"

DH: Mr. Kleiman?

YK: Yes Rabbi Kleiman. Hi how are you doing?

[General introductions and conversation.]

DH: Can you tell me who are your ancestors?

YK: My ancestors go back to eastern Europe. [And] on my father's side I have an ancestry that goes back some three thousand years. As a kohen of the ancient Hebrews.

DH: Can you explain the word *kohen*?

YK: Kohen is translated as *priest*. So, in Jewish teaching in the Bible and the Torah, the kohen is one particular family of one of the tribes, the tribe of Levi. This family of

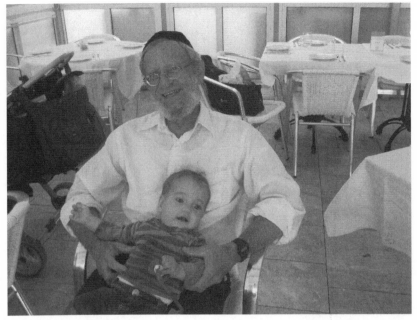

Rabbi Yaakov Kleiman with his newest grandson. Courtesy of Yaakov Kleiman.

the tribe of Levi is from the founder of this dynasty, the kohanim, of Jewish priests. It's Aaron, the brother of Moses.

DH: Do you belong to this family?

YK: Well, the Torah tells us that the sons of Aaron will be the kohanim. These priests will serve in the temple and have certain official jobs to do. They deliver a blessing to the people as part of the prayer service. That's one thing that's continued the whole stretch of three thousand years from the time of Mount Sinai receiving the Torah. That blessing was commanded to the children of Aaron to give to the people daily even though we don't have a temple since two thousand years, a lot of the work of the kohen had to do with the temple service, but the blessing doesn't need the temple. So in every synagogue throughout the world, the kohanim are still doing their job that was dictated some three thousand years ago from the Bible.

DH: From their ancestor?

YK: Connected to that. . . . So how do I know that? Well my father was a kohen. I remember my Bar Mitzvah, all my uncles were there, and we were all kohanim from my father's side, that's certain . . . and I remember that as sort of a click alighted in my . . . adolescence . . . sort of a reminder and a proof as it were that we are connected to this priestly family of the Jewish people.

Yaakov Kleiman Explains *Bar Mitzvah*

The Bar Mitzvah is when you are coming of age into Jewish manhood and you are looking to fulfill all of the commandments of the Torah, not just as a student and a learner but now as a man, as an equal and you accept full responsibility for your choices and behavior.

DH: You're also connected to a lot of other families, wouldn't you agree?

YK: Well everybody is. . . . We're all related to Alexander the Great somehow.

DH: Sure. So how do you choose this one line to identify with, sort of in preference over the other?

YK: It's a direct parental line. Father to son from a hundred generations. The DNA . . . all those things that come up, your questions about ancestry [are] very personal . . . because knowing one's ancestry, especially how you define it through so much history, all the world history, from the ancient Hebrews . . . three thousand three hundred years ago has become the number of years for the receiving of the Torah at Mount Sinai, which we're about to celebrate, actually, tomorrow night at the holiday of Shavuot . . . the holiday of the receiving of the Torah. All of the religious Jewish people will treat the day like Shavuot in no work and special prayers.

DH: When you think of your ancestry or ancestors, are you thinking of individual people with names or are you thinking of it as a cultural group or an ethnic group or some different type of identity?

YK: We are believers in the Torah. We can talk about the specific names that Aaron, brother of Moses, was appointed to be the first high priest and his descendants are this branch known as the kohen—the kohanim.

DH: Do these individuals . . . hold specific significance in your life or in your consciousness?

YK: Yes, yes.

DH: How?

YK: Because a lot of the teachings of the Torah and the written law and the oral traditions that goes with it are so rich, that they make personalities of living beings with spiritual and intellectual influence. The whole Jewish tradition is based on ancestry and continuation of an unbroken chain, not only of culture and religion, but of genetics to a large degree. Even though Judaism is universal, people can convert in and marry in, but the concept is that we are the children of Abraham, Isaac, and Jacob and somehow the twelve tribes; so that's ancestry. It doesn't mean every Jew necessarily goes all the way back, because some convert in, and their children and their descendants . . . it's all a part of the nation, and in general called *the children of Israel* whether it's necessarily genealogically or whether it's conversion, once they are let in, they are part of the children. The teaching is that actually their soul changes and becomes a different identity.

DH: Do you understand their souls as being still alive?

YK: Oh definitely. A soul is part—it's what keeps us upright. You have a corpse and you have a being. The soul animates the flesh. A human being who is alive has a soul and a body is alive. After one passes, we drop the physical body but the soul continues to exist.

DH: Is there communication between you and those living souls?

YK: Only, you know, you see one's dreams . . . when one's physical input is much less so that the mind can wander as it were . . . our teachings of the kabbalah. . . . It has a more universal aspect and it has a higher, holier aspect so parts of the soul . . . often go to the world of souls and in dreams perhaps. In that state you can sometimes learn information and that's part of what dreams are. Dreams are complicated, but one aspect of them is some level of alluding to . . . communicate.

DH: So does it happen that you might be visited by an ancestor in your dreams?

YK: There are stories, but it's a very rare thing. I don't think in our days you see that too much. But certainly in our tradition there's Elijah the Prophet who comes to people who are worthy with certain information that the world needs or something like that.

DH: You've appealed several times to written law and to "our teaching" and those kinds of things. Have you gained your understanding of the nature of your ancestors from specific teaching or have you also gained it from personal experience?

YK: Well . . . I think it's both. Once you know your identity, that's one of the beauties I think of knowing if one's a kohen or [one of the other families] . . . you put out there where are you from? Where did you immigrate from? Spanish culture or Russian culture? These are important connections to our identity. I wasn't born into a religious home and my Judaism was very weak as I was growing up and then I kicked it off pretty much completely while in college and Master's and I travelled and when I was travelling I had certain identity questions. You know, who am I really? Who am I? I'm American, I'm human . . . and then the "Jewish" came up, especially when I travelled in Morocco and sort of had a spiritual awakening or something like that and what came out was . . . an identity that my soul was more significant than my body and the soul was saying, "You're connected to the Jewish people. You're connected!" So I made my way to Israel, so it was a very personal identity crisis I had, and . . . some . . . answer to the identity crisis. Having that epiphany or whatever, something . . . something significant. I came to Israel after that, I spent a year in Europe. But this all led me to coming to Israel, saying, "Okay, you know, I've travelled a while and now I'd like to deal with the question, 'What is a Jew?'"

DH: And do you feel like your ancestors led you to this epiphany?

77

YK: No, no. They're hoping you'll connect, you know, I have a feeling that certain forces . . . I don't know . . . are rooting for you.

DH: [Laughing] I like that.

YK: It's called *Zechut avot*—the merit of your ancestors—*Zechut avot*, and it says a person down the chain . . . can access that, and helps him. . . . But I think to me it was an intellectual journey and a spiritual journey. It wasn't like I was somehow driven or fated to, but I was curious, something woke up in me in my college time and you know, a young adult, I took to travelling and it seemed to be almost a logical conclusion. . . . I say I was looking for truth . . . and I'll keep looking, you know, but I think I found something that seemed to answer most of the questions of what's real, what's true.

DH: And a lot of that seems to center on your ancestry, as part of your identity from what you're saying.

YK: Well, it started with Jewish. And the kohen thing. If I'm part of this nation now I realize that I've got an exalted role here. This is a high-level thing, it's an honor that I think, what can I say, that helped me [work through] some of the questions . . .

DH: Well, now, in experiencing this change . . . would you say that you're contributing to kind of the story or the narrative of your ancestry?

YK: Oh, absolutely.

DH: In what way do you contribute?

YK: Well it's like a chain, and every link in the chain—DNA research backs this up—we have a hundred generations from the time of the founding of the lineage down to the present and every generation is like a link in the chain, you know, father, son, father, son . . . but if somebody goes away from it and doesn't for example, marry the right mate, you know—a kohen is restricted who he can marry, has to marry in the Jewish people, has to marry a girl of certain requirements . . . and if he fails to . . . his children, even male children, lose the title of kohen.

DH: There seems to be two parallel themes here in a sense: DNA or the biological on the one hand and on the other something more spiritual, or possibly cultural? Could you explain the relationship between those two things?

YK: Each reinforces the other, that's the beauty of it. You know, looking for holism, we're looking for unity . . . the concept [that] God is one.

DH: You mentioned earlier that you were becoming a part of your ancestry and the narrative of ancestry. Would this also be true for somebody who doesn't have descendants?

YK: Well . . . he has ancestors but he is not able to keep it going . . . that's something, you know . . . bordering on the tragic. Ancestry is important to us, it's important because we're part of something significant.

DH: If you include in the community of your ancestors people from whom you're not directly descended, then wouldn't it also follow that people who don't have descent could also be linked?

YK: Yes, I mean, every life is significant, certainly! But the concept of passing on one's experience whether it's just genetic or more than that . . . being a father, being the next generation's teacher giving over what you've accumulated in your experience seems to be a significant part of what life is about. [If] a person is unable or misses out on that . . . he can have a fulfilled life otherwise as well.

DH: Are experiences and learning passed down genetically? Or are they passed on through teaching and intellectual activity?

YK: Some things are passed on genetically, even some aspects of character, you know, we see. Intellect or at least intellectual potential to some degree is also. But the content and the lifestyle and everything of course . . . is something that's from experience and teaching [or] socialization.

DH: When we're talking about ancestry and spirit and religion and law and all these things coming together, it sounds as if ancestry or extended family is something that is acknowledged or recognized by God.

YK: That's a good point. That's a very true point. It means that it's significant to God because we have lists within the Torah, in this week's reading! The whole Book of Chronicles is a list of "A begat B, and B begat C. . ." and really that's what, ultimately ancestry is. And I know by the Torah, the Hebrew Bible, that it is significant . . . and son of whom had this many sons, this many daughters . . . so that keeping that lineage straight, there's a significance to that. You know, but on the other side, this whole discussion is universality because we really are all mankind, all together, all in this together and, you know, black, brown, white, yellow, rainbow, you know, we're all humanity. And even DNA says that . . . what is it 99.9 similar? It's only a few thousand, a few hundred thousand nucleotides that make us different.

DH: Could you tell me a little something more about your own personal biography? Your education, you said that you've lived in Israel for thirty years.

YK: I grew up in Baltimore, I went to college in Philadelphia at the University of Pennsylvania. I got a degree in social sciences . . . interested in urban studies . . . and then . . . I took to travelling and . . . then I came to study here in Europe, then came to Israel and decided to go to what's called a yeshiva. A yeshiva is a college of Jewish study, Talmudic studies typically.

DH: Is that what led you to the DNA research and genealogy?

YK: Yes, I did a book called *DNA and Tradition.**

---

*Yaakov Kleiman, *DNA and Tradition: The Genetic Link to the Ancient Hebrews* (New York: Devora, 2004).

DH: Mmhmm, and you participate in conferences and that sort of thing?

YK: Yeah, I do. I lecture on it. I have a PowerPoint and I give it over to schools and to organizations and what not.

DH: This is a topic that is very interesting to people and important to them as well.

YK: The discussion of ancestry is a very rich subject. And that's the thing, because, like you said . . . there's a drive to know who we are and ancestry is the key to it. . . . Past is prologue.

MAKING ANCESTORS BEYOND GENETICS: FRIENDS, TEACHERS, AND FICTIVE KIN

Interviewees describe their ancestral identities broadly, commonly expanding them far beyond genetics. This is something of an irony, since the idea of identifying ancestors is often associated with the principle of exclusive groups, privileged lineages, and so on. But all interviewees accept nongenealogical ancestors into their ancestral communities and narratives—in practice as well as in principle—and some extend ancestry to friends, associates, and other people of influence. And, as has been shown, some interviewees consider all humanity, all life, or all parts of the universe to be their ancestors.

Friends are important contributors to community, village, family, and spiritual life and might contribute to a family identity as much as any other acquaintance. If an adopted parent, in-law, or second spouse becomes an ancestor, why not also an intimate friend? Alexandra Senfft explains,

> Yes, I think [family] are the people closest to you in your life. [Family] are the people you grow up with and you have to deal with . . . friends can replace family and colleagues or . . . you can find different support networks. [There exists] a love relation to friends or very close relation to colleagues. . . . I would not argue that family is the last word. I have a lot of friends that I would consider a large family so to say.

It is not unusual for interviewees to discuss "making" family and ancestors similar to the way Alexandra Senfft describes friends becoming family, or drawing from other types of associations.

Henrietta Mann relates that people join the hearted-alike people through participation in specific customs of her tribe. Nongenealogical Cheyenne might be counted among her ancestors by virtue of marriage, adoption, or invitation or participation in the Peyote Church. Cheyenne people, says Dr. Mann, "make relatives," mirroring interviewee Leon Dixon's observation that "some people are adopted but all [people] adopt ancestors." An adoption might occur during an ancestor's lifetime or it might happen without an ancestor's knowledge, perhaps even generations after his or her death.

Leon Dixon includes among his ancestors people who have influenced him intellectually, including some who were not his genealogical relations and who he never personally met. Dixon refers to such ancestors as *fictive kin* and he compares the adoption of fictive ancestors to family adoption. Dixon's own fictive kin are people he has come to know through their writings and reputations, including W. E. B. Du Bois, for example, whose work guides Dixon, nurtures him, and contributes to Dixon's identity much the same as might a good uncle or a loving grandfather. Dixon honors W. E. B. Du Bois as his own relation, his own ancestor, perhaps similar to the way Henrietta Mann describes Cheyenne people being hearted alike. "If you read their books," Dixon explains, "the spirit resonates—they come to me in a sense. Not ghosts . . . [but] as long as somebody keeps calling their name, their spirit is still around."

Leon Dixon is not the only interviewee who discusses drawing ancestors from intellectual and cultural sources. Simon Jacobson suggests a student might honor a highly respected teacher or other mentor even more than a genealogical ancestor by reading and following the mentor's intellectual work and the student might also adopt the mentor as an ancestor. Such ancestors would be respected and honored through imitation, teaching, carrying on their traditions and honoring their sacrifices; they are sanctified in the sense that a descendant listens to them, remembers them, repeats their words, follows their examples, and shapes their ideas into realities. The intellectual descendant keeps them and their ideas "alive." Jacobson says, "So, you can have ancestry that's spiritual without biological. Biological without spiritual, or both!"

Leon Dixon and Simon Jacobson construct their own ancestries selectively, in the belief that ancestries should be inclusive, at some discretion of the descendant. Their selection processes are not arbitrary, but occur organically through shared work, values, and culture. Fictive kin are *made* through shared efforts, not through mere wishing. The descended build their ancestries as models for their own behavior and belief, not only genetic models but as constructed, moral ancestries, ethical traditions shaped by those who came before them, those whose ideas and principles they hope to advance into the future, just as any family or tribe would strive to perpetuate itself into the future.

Dixon and Jacobson enlarge conventional categories of ancestry through the inclusion of cultural and intellectual figures. Interviewee and genealogist Thomas Benjamin Hertzel also constructs ancestry broadly and inclusively, if from a different angle from those of Dixon and Jacobson. Hertzel expands his genetic ancestry by reaching as far into the historical record as his sources can carry him.

I've traced my family back to England, Medieval England. And that was kind of gratifying to be able to make the leap from immigrant to specific culture. But then in pursuing that, it splinters and then you discover, well the ancestors from England they're also Danes and they're French and they're Romans. And . . . what's England? It [ancestry] has to start disseminating that, and figuring out where those people came from, and once you go, say to France then you discover that, well, the French, they're Burgundians, they're Gauls, and they're Celts, and that gets disseminated. And I find all of that kind of cultural history that starts and melds and then moves and then meets up with others and then joins, the whole thing is interesting to me. All of it!

Tracing any genealogy back in time, there are points where culture and genetics part ways, people join "other" cultures and "other" genetic lines, to perhaps meet up again generations later—as old cousins, reunited. The ancestral community grows and integrates, diverges, and digresses. Labels identifying people, tribes, families, and ancestries cease to hold absolute significance.

Thomas Benjamin Hertzel. Courtesy of Thomas Benjamin Hertzel.

Interviewee Darold Treffert expands definitions of genetic ancestry to include and recognize all those categories of ancestry Hertzel outlined and still more. Treffert takes Hertzel's incredible networks of ancient Gauls and Celts another step further, to an understanding of ancestry that might be called "genetically expansive." Drawing from his expertise in genetics, Treffert explains his personal ancestry in a way that it reaches as far as the scientific information will take him.

With all my more recent work with genetic memory [and] because of savant syndrome, I've broadened considerably when I'm thinking about ancestry—not just my family but in a broader sense. . . . Our DNA is much broader than our traditional thinking. My ancestors are from Germany. Well, where are my German ancestors from? Well, it turns out they were from France, and if we go back and look at some of the DNA, it crosses the usual boundaries that we think about. Some of the work that's been done just recently with the DNA in genetics . . . and looking at ancestry. . . . First of all finding out that DNA is capable of astronomical storage in a small amount of DNA . . . and as they've gone back with DNA testing, one finds that most of us are three percent Neanderthal or some others way back . . . as you begin to trace back with DNA, it's much broader than our traditional thinking.

Treffert's construct of ancestry extends so far that it begins to reach the same expansive range as Dr. Mann's, even if the initial basis for Treffert's is perhaps less philosophical than scientific, Dr. Mann's perhaps the reverse. But their conclusions regarding relatedness endorse each other. Dixon, Jacobson, Mann, Treffert, and Hertzel connect to incredible communities of ancestral identity that reach far beyond ordinary genealogy and family genetics. Yet their expansion and inclusivity emanate profound senses of personal connections and identity of the individual to his or her ancestors. Great spaces between ancestor and descendant are effortlessly traversed in mind and spirit.

Interviewees enrich the concept of "where I come from" far beyond the mechanics of a multigenerational family tree. By allowing their ancestries to transcend local associations drawn from local memories, these interviewees open notions of ancestry to new engagements, new worlds of relatedness, and new dimensions. From Mann to Treffert, interviewees establish ancestry as intimate, personal links to a moral and ethical universe, ancestry as an ideology, a world of intellectual and spiritual meaning. Undoubtedly we arrive on this Earth as heirs to the material work of our grandmothers and grandfathers but, following the thinking of Dixon, Jacobson, Mann, Treffert, and Hertzel, we can say we are heirs also to how our predecessors lived, what they ate, whom they loved, where they walked, what they believed in, and who they befriended. It seems like a heavy responsibility, to offer our own lives similarly to future generations, to know that our own lives will one day be adopted into the survival, the identities, and the ideas of those who look to our models for their models. We are making the future just as our ancestors made our present.

INTERVIEW WITH LEON DIXON

"On the Shoulders of Giants"

DH: Good day Mr. Dixon, can you tell me what is your connection to the W. E. B. Du Bois Center?

LD: One of the cofounders and head of the Math Department.

DH: And, who are your ancestors?

LD: Well, I was raised by my grandmother and [being African American] I have heard her tell me stories of her grandmother who was a slave you know, and of her ancestors who fought at the war and so forth, on both sides of my family. So I think about those who went along before me to make it possible for me to be where I am.

DH: You include specific people in your ancestors, your grandmother, then you also mention groups of people such as slaves and others. Are you thinking of ancestors as specific people or more by groups?

LD: A little bit of both, you know, I don't know my great-grandparents but I know of them. One of them is the founder of one of the local churches here . . .

DH: In Kansas City?

LD: In Kansas City . . . of course I hear stories about that; I don't know him, I know his wife, which is my great-grandmother but it was my grandfather that actually did that. He passed before I was of any age. On one side of my family, I've heard stories like one of my grandmother's brothers—which would be one of my uncles—knew the Dalton brothers and he had a farm, you know like Jesse James? And the Dalton brothers used to rob banks or whatever and they'd ride in and stow money on his farm! Come back years later and get it. Those are stories that I grow up hearing and I heard stories from my grandmother how one side of my family owned a lot of land in Galveston, Texas, but it was confiscated and she went down there to try to get it but she was unsuccessful. I heard stories how we started out in Texas and then we ended up in Missouri.

DH: Most of the stories you heard, did you hear them from your grandmother?

LD: Well, from my grandparents. I had two grandmothers. One [story] about the Dalton brothers came from one grandmother. The one [story] that came from Texas

*Leon Dixon. Courtesy
Tiffany Matson
Photography.*

came from the other grandmother. One time I even had documentation—I lost it—where she went down there to go to court to try to get that stuff sued. And then I heard stories of her father—grandfather you know, how he ended up in Missouri. So I've heard the stories.

DH: It sounds like the stories are not all necessarily about direct line ancestors.

LD: Well, yeah, some of them are and some of them—like those who fought in the Civil War—were great-great-grandfathers. They would be direct. But I heard about them from uncles and cousins.

DH: Would you include uncles as your ancestors?

LD: What I think is along two lines, I think like *direct descendants* if I want to be . . . literal, and then I think of a group, you know like a whole body of them.

DH: When you think of the whole body of them how do you define that?

LD: I'm fairly well read in African American history and when I look back . . . I'm no kin to Frederick Douglass, but I look at him as an ancestor. Or Harriet Tubman. Although I'm not kin to them. But they would be in the collective.

DH: In what sense do you think of them as ancestors?

LD: Let me say this. I'm going to go way back on you. I saw a guy on TV making this argument. . . . The guy wrote a book [about slave ships] and I was watching him on C-Span 2. I bought and read the book but in the discussion he made the comment that if the true stories of African Americans could be really told, and be put out there, it would rival all the epics of history. So when I look at ancestors, I look at all those that came before me and made it possible for my generation to be where it is now. Now, having said that, you talk about ancestors. One of the things he points out in the book was that in Africa there were some trials, fights, and all that kind of stuff but once they got on that slave ship, they were literally and physically in the same boat! Now, what we created then is what he termed *fictive kin*. Meaning that, husbands and wives, brothers and sisters were separated so we created fictive kin and I argue that that's the reason why to this day we call each other "brothers and sisters." Our real brothers were gone. So we had to adopt.

DH: Do you consider those people on those ships to be your fictive kin?

LD: Yes!

DH: Is fictive kin more than symbolic?

LD: I'm going to say yes. It's kind of like, if you are an adopted child, is that your mother?

DH: Do the ancestors in those stories carry moral messages?

LD: Yeah, moral messages, cultural messages . . . I'm going to say cultural messages. It's really kind of strong in the African American community. See, I had friends of my parents who I considered aunts. They weren't aunts but they were so close to family that they were like aunts. Sometimes we would call them aunts, at least my generation and older; that may not be so much nowadays.

DH: Is this changing?

LD: I think this is changing now but in segregation days we were all in the same area. I mean lived in the same area, we were a closer-knit community than we are now and there was a lot of that. I think that's one of the problems with the schools. You know when I was growing up, everybody knew the teacher in the schools. . . . I went to the school and one of the teachers went to the school and knew my mother and my father so if he said I did it, I did it [laughing]!

DH: What is your relationship to the historical community? Some of those people came to you through stories . . .

LD: It's a story but it's also a lived story . . . this is a little sad but I remember my grandmother had a sister and I referred to this lady as "her other sister." She was her friend but I referred to her as her sister because they were so close. This lady had authority over me like my own relatives did. So you hear their stories but they were actually true!

DH: Do you have a continuing relationship with other people in your past including those you never know?

LD: Most of them are deceased but I'm going to say yes. Some people who are mentors to you, they are not your blood relatives you know, but from a cultural, community point of view, they take you under their wings and they work with you. You know like if you go off to college, you have a thesis professor, well how close you are? You take certain fields that are expressive, like the arts. . . . I hear a lot of people talk about Quincy Jones like that, musicians. You hear stuff like that and you hear Quincy Jones talk about the people who did him that way.

DH: What about the people you didn't meet? Those who . . .

LD: I look at them as ancestors too! They are more like spiritual ancestors, if that makes sense. They set the tone for what was to follow. And you follow in their footsteps.

DH: Beyond following their examples, do you suppose you have an ongoing relationship with those people today? Even those who you never met?

LD: I'm going to say yes, in a spiritual type of sense, because—I think it was Newton who made the comment that, "If I've seen further than others, it's because I stood on the shoulders of giants." Did he know the giants? No, but it was like they were ancestors, if you follow where I'm going with this.

DH: In a personal way also?

LD: Whatever field you're in, like in my case it was math I majored in. Like I didn't know any of the great mathematicians but in a professional sense they were like my ancestors.

DH: In the sense of your person, yes they did things to help you develop in many ways, but what about something more tangible than that? Are they continuing to influence you in the sense that they are really there? Or did they just leave a body of work for you?

LD: I don't know how to answer that. They were there! They're not now, they're dead and gone but their work's still there. Like how many times do we quote authors or politicians or whatever? People still quote Kennedy and George Washington and all of them so you know, people call George Washington "Father of the country." Well, was he your father? No, but you see, for me some of the things they did . . . set patterns and traditions and so forth that carry on to this day. Does that make sense?

DH: Sure, sure. Is that all?

LD: Well, when I read Frederick Douglass, W. E. B. Du Bois, and I could name several of them, and I read their biographies and some of their thoughts and so forth, some of that stuff resonates with me today. Did I know them personally? No, but I felt touched by their life stories and some of the things they had to say and some of the insights they laid out that I even use to this day!

DH: So you wouldn't say that the spirits of those people are still alive, communing with you?

LD: Well, yeah, it depends on how you say that. Like they came to me in a dream? No, I'm not saying like a ghost showed up and stuff like that but if you read their books, their spirit comes through the readings. That's the sense that I'm saying that. You know, like Frederick Douglass said, "Power concedes nothing without a demand." Well, did he tell me that personally? No, but when I read that, it resonated with me and that's a part of my thinking, so to speak.

DH: But you had to do the work to get to that point. They didn't bring it to you, they left it for you . . .

LD: . . . left it . . .

DH: . . . and you had to study for it.

LD: Yeah, and my mother would tell me things, that they brought to me because we shared time and space together, like my mother used to say things like "stick by people that stick by you." Now, she's dead and gone and every now and then some things come up and that resonates. . . . A lot of artists have sayings and songs that resonate with you to this day. Like Billie Holiday, "God bless the child that got it on." Now did she tell me that personally? No, but I heard that song over and over and that statement has resonated.

DH: And your relationship to Billie Holiday and the others, it's intellectual . . .

LD: It's intelléctual and it's emotional too.

DH: It's also emotional. Is your relationship to your direct line ancestors—beyond the people who raised you—any different from that?

LD: Like my great great-grandparents who I've heard stories about?

DH: Exactly. Is your relationship to those people any different from your relationship to Billie Holiday? Is there a different quality to what your great-grandfather left you than . . .

LD: Well you know, not in the [same] depth as say if I read an autobiography of Frederick Douglass or anybody for that matter . . . my great-grandfather who's passed, I'm not ever going to know that much about him. Or her. I get little tidbits from time to time but you can always pick up that biography and re-read it. . . .

DH: Do you feel a responsibility towards those people who did things that have come down to you?

LD: Yes, a responsibility and all of that. Like for example, I had a friend of mine and we were classmates and he was real proud of his mother and real grateful for helping him get through college and all that and I remember talking to him one evening and he was saying he wanted to pay her back and I said, "You can't pay her back." I said, "The way you pay your mother back is you do a good job of raising your kids."

DH: Is there reciprocity between the living and the dead where the living can do things for their ancestors like praying for them . . .

LD: No, I'm not into that because . . . I can't get to that because once they're dead they're gone. Now their memory lives . . . there's an ancient African proverb . . . and it said, "As long as somebody can call their name, their spirits are still around." So if you know the name of Frederick Douglass, his spirit is still here, his writings are still here, and I could name other people, you know they say the same thing about Abraham Lincoln, there are others, Geronimo, whatever.

DH: But is the person dependent on the memory? When the memory is gone, the person is gone?

LD: I'm going to say yes and no. Because you see your triple great-grandfather is gone but if he wasn't around, you wouldn't be around. So, the specifics of it are not there, but yes, he's still there.

DH: What about remembering ancestors who didn't do such good things? Not all the people on that ship were good . . .

LD: I take what one of my uncles used to say, "You have to take your bitters and your sweets." You get some of them both. Go far enough back and you'll find somebody, some ancestor you're not too proud of. And you might find one you're extremely proud of. You have to take your bitters and your sweets.

DH: Don't just ignore the bad?

LD: I don't think you have to account for it but I'm going to use the expression *acknowledge it*. But I don't feel responsible for it. You know, if my father was a criminal and I'm a Baptist preacher, I don't feel like I'm responsible for what my father did.

[Discussion about the principles of reparations for African Americans. Mr. Dixon says it is not his expertise.]

LD: [Ancestors] should be more than honored. They should be studied and understood. I'm reading a book now that is talking about what climate does and the global climate and all that and I was reading about a situation in Africa where due to the climate the crops aren't growing and the cattle are dying, so the people are ending up stealing and robbing each other. Well, I understand both sides. Now, is what they're doing right? No, but I see why this side's doing what it's doing and I see why that side's doing what it's doing . . .

DH: In the end, what is the significance of studying ancestry?

LD: Are you familiar with Richard Feynman, Nobel Prize–winning mathematician and all that? He said when his father was a high school physics teacher and his mother was carrying him, his father said, "If he's a boy, he's going to be a scientist." And he tells a story when he was on a baby high chair and his father put something, like he put two blue dominoes and one white one, and he said "I'm trying to get him to understand patterns." So, back to your question, when I'm looking at history and I'm studying history, I'm looking for patterns. Why people do the things they do? What causes things to happen? How are they best addressed? So you look for those patterns.

4

EVERY PERSON
IS AN ANCESTOR,
A DESCENDANT,
AND AN INDIVIDUAL

Two points concerning ancestors and descendants seem plain enough. First, all people are descendants because people descend from other people and inherit cultural identities. And second, when people have children they become ancestors. But when interviewees maintain that their ancestors include cultural, intellectual, and other predecessors from whom they are not genetically descended, they introduce the possibility of a third point, expressed by nearly all interviewees: With or without children, all people are ancestors. Through living, working, and sharing life, people organically build relationships and legacies that shape future people and societies. The most isolated monk and the most prolific biological parent participate in the world and help mold their worlds into what they are becoming.

The position that all people are both descendant and ancestor is nearly universally accepted among the interviewees. Yaakov Kleiman comes the closest to offering an exception. Kleiman readily acknowledges the importance of cultural ancestors but he is also confident that—even apart from medical issues—a genetic ancestry carries unique significance.

DH: You mentioned earlier that you are becoming a part of your own ancestry and contribute to its narrative. Would this also be true for somebody who doesn't have children?

YK: Well . . . he has ancestors but he is not able to keep it going . . . that's something, you know . . . bordering on the tragic. Ancestry is important to us; it's important because we're part of something significant.

DH: Since you include in the community of your ancestors . . . people from whom you are not directly descended, would it follow that people who don't have genetic descent are also ancestors?

YK: Yeah, I mean, every life is significant certainly. But the concept of passing on one's experience whether it's just genetic or more than that . . . being a father, being the next generation's teacher, giving over what you've accumulated in your experience seems to be a significant part of what life is about.

DH: Are there kinds of experiences and learning . . . which are passed on genetically? Or are those things only passed along through teaching and through intellectual activity?

YK: Some things are passed on genetically, even some aspects of character, we see. Intellect or at least intellectual potential to some degree is also. But the content and the lifestyle and everything . . . is something from experience and teaching [or] socialization.

Stopping short of naming all people ancestors, Kleiman affirms the lasting contributions to identity and society, of those who do not carry on genetic lines.

For the majority of the other interviewees, there is rarely any kind of natural hierarchy of genetic over cultural ancestors. Glenda Mattoon says, "The person who wrote the definitive work [on the Mattoon family] had no children. But he wrote the book because they're all [related]. Every Mattoon in the United States is related." Cultural ancestors might stand more prominently in a family's history than do some genealogical ancestors, even among families of interviewees who do not explicitly recognize models like Leon Dixon's fictive kin.

Notwithstanding the great influence of genetics and culture on a person's life, perceptions, and behavior, interviewees agree that a descendant is also an individual and takes some responsibility for his or her own personal choices. Referring to the influence of DNA on his personality, Muatasem Ubeidat says he is a "genetic blend" of his mother and father and his inherited genes influence the way he looks and behaves. But in the end he says, "I still can make my own choices."

Janna Thompson agrees that DNA delivers propensities; but, like Ubeidat, Thompson says the behavior and character of each individual is determined less by genetics than by free will.

DNA plays a role in forming who you are but they don't give you something like a direction in life and a sense that, what you're going to do with yourself, what kind of person you're going to make yourself in to—they'll [ancestors] play a role in all that but your own decisions play a much greater role in who you actually become.

Research into the influence of DNA advances steadily and may eventually answer many of the questions regarding the impact of nature and nurture on personality, identity, and forming who we are. But for now, the individual is still perceived to carry a great deal of authority to shape his own identity and to construct her own personal narrative, ancestral and otherwise.

INTERVIEW WITH STANLEY AKITA FUKE

"When I Meditate"

DH: May I ask your name?

SF: My first name is Stanley and my middle name, which was given to me at birth, was called Akita, and then my last name is Fuke and my name started back in the 1500s. I have a long history that has been recorded up until today. And it's because my original ancestors came from China, in the 1500s as a missionary, a Buddhist missionary. So, then they began a particular sect. The original one started a mission in southern Japan—Buddhists—and they had a *Fuke* sect in Japan until the Tokugawa came in and they banned the sect because they thought that the sect was getting a little too strong and too many of those warriors joined the sect, the Zen sect. And then—so my family has lived in Japan until the 1800s, the last part of the 1800s, at that time my grandfather on my father's side was—they're all scholars and Samurais and they were sent to Hawaii to educate the plantation children in the Japanese language and culture. That was back in the 1800s, late 1800s.

DH: Can you tell me your occupation?

SF: I was the Director of School Libraries for the Clark County School District, which is here, and I supervise over 360 library and school librarians, and I have a staff of six.

DH: And your first language?

SF: My primary language—well I have this chop suey language, my first language—I was born and raised in Hawaii and so I was conversant in English but not the real English, it's pidgin English, and also in Japanese.

[Discussion about the word *ancestry* in various languages]

SF: . . . so when I'm with you I'm speaking the King's English. And when I'm with my group of friends, which we just did last weekend, we spoke pidgin English. And the language comes right back to you again. . . . English is the basic language and then you have all these other words that come in from different languages.

DH: Can you tell me who are your ancestors?

Stanley Akita Fuke. Courtesy of Stanley Fuke.

SF: Who are they? On my father's side, it's Fuke, and they came from the southern part of Japan.

And my mother's side came from Hiroshima and they have since all deceased from the atomic bomb. . . . They died during the atomic bomb. So on my mother's side there is no family left.

DH: You are identifying your ancestors by family name?

SF: By family name, but also we came from the Kumamoto area of Japan so we also identify with the Kumamoto.*

DH: Is Kumamoto a place, a people . . .

SF: It's a place. Historically, the Kyushu, the bottom island (not way towards Okinawa) but the bottom of the four islands, that area is called Kyushu, and the district in Kyushu is called Kumamoto, the southernmost area of Kyushu.

DH: Do you think of *place* as part of your ancestry?

SF: Yes. Number one, it's culturally and language. There are different dialects in Japan and so the dialect I am most conversant in is Kyushu.

DH: How is language part of your ancestry?

SF: When we were growing up we were taught the philosophy of the Buddhist and also Japanese. We didn't dare shame our families growing up.

DH: Would you say the place is an ancestor to you?

SF: The places where our ancestors came from.

DH: In what way is culture an ancestor?

SF: I haven't really defined it in my mind . . . but the culture also determines how you were raised. . . . You were basically [from] the German culture so you were raised according to a German philosophy of a household. And you follow the philosophy of a German family. And your upbringing was probably similar to mine, but there were different aspects of it. So, I was raised in the Japanese culture where you respect your elders and your grandparents and you know, you have to listen to your grandparents and your entire family.

DH: How is the philosophy an ancestor?

SF: Because it's passed down through the generations.

DH: It sounds like you're saying that ancestry is both culture and genealogy.

SF: Correct.

DH: Because you mentioned your parents, your grandparents, but you also mentioned the culture. In terms of the people, would you include people who were not part of your direct line as ancestors?

---

*Kumamoto is a city and prefecture of southern Japan, on the island of Kyushu. Like many regions of Japan, Kumamoto has a distinct culture and history.

SF: With friends, you have the similar cultural background. I was raised on a sugar plantation in Hawaii, on the big island. And we were in the Japanese camp and we all had similar ancestry backgrounds, so the same culturally and we were raised the same way.

DH: Would you consider the ancestors of your friends also your ancestors?

SF: Culturally, yes, not by bloodline but culturally, yes.

DH: Do you make a distinction between the two?

SF: Yes.

DH: What is the distinction?

SF: I don't know. I'll have to think about that. [Pauses to consider] The distinction . . . I'm just trying to look at some families that I was raised with . . . and my own family . . . we all share the similar philosophy of life, of living, even though they have a different interpretation of it in each family.

DH: Would you include any nongenealogical people as your specific ancestors?

SF: It depends on how you're defining ancestors. If you're defining ancestors as genetic, bloodline . . .

DH: Within your bloodline could there be people who are not genealogically related to you? For example, could there be an adopted person in there?

SF: Yes, for example we have had in our family, you know when people are having a difficult time raising their children, they would ask someone else to take care of their child and adopt them as their own, and they follow the same cultural leaning or background.

DH: Culturally, yes, but could that child then claim the adopted parents as his or her ancestors?

SF: Not in bloodline, but culturally, yes.

DH: Some of the Korean people I've spoken with have told me that when the women in the family married, they adopted the husband's family as their own ancestors.

SF: That's cultural.

DH: They didn't make those distinctions.

SF: But to me there's blood—there's bloodline, and then there're culture.

DH: Are you not also saying that an adopted person could adopt into the bloodline?

SF: They can't.

DH: So bloodline is scientific, genetic . . .

SF: In my . . . thinking.

DH: Does the bloodline have any significance by itself without the cultural aspect?

SF: I'm thinking back also. I've had some ancestors say about three or four generations back in the eighteen hundreds where they did not have a male heir to take that line so the adopted child to take over on the bloodline because they didn't have any male child.

DH: So not all of your genetic ancestors are actually genetic ancestors?

SF: Correct . . . so sometimes the lines get a little blurry.

DH: And when that person is adopted in, it brings an entirely new . . .

SF: Correct. It happens in my family. We have charts that delineate because we didn't have any male to go through that line. Because my family was not a commoner. My family line came from . . . when Tokugawa took over the ruler of all of Japan, he had a big battle with another family called Toyotomi. And we belong to the Toyotomo family. We were vassals of Lords in that family. And they had lost that war and they had to move from Kyoto to southern Japan. And this is where my bloodline came from.

DH: So does the genetic have any significance apart from the cultural?

SF: It would be nice to have it tested in your blood. How much of you are together with the others.

DH: Would that have any greater significance?

SF: I don't know. It's more culture than anything else, when you're brought in to this group.

DH: Do you think of animals as any part of your ancestry?

SF: Animals? I don't understand that.

DH: Are you related to other living creatures besides humans?

SF: I don't really know. Are you talking about Adam and Eve back down in Africa? That we're all related to a single woman? I believe we are.

DH: And would that be both cultural and genetic?

SF: Because there were, like three or four women that they discovered that had the same DNA that is scattered over to eastern Europe and western Europe and to Asia.

DH: If that is true, then you would be descended from all humanity?

SF: Right.

DH: Then are you also related to other creatures or to previous creatures?

SF: I'm a monkey! [Both laugh]

DH: Or it could be all life descended from . . .

SF: The ocean? . . . Like if you're a Christian . . . Adam and Eve were placed on this Earth and from that came the DNA . . . I've read the study of man when they talked about those four or five women . . .

DH: If you had to name a starting point for all of your ancestors, it sounds like it would be Africa?

SF: I started where everybody else started. And when you're killing another human being, it's like you're killing your brother and sister!

DH: Is God in there? Are you descended from God?

SF: No.

DH: Are ancestors closer to God than you are?

SF: I always believed in the afterlife and I always believed in reincarnation. So, are we closer to God? I have no idea. And who is God?

DH: That is up to you. [Laughing] People answer according to their own belief.

SF: And you really can't answer that unless you die and come back!

DH: Do you have a relationship to your ancestors today?

SF: Yes, I pray to them.

DH: Can you tell me about praying to them, what do you pray to them?

SF: I don't ask for anything. I just recognize who they were, of those I can remember. . . . I can't think about or meditate about the others that I don't know about. But I think about or meditate about my immediate grandparents and my parents. I think about them as I meditate. This is why the Buddhists have the Obon. What it is, is recognizing your ancestors that have lived before. My mother and my grandmother used to say to me, "You need to dance!" I said, "Why?" "Because it makes you remember all of us that have gone by."

DH: When did your grandmother say that?

SF: Oh, about 1950. "Just go out and dance for us so you'll remember us." And you know, I remember that all the time. So, it's in my mind and when I do this Obon, no matter how rickety and crippled I am, I go out there . . . it's just . . . memory.

DH: When you pray to your ancestors, do they hear you?

SF: I don't pray that way. All I do is remember them. If I can remember their faces, I do; if I can remember their thoughts, I do. But I'm not praying to them like "Oh please help me I need to win the lottery." [Laughs]

DH: When you do remember them, do you speak to them?

SF: Not necessarily.

DH: Do you sometimes?

SF: You know I conjure images that I think of what they look like.

DH: And when you do that, do you sometimes speak to them?

SF: Sometimes I . . . this is getting personal but . . . sometimes I ask if they are ok.

DH: And when you ask, are they aware you're speaking to them?

SF: I don't know. All I know is people that have gone by . . . I just have this strong feeling that they're around us. I imagine that they're around and sometimes I have a feeling that they're around me . . . I just think they're around . . . spiritually.

DH: Do you believe that they are aware of you?

SF: I really believe that because sometimes when you're feeling down and . . . all of a sudden you feel they're there with you and it gives you solace.

DH: So, they might be there with you, and also they care for you still?

SF: I like to think that. That's why . . . in the Christian religion they talk about the soul of ghosts, it's the same thing!

DH: Can you explain why they care about you?

SF: I guess they have feelings for them, they want to make sure that your soul is settled.

DH: Are the feelings they have related to the genetics or to the culture?

SF: I think it's cultural. You know when you really feel—in the Buddhist religion they really emphasize compassion. When you have compassion for someone, regardless if you know them or know them really well and you find them, they're a little lost. And the compassion makes you feel—"I'm okay."

DH: And that compassion could come from Grandma?

SF: It comes from somewhere. Of course, since I'm alone, you feel this—and also you feel very settled.

DH: Is there any way you can return this compassion?

SF: By thinking about them! Recognizing that they're there.

DH: How does that . . . have meaning for them? That you continue to care about them and remember them?

SF: Because you remember them. . . . They're in the front of your mind, you're thinking about them; whether in a loving manner or a hateful manner, you're still thinking about them. . . . And that's a good thing, that you're remembered. You wouldn't just want to lay there and have nobody remember you at all!

DH: And that could happen with any relationship?

SF: It could happen with anyone.

DH: Not dependent on the genetic relationship?

SF: It's the culture too because you know, religious culture. . . . For an example, I just have a feeling . . . if I had passed on and I have a feeling that you're not that well, and someone comes and says, "You're okay." [Speaking very softly]

DH: Has that happened to you?

SF: Yes.

DH: And when it does, do you always know who the person is?

SF: Yes.

DH: Have you ever seen the person?

SF: Not with my eyes.

DH: You know who the person is but the memory fills in the blanks?

SF: Yes.

DH: Are you awake when that happens or are you asleep?

SF: Both.

DH: Is there some sense of those experiences being different from other more usual dreams?

SF: Yes, there is. You see, I had a boyfriend, a lover for forty years—he's recently passed—and we had two dogs. And whenever I knew he was around, the dogs were well aware. It could be in the middle of the night the dogs would get out of bed and we'd look in a certain spot . . . and I'd hear him talking (you know we're getting metaphysical here!) and sometimes I walk somewhere and . . . Oh! I'd see him there. And so do the dogs. And he told me, after he passed away, which one of his dogs was going to die first . . . and I heard him say, "and take care of such and such," and which one is joining me first. And he told me and it's so true. I firmly believe that.

DH: When you see him, you say you re-create him in your mind, not really seeing him.

SF: But I know he's there. In fact, when my grandmother passed away, it was 1951 or '52, I was really young at that time . . . but I told my mother before my grandmother passed—you know my mother was crying, she was really missing her mother. So I told her, "You know, Grandmother told me, Grandmother came to me and you should be happy because everything is fine now."

DH: You said that?

SF: I said that. I was like four or five years old. I remember it.

DH: Do you remember Grandmother telling you that?

SF: Yes.

DH: How did she tell you?

SF: I could just feel it. And, I told it to my mother and my mother was very happy!

Another time I was at college in Iowa—back in the sixties—my father's mother passed away. I didn't know. But that night I just lay there just staring, and all of a sudden I was just talking to her and I was telling her about the college in Iowa and for some reason I had in my mind taken her all through campus and showed her . . . Cedar Falls. Then I knew the next day when my father called and said that she had passed away, I said, "I know."

[Discussion about Iowa universities and towns]

DH: It seems like these experiences are not dependent on a genetic relationship.

SF: No. [Meaning, he affirms]

DH: Have they all been good experiences? I asked another interviewee if love has something to do with the transcendence of life and death and he answered, "Absolutely! And sometimes hate!"

SF: All of them have [been positive], and sometimes it's a warning. You just stop for a minute, and they say, "Oh!" And you don't do that.

DH: Do you know who it is, who says that?

SF: I don't know. It's hard you know when you're driving . . . "Oh my God. I can't do this," and you stop and turn around.

DH: Do you agree that everybody is an ancestor?

SF: That is correct. You know we're all connected!

DH: So you agree that people without children are also ancestors?

SF: Yes. I'm connected to you somewhere and that's where we are together.

DH: And you also have descendants, and everyone has descendants, and people who die young also have descendants?

SF: Yes, absolutely.

DH: Can you tell me something about the Obon? When you dance? What is your relationship or your state of being when you dance?

SF: [Laughs.] I'm walking now because I'm getting older. But I still go. And a lot of times in my mind's eye, a lot of the motions are repetitive. You're going around in a circle, doing this repetitive motion, sort of like . . . almost like in a trance. Dancing, and . . . [stamping his feet on the floor] just happy.

DH: Do you do it for your ancestors?

SF: [Laughs] I'm supposed to but you know, it's fun to get together with others.

DH: Do you know the story of the origins of the Obon, that an important disciple of Buddha saw his mother, and she was . . .

SF: . . . in hell . . .

DH: . . . and he was terrified . . . and he ran to Buddha . . .

SF: Correct.

DH: And he did good things and his mother was released.

SF: All those stories were passed down from generation to generation. My grandmother told me that story.

DH: Did she tell you the story as if it were a true story?

SF: When you're four or five, everything they tell you is true! [Laughter] You have a tendency to believe.

DH: Would you say the story is true? And when the story was originally told, did those who told it believe it to be true? That it really was his mother he saw in his dream. Or, was it a fabrication of his mother, or a metaphor for his mother, or what?

SF: Well, it's like . . . people have a tendency . . . when you're a child, to believe it. Like, if you're a Christian, do you believe Jesus woke up three days after he was put up on the cross. We as human beings like to believe . . . and it makes you feel better to believe there is something there . . . after life. We are very egotistical. . . . People like to believe, don't you agree? To think that we're something special, above the animals . . . but animals go to heaven too. . . . I believe that, like our pets and stuff? They're there. I believe I'm going to see my little dog when I die.

DH: Because you loved that dog and the dog loved you?

SF: Well, not the mean ones running around out in the street! [Laughs]

DH: Because you're related to that dog?

SF: Yes, I am! . . . But we're kind of veering off to cultural more than bloodline. . . . In my culture, there's a lot of ancestor worship. We do. We pray to them, we think about them, we light incense, I have a little temple in my bedroom, and you think about them. Like when I went back to Japan, we got a small group of people who are still left from my clan or group of ancestors. And we went to a little cemetery which is on the top of a hill in a little town called Ashikita and all of the Fukes were buried up there. And I thought, "Oh my God, how could they carry all the way up there?" But no, they were cremated; their remains were placed in those tombs. And I thought, "Why are they put on the top of the hill?" Because of arable land and the higher it is, the more honored your ancestors were. That's why. They were highly revered.

5

THE ANCESTRAL NARRATIVE

People are borne not only of corporeal people; they are cultivated, nourished, and comprehend themselves from inherited languages, food, music, rituals and other traditions, water, wine, bread, spirit, earth, landscapes, air, fire, and all sorts of environmental circumstances. The thirty-four interviewees describe themselves as descending not only from the DNA of their parents and grandparents, but descending from complex cultural, spiritual, and ecological identities. Descent includes ideas, words, and all those aspects of the cultural world into which a person is born. The sum of a descendant's inherited legacies and constructed remembrances of ancestral people and ways creates an *ancestral narrative*.

Ancestral narratives integrate written, oral, and ritualistic remembrances and include stories, historical records, artistic and religious performances, artwork, music, and any other customs and behaviors that celebrate or remember ancestors. A narrative naturally begins with the essential details of personal names and places, birth and death dates, and other historical facts. But an ancestral narrative is not limited to two-dimensional information any more than were the lives of the ancestors themselves limited to names and dates. Ancestral narratives proceed from details to greater things—to transmit the deeper qualities of those names and dates and to enrich them with meaning. Narratives display the ethos, the identity, the character of an ancestral body, as adopted and interpreted by descendants. Narratives provide ways of organizing and reproducing identity, transmitted along the stories and all those things "my people" did, said, made, and left for us.

Stanley Fuke's brief statement describing his ancestral background shows how complex, profound, and deep a seemingly ordinary narrative of ancestors and ancestry can be. Fuke builds his inherited identity from a cosmology of sources, beginning with the family name Fuke.

> My first name is Stanley and my middle name, which was given to me at birth was called Akita, and then my last name is Fuke. My name started back in the 1500s. I have a long history that has been recorded up until today . . . my original ancestors came from China, in the 1500s as a missionary, a Buddhist missionary. So, then they began a particular sect. The original one came and started a mission in southern Japan—Buddhists—and they had a Fuke sect in Japan until the Tokugawa came in and they banned the sect because they thought that the sect was getting a little too strong and too many of those warriors joined the sect, the Zen sect. . . . So my family lived in Japan until the 1800s. My grandfather on my father's side was—they're all scholars and Samurai and they were sent to Hawaii to educate the plantation children in the Japanese language and culture. That was back in the 1800s, late 1800s. . . . We also identify with the Kumamoto area. . . .When we were growing up, we were taught the philosophy of the Buddhist and also of the Japanese. We wouldn't dare to shame our families.

In this brief passage, Mr. Fuke shows the richness of an ancestral narrative. His ancestral geography associates him with particular places in the world, the names of which carry significance beyond the geographical. He names China, southern Japan, and Hawaii, all of which are now important ancestral places. The Kumumoto region of Japan and the sugar plantation of his childhood particularize this geography, which lead his life down through the generations into his present-day home in Nevada. Fuke identifies his ancestral times more broadly, by mentioning "original ancestors," the 1500s, the Tokugawa period, the 1800s, and his own early years with his friends and family. These establish Fuke's ancestral positions in time; they clarify the intersections of his modern identity with historical communities, languages, and ethics. Each one of these time and place markers provides a reference, a vocabulary of family idiom that signals attributes of his family's and his own self-understanding.

So too do Fuke's cultural references display the complexity and depth packed into this brief introduction. Warriors, scholars, and missionaries, Samurai, Zen Buddhists, educators, philosophers, and bearers of traditional Japanese culture build Mr. Fuke's ancestral ethos, an ethos he perpetuates by recounting his story. Every person, profession, and quality he mentions is worthy of its own story, each one bears a profound family significance and reveals a rich and colorful idea Fuke shares with his ancestors.

Stanley Fuke's opening statement is a testimonial to his ancestral values, his ancestor's pride and purpose. By identifying with these people and their values,

Stanley Fuke and relatives at a family site. Courtesy of Stanley Fuke.

Mr. Fuke assumes a responsibility to perpetuate the family's positive qualities, its nobility, professionalism, and dignity. Fuke's ancestors were proud, educated, loyal, and tightly knit. He conveys all of this in a single oral paragraph. How richly an ancestral narrative constructs identity! And how much more than just a word is wrapped inside a name.

Ancestral narratives are dynamic and complex in their character and also in their origins. Narratives grow from varieties of sources, public and personal, with an individual descendant working as a kind of editor-in-chief to "complete" the project, at least for the time being. Grandmothers, grandfathers, family genealogists, and tribal or other elders are often primary in defining and constructing narratives through the telling of stories and by acting out rituals and practices. Peter Grant says his mother related family stories to him, "so I suppose one of her relatives told her . . . it's an oral tradition."

Stan Fuke describes songs he and the other children of Japanese emigrant families in Hawaii were taught by their elders to help them learn about the culture and people they left behind.

SF: Our parents were so insistent for us to learn these Japanese tales, Japanese songs that tell us about the valor and the courage and strength. This is one way that our parents passed down the culture.

DH: Do you remember any in particular that you really enjoyed?

SF: Yes, I remember *The Peach Boy*, a story about an older couple that wanted to have a child. And they found this peach. And when they opened the peach, instead of a pit, out came this young boy . . . and so they raised this child and the child became brave and strong, and protected the old couple.

DH: Do you remember the lyrics?

SF: Well, it's called *Momotaro-san*. . . . There are many [songs].

DH: When you meet your friends and family in Japan, do they also know these songs?

SF: Yes, as a matter of fact, there was a mother there [on a recent visit to Japan] teaching her child one of the songs, that one called "The Spring Is Coming," *Haru ga Kita*. . . . It was the same song, same melody, same words. It carries through your history, your cultural history.

DH: What were some of the other themes of the songs?

SF: The seasons, even though in Hawaii there aren't any seasons, we still just loved the songs.

DH: Did all the children know those songs?

SF : If they were Japanese, they did.*

There are also many "outside" sources that contribute to an understanding of one's ancestry, including public, professional, and historical sources. Alexandra Senfft learned from a school textbook about her grandfather's complicity with Nazi atrocities, his subsequent trial, and his public execution, which came to stand as one of the defining features of her ancestral narrative. Daniel Essim's sister and he learned about a particular ancestor when they discovered some old photographs. Glenda Mattoon describes how in the course of her genealogical research she frequently shares information with colleagues because one genealogy intersects with another and when one finds something of interest to the other, they exchange news. All these exchanges and sources intersect with family stories and practices to verify and build larger narratives.

A narrative is co-authored between ancestors and descendants, a joint project connecting the two groups. Several interviewees suggest that even after they have passed away, ancestors themselves might contribute to the development of their own narratives. Interviewee David Dollahite describes the spirit of his deceased grandmother visiting him, bearing a message of importance to the family narrative.

---

*From a telephone conversation following up on Mr. Fuke's interview.

DD: I wake up in the night and standing next to my bed is an older woman in a flower dress who I did not know. I didn't recognize who it was. . . . And she never spoke, I just knew—I knew that this was my grandmother and I was three when she died . . . and the question that my grandmother asked me was, "What about me? What about my family?" In other words, she knew that I had been focused wholly on my father's father's father's father, all the way back . . . I could have done some research on her line but I hadn't and so the question was, "What about me?" And it was very powerfully and indelibly imprinted in me and then my little daughter Rachel came running into our bedroom, this was in the middle of the night, and she came around my side—normally she would have gone to her mother.

DH: You were still awake?

DD: I was . . . my grandmother was still there and my daughter ran through the spirit of my grandmother and as she did so my grandmother disappeared or was beamed up or however you want to think about it. My daughter ran, she ran through the spirit of my grandmother and she ran and she hugged me and she said, "Daddy, I'm scared," and I said, "Why?" She said, "Because there was a woman in my room looking at me and I didn't know who it is," and I said, "It's okay, honey. That's your great-grandma."

Even from the beyond, David Dollahite's grandmother spoke on behalf of her side of the family, who expected to be included in the ancestral narrative. Ancestors care not only for the people in their descent, but for the culture of their descent as well.

Interviewee Lee Guem Ok reports that when she married, she adopted her husband's ancestors as her own. The new bride did not abandon her genetic ancestors but once she entered her new family, she performed remembrances and rituals preferentially for her in-laws. Hwang Jeong Soon also underwent such a transformation. "Before marriage," she relates, "Hwangs are my only ancestors. After marriage, Hwangs and Parks are my ancestors. However, I more respect Park ancestors since I'm married to my husband who has the last name Park."

Lee Guem Ok found it emotionally difficult to shift from one family of ancestors to another, but her belief as well as Korean customs dictated the shift. Lee Guem explains that her new ancestors arrived to help her adjust. The spirits comforted her, as they welcomed her into the new community. Her mother-in-law in particular visited with a friendly, maternal message.

When I got Jack's father [i.e., was married] in Junra Province, my mother-in-law visited my dream. At that time, something bad had happened to my husband and I cried over and over, staying up all night. After I finally fell asleep, she patted me on my head to console me. After the dream, I went to the market to do business and I made lots of money. It was a very lucky day!

When she joined her new family, the young bride gained not only new ancestors, but a new narrative as well. Her own marriage marked an important event in the narrative. Lee Guem contributed to the new family's narrative by joining the family but also by eventually bringing Park children into the world, tending the graves of the dead, learning the Park's stories, and honoring her new line of ancestors. Her transition from one family to the other demanded a collective effort—her natural parents, her new husband, her married parents, and even the ancestors, in the person of the deceased mother-in-law, worked together with the young woman to fulfill her incorporation into the community, and to sanctify the new order.

According to Lee Guem Ok's story, the integration of new descendants affects a large community, ancestral, spiritual, physical, past, present, and future, similar to Yaakov Kleiman's description of converts into the Jewish community, whose "souls change." David Dollahite's bedside experience suggests similar or parallel principles at work. Where there is belief in a spiritual universe, the nature of an ancestral relationship and connection is spiritual and the entry of a new member represents a phenomenon of spiritual significance.

The spirits of Henrietta Mann's grandfathers visited her world to encourage her before an important public presentation. Charles Sleeper's ancestors visit during times of stress. Lee Guem Ok's mother-in-law comes to comfort her. In all these cases, interviewees describe ancestors showing concern for the lives and actions of descendants. Such stories and experiences of ancestors become themselves part of ancestral narratives, which in turn shape evolving family legacies and identities.

Daniel Essim relates that his sister was living in Gabon, Africa, when a great-uncle she had not known during the uncle's lifetime visited her in a dream. "He said to her, 'Are you not the daughter of my sister? I want you to go back to Cameroon.' She said he came to her in person. Someone who died fifty years ago! They are helping us!"

Essim's sister indeed returned to Cameroon following the dream and her move and the event that prompted her move became part of her and her family's story. Sister's dream and return to Cameroon is now part of a familial-ancestral narrative and are becoming part of an evolving narrative and moral: the ancestors care about you. "God can work through the ancestors. Remember them!"

As with any story, idiom plays an important role in defining the deeper meanings of narratives. Values and identity emerge not only through literal meanings, names, dates, and so forth but also through intonations, nuance, political subtexts, and coded language. Interviewee Muatasem Ubeidat reports that his family's narrative arises from a complex of sources and, through selection and omission, teaches lessons about many things, including gender. He relates that the Ubeidats

> came originally from Saudi Arabia. . . . Three or four people migrated from there to the Jordan Valley or river area, currently Jordan. . . . Who they were, how they looked, how many men how many women I have no clue but they said "three or four men!" What about women I don't know. . . . Probably ten or more generations back. . . . The Middle Eastern culture is men-dominated. . . . Therefore, probably in any family tree you'll find more men than women. . . . All our generations made the selections of names and narratives.

Men tell the stories in which men dominate, predominate, lead, and rule, constructing patriarchal identities, values, and prejudices. Not only patriarchal lessons permeate the Ubeidat narrative, but tribal prejudices, morality lessons, political suggestions, and values wide and deep influence the selection and "editing" of an ancestral narrative.

In the end, however, after adapting to cultural, genetic, and personal experiences, a descendant is the ultimate arbiter of his or her own narrative. Given the information and stories available to him, Muatasem Ubeidat concludes, like many others, that "I define my own ancestors." As descendant he chooses which particular family lines his narrative will follow, which stories to repeat and how to repeat them, which tribes to identify as his own, and which individuals and stories to advocate and which to diminish. He hears the patriarchal narrative and interprets it in its context. He understands that a narrator chooses the tone and tenor of the stories, of their telling, of the enthusiasm for one ritual or one ancestor over another, and even of the sincerity of elements within his narrative.

Although a descendant remains a narrative's "editor in chief," most sources of narratives originate outside a descendant's control. Many factors contribute to the evolution of a narrative and identity, whether personal or collectively ancestral. Interviewee Janna Thompson explains that ancestral and other personal identities are indeed constructed but,

> they aren't constructed just according to our will . . . individuals are just born in a particular place, a particular time, they are very dependent when they are young, how their parents bring them up, they learn who they are long before they are actually able to construct anything consciously. Who they are has to do with their relations to people around them who are already influenced by people of the past. So, in that way there is nothing imaginary about these connections . . . it [identity and ancestral connections] is natural, even universal.

A descendant inherits many aspects of identity, learns other aspects, and develops a narrative through variable processes of integration and editing.

Some terms of identity and narrative arise from unsurprising sources, grandmothers of course, DNA, language and so on. But other sources, less intimate than these, come from general and institutional circumstances. Many Americans have family stories about names being changed because immigration officers or clerks could neither spell nor pronounce family names from Poland, India, or Vietnam. Those singular events might even begin a process of the development of a family identity, such as a process of "Americanization."

Interviewee Chief Charles Sleeper, who identifies principally as Arapaho but who has family lines and ties through many tribal and other groups, discounts his own initiative in the selection of his Arapaho identity. "I was born into it! I didn't make myself an Arapaho," he says. "Who made me an Arapaho? The BIA made me an Arapaho! That's how they interpreted my lineage!" An ancestral identity in fact comes to a descendant along many paths—cultural, geographical, even administrative.

Many details that fill ancestral narratives emerge from the personal experiences of a descendant. The testimonies of several interviewees show that when a descendant has had an intimate or loving relationship to an ancestor in life, that ancestor is far more likely to appear prominently in the descendant's narrative. This broad rule defies genealogical station and family position. An adopted father who was loved in life for example is more likely to stand as an important ancestor than is a biological father who was barely known. Ancestors and descendants work cooperatively—kindness and love in this generation leads to kindness and love in the next.

INTERVIEW WITH JEFF LIVINGSTON

"To Live That Kind of Life"

DH: Can you tell me about yourself?

JL: I'm Jeff Livingston. I'm about fifty years old. I have a wife, I've been married for twenty-six years this June. I have four kids, three boys and a girl. My girl is the youngest. My oldest is twenty-five and my youngest is seventeen. They are anywhere between there. My grandparents are all passed away, my parents are still living.

DH: Did you know your grandparents?

JL: Yes. I knew my great-great-grandmothers, one of them on each side of my family.

DH: Great-great?

JL: My great-grandmothers. My wife knew her great-great. I was probably in high school when my last great-grandmother died so I didn't get to spend enough time but I spent more than the usual time with my grandparents and great-grandparents. That was always one of the things that I was brought up [to do], to spend time with family. That was important to be around family.

DH: Do you still have something to do with family beyond your wife and children? Family research or anything like that?

JL: Yeah, it's a little hard living where we are to get out to see my wife's side of the family. They live in Ohio, we get out there maybe once a year. Thanksgiving and things.

DH: And when you go there do they have family reunions?

JL: No, but it's just kind of—yeah, family get-togethers. It's not like a reunion. Everybody gets together. Family was big on my wife's side too. I live in the community where my parents live, my grandson, one grandson, and my kids . . . so we have four generations all living basically together.

DH: When you say live together, do you work together?

JL: We farm the same farm.

DH: How long has that been going on?

JL: We moved out here to the farm in 1988. Before that my dad and I ran a welding business together.

DH: In southern Iowa?

JL: Yes. And I've lived here since I was in third grade, nineteen seventy-something.

DH: When you made the decision to come out here in 1988 was it a group decision? Did you sit down together and discuss it?

JL: Yeah, our church group decided that we wanted to have property and basically start living our religion more. And my whole family was basically the ones that came out and were behind it.

DH: When you say family, does that mean the same thing as ancestors?

JL: Yeah, family to me is more the people that are still alive. Ancestry is the people that have passed on, further back in history.

DH: Can you describe your ancestry to me?

JL: I guess the way I look at it is ancestors is part of who you are because you build on a foundation of who they were and they pass on traits and those traits keep building and

Jeff Livingston with family. Courtesy of Jeff Livingston.

building. And . . . each person has a chance to weed out the bad traits, I suppose but there's family traits that I can see as I've studied my family and watched them. I can see that there's certain traits that are family traits and I think that come from my ancestry. So I think ancestry is who a person is in terms of where they've gotten their personality. They can develop their own personality of course . . . there's traits that build from a family down though the line.

DH: So when you think of your ancestors and your ancestry, how far would you extend that horizontally? In other words, would you include in your ancestors people who are not your direct-line ancestors?

JL: Not necessarily. I wouldn't consider my ancestors, but there's a respect I've had taught to me for older people and I can use qualities they had in their lives as something I can build my life, I can take on. So they can influence me the same way that my family has but it's more of a choice, something I have to decide to take on where people in my ancestry, my family have . . . it's something that I inherited without knowing it. . . . It's not something I chose. I could choose to not be like something in my family but some things I just inherit.

DH: There are people who are raised by people who are not their direct family, adopted children. They wouldn't have a choice but could family mean the same thing to them as it means to you?

JL: Yeah. I have an adopted brother who's Klamath Indian and he was raised by my parents. He has some of the same characteristics as the family traits. Yet he has his own, I don't think it's all environmental. I don't know how to explain why it wouldn't be all environmental in terms of how you're raised but I think there's some that's inherited and I don't know how to explain that scientifically.

DH: So when you say ancestry . . . do you limit that? Do you limit it to genealogy?

JL: I would say genealogy probably. I can go back seven generations in terms of my known family.

DH: And with the people who are not included in your direct line but are still fairly closely related to you like uncles and cousins and aunts?

JL: I would consider them part of my ancestry. I guess when I was thinking of people that aren't, like there was a lady when I was a young parent, I was married she was like ninety-something years old and I used to go visit her just to hear stories and be around her and hear her talk, just because there's something there that I can get from her that was a benefit, it was a good time to be around an old person, they've lived their life long and . . . reveal what their life was to them. So, she wasn't . . . I wouldn't consider her one of my ancestors but she was someone that was worth knowing.

DH: And could you choose to, could you elect to include her in your ancestry if you wanted? Is that up to you or is that something, is that . . . ?

JL: No, there's lots of people I've considered to be like a grandmother or grandfather that weren't related. And I can see that.

DH: People marry in. They're not initially related; they become related.

JL: I would consider someone that marries in just as much a part of the family.

DH: So how expansive would you make ancestry? And when we say ancestry, are we talking about the same thing as family?

JL: Yes.

DH: How expansive then would you make ancestry? Where would you draw the line?

JL: I wouldn't. I would say there wouldn't be a line in terms of . . . it's just a spider web back to whoever married into the family, whoever was a part of the family. Just as you go back it gets bigger and wider until who knows how big it gets.

DH: Right, exactly. What about bad people? You said something about choosing good people, and model after good people.

JL: No, they're still your ancestors whether they're good, bad, ugly, whatever. They're still your ancestors and that's part of life.

DH: And what do you do with that?

JL: Well, I have an uncle on my dad's side that I would consider one of those black sheep kind of the family. He's fifty, almost sixty years old, never worked a job in his life. Trying to get on welfare and he's on drugs and getting out of jail and all that. My brother once said that he shakes his hand when he needs to because he's kin and that's it. You know, so I respect him, I don't have overly amount of stuff to do with him because he's not the kind of person I want to be around. But he's still family and he still deserves that much respect and politeness.

DH: Can you explain why that is? Because if he were the guy down the street you knew when you were little, you probably wouldn't even shake his hand.

JL: No, there is a difference. I think it's . . . it's hard to say. I think it's just because I was taught that you respect your elders and that, first of all I can understand some reasons why he was that way. How he was raised and all that and that I guess, I have a little more compassion on him. Although I know that he had to choose what he's chosen. Still, there's a respect there just because he's family.

DH: When you say "respect," what kind of respect do you show family who have passed on?

JL: I don't know in terms of what you're asking . . . I don't necessarily, we don't, I don't visit their graves or anything like that. I don't personally do anything that shows respect or disrespect. Just kind of they're gone and off to the next life or whatever. I mean we have lots of memories and tell stories, family stories, things about them and I suppose that's a way of showing respect. I tell lots of stories that my granddad did and I tell my boys and kids about it and they'll probably tell their kids and it just passes on down the line. Then I think that's part of how you bring the family history, there's something that gives a child some feeling of belonging to something. So there's not just, not lost . . . all they did. This family history keeps coming with you because of those stories. So that's one of the traits of my family is we tell stories a lot about our family.

DH: The good and the bad?

JL: Yeah, yeah.

DH: And have you celebrated funerals for people who have died?

JL: Yes. We mostly, we do it a little bit differently.

DH: When you say "we," what do you mean?

JL: Our community. And I think it's a real good way.

DH: What is?

JL: I think it's a real good way to do it. We did this when my grandmother died. Before she died, before . . . she had cancer, before she got to be too far gone mentally, we got everybody, all her family around and told her what she meant to us and how she impacted our lives. And shared all that with her, what it meant to her, to us.

DH: That had to be very difficult.

JL: And then the funeral, after someone dies . . . this was before the person had died, for the people that are still alive . . . so in the funeral we get around and we talk about that again and we talk about how to deal with death. So the, by getting all that out ahead of time and explaining what the person's life means to you, you're actually explaining to them. So to me, that means something to be able to say that to the person before they die because that's part of how you deal with them dying and how they deal with dying.

DH: Then . . . it sounds like you're saying that funerals are for the living.

JL: Yes. Well the dead person, it isn't doing anything for them.

DH: There are people that believe that funerals are for the dead, they help the dead along the way.

JL: Yeah, and I can understand that.

DH: But you would say not in your case?

JL: I would say my belief is when they die, they're off doing bigger and better things hopefully . . . so I really don't know what it does for . . . in my beliefs it doesn't really do a whole lot for the person that died. It's mainly to help people that are still here.

DH: Do you believe that people who, family members and otherwise, that those family members who died still have souls?

JL: Yes.

DH: And the souls are living?

JL: Yeah. In fact I've . . . I've never personally felt like I've—how you say, contact, not contact, but my dad has felt things about some of his ancestors that his family has gone on. And he thinks they are and I think, I've never really personally felt that but I believe that some of the . . .

DH: Are you saying that you don't discount it necessarily?

JL: I don't discount it. I've never personally experienced that. But I do believe that they can be involved to some extent, at least on a spiritual level with our lives now.

DH: Can you speculate about that a little bit more?

JL: I would say they, well like for example, my dad was at a real low spot in his life and he was ministering to people up in, native peoples up in Alberta. He was doing a suicide workshop and all of the feelings of how bad it was with the natives in terms of all the suicides, he got real down and he was walking along the road and . . . it was the middle of the winter and it was real, real cold and he just had a t-shirt on or a light shirt and he just was so down and he didn't care whether he died or not and thought about suicide himself. And he said that his grandfather came and told him to take the next ride that came along because he was declining rides on the road. And his love for his grandfather snapped him, made him realize, "Whoa, what am I doing?" And so he took the next ride and got over it. But that's the story he tells and the spirit of his grandfather came to him and told him, "Take the next ride." So I think that people that have passed on are aware of what we're doing and I think they can have some kind of influence like that. I don't know exactly how.

DH: It sounds like your father believes and you don't deny that this really was your grandfather.

JL: Yeah, yeah.

DH: If those stories are true, then there would be some special connection between your father and that man.

JL: Yes and there was in this life, too.

DH: There was in this life. And I guess that kind of leads to my question that, would you suppose that whatever special connection is there would be dependent on the way things went in this life?

JL: Yeah, to some extent.

DH: Did you say your brother is adopted?

JL: Yes.

DH: Could that happen to your brother and his father? The man who raised him?

JL: Yes, I would think so.

DH: So if this is some recognition of God of the relationship between those people, assuming that there's something like that going on, it wouldn't necessarily be a recognition of genealogy . . .

JL: No.

DH: . . . it would be a recognition of something else.

JL: Right and I think that someone can be someone's parents regardless of their bloodline or something. I think adopting . . . parenting, a lot of parenting is how you feel about your children and I think that that relationship, if you have that kind of relationship, parent-child relationship with anybody I think it kind of takes on that kind of element of feeling as parents. So you can feel like someone is your parent and have that same kind of relationship even though they're not really.

DH: Although in a way you're suggesting it's more of a feeling.

JL: Yes.

DH: It would be that person really is your parent in a sense.

JL: Well, yeah yeah. That's what I'm saying.

DH: Would that be going too far?

JL: No, I'm saying I guess when I say "feeling," that's what makes it real. It is how you feel.

DH: Right. In which case then it sounds like family would be something that you do make. You can bring people into your family.

JL: Yes. Because I would consider my brother who's adopted part of my family.

DH: Can you kick people out of your family?

JL: I don't think so, that'd be harder. I think it's easier to bring them in than it is to kick them out.

DH: Right.

JL: Now, if someone is adopted or not adopted formally but where you have a relationship with someone who's like a brother or sister and they're not really your brother or sister or your parents or grandparents or something, I think if that relationship . . . something happened there, I think you could kind of lose that relationship but not be the same as if it was a bloodline or formally adopted.

DH: It seems to be true. Telling stories and keeping memories alive of the ancestors which you said you do does seem like, I don't know if you would call it a ritual but it does seem like a form of practice of respect.

JL: Yes.

DH: And of honor. And is the respect and honor intended simply as a lesson? "Here's how Grandpa did it, Grandmother worked hard, you work hard." Or is it really honoring the quality of the person?

JL: I would say in my case, from when I've met with my family, it's never a lesson. In terms of formally . . .

DH: Never a lesson?

JL: It's never formally, "You need to do this because Grandpa did this." It's always honoring them, making a hero out of them kind of them. It's never, "You do this because this is the way the family does it." I was never raised that way, I didn't raise my children that way. People have their own, they can make their own vices to do something different than the family but I think the stories are aimed at helping children know who their grandparents were or, especially when they get to know them when they're older. And it's like making a hero out of them, giving them something as a role model that they didn't have—like my kids never knew my granddad on my dad's side and my dad and I both tell stories about him and the things he did. He was brave and all different stuff like that and it kind of gives them a sense of belonging, a sense they have something in their past they can emulate. So it's kind of a lesson but it's never, "You need to do this because . . ."

DH: Is there a religious dimension to that?

JL: I would say no.

DH: Is there a religious dimension to the family? To the idea of family? The sanctity of family?

JL: No, I would say no. As I think about that I guess that's surprising. But as I put religion into everything else, in terms of my family, in terms of those kind of stories and things I would say no, that's not a part of the religious beliefs.

DH: But it does sound like it's a strong part of . . . of your identity?

JL: Yes.

DH: Do you think that a person holds any responsibility for the ill behavior of his grandfather?

JL: No, I don't think that the. . . I know it's scriptural that the sins of the fathers are answered on the sins of the children. I don't believe it like that, I think that . . . the way I view that is the family traits that someone chooses to have, those can be passed down to the children and if those are bad traits then they can inherit that but they still have the ability to decide not to do that. So like my uncle's children, they can decide to better themselves even though they were raised like they were and they can better themselves and not do what their father did. And I think they have. So when I view that scripturally, says "His sins are on the hands of his children," is that it's what's inherited in terms of what they learned as a child and if they don't change something then it's going to continue on down the line.

DH: Can you do anything spiritually for ancestors? Kind of the reverse in the way that your grandfather visited your father and helped him to get up.

JL: I don't know, I've never had any experiences with that. I've never thought about it. . . . I know my grandmother prayed for her stepfather . . . no it was the other way, it's her father and her stepmother. She prayed for them, that they would learn something in that but I have never approached that myself. I don't know, I can't say that it's impossible and I can't say that it's possible. I have no feelings on that.

DH: Do you have any expectation at all about the future? You'll die someday and what to do . . . do you have any expectation or hopes about the way that you are honored or remembered?

JL: I hope that my children and grandchildren tell stories about me. I hope I can live the kind of life that produces stories.

ANCESTRAL NARRATIVE AS MYTH

Myths are the authentic meanings and messages of a narrative. They are transmitted through the "ways" of a people and include much more than stories; they
are contained within the behaviors and ways of a people's identity and ethos.
Myths educate a society about "who we are" and "who we are not." Ancestral
myths are communicated as the practices and ways that recall the things a
people share with their ancestors.

Ancestral myths are neither necessarily true nor false; they are instead maintained to teach and convey values, performing in three dimensions the living
body of a culture and a people. Myth-making happens at the cemeteries, the
temples, and the family gatherings of the living. Myths inhabit the dreams, the
languages, and the political customs of descendants. Myths define and justify
ways of life and ways of being, through honoring and reproducing ancestral
languages, cultures, and behaviors. Through myth, historical ancestors become
more than people; they become constructs of meaning.

Myths transform names and dates from the narrated past into the identities
of a People. Along with historical elements, there are elements and actors in any
ancestral narrative that are symbolic, larger than life, or that carry values special
to descended groups. Individual ancestors are celebrated or despised for the
meanings they represent, and their lives become for descendants lessons of
failure, suffering, sacrifice, and other morals.

David Gelsenliter mythologizes his ancestors when he progresses from a simple, historical, genealogical description of his ancestry, to a value-filled, honor-
ific description. "My ancestors were hardworking, loyal, and conscientious," he
says. "They were Germans." More than mere genetically German, his father's
people represent principles; they were people named for their values, revered
for their values, and now emulated for their values. The myth of Gelsenliter's
description lies not so much in the national identification as in the national
character he constructs and claims as his own, his father's, and his ancestors'.

Gelsenliter's narrative sets up the "German people" as but a backdrop for
the larger than life character of the father who is the only real creative force
Gelsenliter names in his interview. For, while he acknowledges he inherited
culture and values from a national or ethnic community of ancestors, the father's
unique greatness was singular and "came from within" the father, from the character of the man himself. This one person dominates Gelsenliter's narrative so
completely, the father becomes almost a kind of Rootman, only one generation
removed from the present. The single ancestor embodies the identity of the
whole ancestry.

DH: Do you identify with people who came before him?

DG: No.

DH: Grandfather, great-grandfather?

DG: No.

Gelsenliter hopes his children will also hold "deep feelings" for the father—their grandfather—and teaches them thus.

Jean Neal's narrative develops a mythology from the names of her ancestral groups and the modern connotations those titles convey. Her selection raises complex cultural identifiers and subtexts.

JN: I am a Black-Sioux-French-Indian. I'm Black, Sioux, Indian, and I'm French. I'm all of that.

DH: How have you chosen to identify with those lines?

JN: Because those are the ones my parents let me know: "This is who you are!"

Black, Sioux, French, or Indian, each of these groups is historically heterogeneous in every way—culturally, linguistically, and genetically and they cannot be historically contained by their titles. But that is not the point of naming them. Rather, Jean Neal's use of the tribal and national identifiers carries messages of the perceived values of Indian, French, Black, and Sioux as well as an indicator of the complexity and multiplicity of her background. There is a romantic feel to the blending of these great people and their cultural ways into a single, descended line. Jean Neal describes herself as the sum of all those ways. Historically, Neal's four ancestral people were dynamic, migratory, and intermingled with many other tribes and people. Their modern identities have changed from what they once were. But in the modern vernacular, and in Jean Neal's tone and context, the names of the four groups carry meanings spun with the threads of the ideals those names elicit.

Yaakov Kleiman's personal story demonstrates the importance to his ancestral identity of a word and a name, enlarged to mythic dimensions.

In travelling I had certain identity questions. You know, who am I really? Who am I? I'm American, I'm human. And then *Jewish* came up, especially when I travelled. . . . I actually travelled in Morocco and sort of had a spiritual awakening or something like that and what came out was . . . [the] identity of my soul was more significant than my body and the soul was saying, "You're connected to the

Jewish people." So I made my way to Israel . . . it was a very personal identity crisis. . . . Having that epiphany or whatever, something . . . significant . . . and now I'd like to deal with the question, "What is a Jew?"

Understanding himself to be a Jew, and to better understand who he was, Kleiman needed to understand what and who is a Jew. That knowledge would shape his identity into a Jewish identity. The individual joins the many, becoming one of the group and eventually the group will find expression in the individual, the Jew in the man and the man among the Jews.

Yaakov Kleiman's path of self-discovery and identity parallels those of other interviewees, who have also sought their identities from ancestral myths and narratives, different in content from Kleiman's but with similar goals. Interviewee Jason Felihkatubbe discovers his personal identity by learning about the ways of his Choctaw ancestors.

JF: Well, for me it [ancestry] is about who we are. It's about our culture, our ethics, our thinking you know in the present because those are all ideas and stuff that were passed down. That speaks to who we are today.

DH: When you say "we," who are you referring to?

JF: You know, all people in general [laughs], everybody in the present.

Felihkatubbe generously offers that all people in fact have myths of ancestry with which to identify.

Loubert Trahan's ancestral narrative identifies "the way of life that is the family," as he forges the historical and moral narratives of his Acadian and Cajun ancestors. Trahan says he, his ancestors, and his descendants promote traditional values through the meticulous maintenance of their ancestors' stories, customs, and traditions. Continuing their "way of life" is a living myth, and testament to the ancestor's success, dedicated to the great example of his Acadian predecessors.

> Well, the way of life that is the family is the most important part of the family, you know. Keeping the family together, having our meals together, practicing our religious faith . . . ongoing and I guess going by the good Lord's word.

The ancestral narrative embodies the heritage of Trahan's people, expressed and maintained through a group assent to mythologized ancestral behaviors, values, and experiences. When he researches, recites stories, organizes family reunions, prays, or sits down to dinner, Trahan essentially furthers his own ancestral identity by "keeping" and "practicing" like they did. He is a player in his own ancestral performance. By mythologizing the ancestors and following their good examples, he essentially meets the ancestors inside the myths—Trahan enters the myths of his people and there he mythologizes his own life.

Interviewees such as Leon Dixon and Simon Jacobson who claim fictive or intellectual ancestors create ancestral myths through narrative in much the same way as do Trahan, Kleiman, and Felihkatubbe. Dixon's "fictive kin" represent his personal association with particular cultural traditions and ideas, which Dixon—like Jacobson—studies and teaches, keeping great ideas and work alive. The heritage Dixon adopts is also similar to tribal and national ancestral narratives in its cultural advocacy.

Descendants incorporate themselves into their ancestral communities by practicing the culture of their ancestors. Culture transcends an individual in one place and time by linking him to people in a different place and time. Loubert Trahan describes the culture of his people as "something more or less inbred into the ones that came here [Louisiana] in the 1780s." Trahan describes an Acadian work ethic, respect for tradition, and adaptability as the qualities that continue to this day among his people as the markers of his ancestral culture. The foundations of today's values and traditions were famously laid centuries before.

Writing ancestral narratives as myths allows descendants to evaluate their own experiences through the experiences of others. An ancestral association provides an intimate context to teach the lessons and values of ancestors. Ancestors mythologized are mythologies personalized. Simon Jacobson says,

> When I was in high school we always used to ask our history teacher, "Why study history?" And we never got a decent answer. But then later in life I realized we study history to understand ourselves and you see yourself in different contexts, it allows us to understand ourselves better and our future better . . . studying that which came before us helps us be more objective about ourselves . . . as soon as you look at history, you look back at our roots, and ancestry is [to say] okay, my grandparents, they had similar aspirations to me, but they didn't have the same opportunities. I think wisdom is based on a cumulative knowledge. . . . We're like links in a chain.

Jacobson places the beginning of the "chain" at creation and the Creator. Identifying with ancestral ways is a path to defining the "I" in a grand universal mythology.

INTERVIEW WITH DR. DAVID DOLLAHITE

"The Story Goes a Little Deeper"

[Following personal introductions and conversation about research, students, and university life, Dollahite explains that in his research as a family historian, he interviews people from many religious backgrounds and has heard many say that "what they're doing is a part of a long legacy, a part of a long set of values, beliefs and behaviors. I can't tell you how many Jewish folks interviewed would tell you something like 'I don't want to be the person that breaks five thousand years of history. I don't want to be that. I want to be a good strong link in this chain.'"]

DH: And why is that?

DD: Yeah, the stuff you are dealing with is very deep, very profound. It connects with faith and family, and identity, and the soul, and it's very deep stuff. So, I'm assuming, you—like me—feel like when you are in the middle of these interviews . . . what a great job to get to interview people about stuff that really matters deeply to people, not just as some politics matters or like sports matters but what really matters to people is their faith and their family and their heritage and their legacy is all wrapped up in that. But, and just so I'm clear about this, you don't want me to talk from a scholarly perspective or from an LDS perspective but just from my own personal family?

DH: Right, and as much as that's informed by one perspective or another, that's up to you.

DD: Okay.

DH: But yes, my first question is, who are your ancestors?

DD: That's interesting, the name Dollahite—as I was growing up in California people would say, "So where's Dollahite from?" and I said, "I don't know." And I'd ask my parents and they'd say, "Well someone thought that maybe it was Dutch or German because it sounds kind of German—Dollahite." So I grew up thinking that my ancestors were probably German or Dutch. And then I joined the Mormon church, moved to Utah and one of the people I met here was my great aunt by marriage who is a very old person, at that time—she was probably in her seventies at that time I think—and she was the family genealogist. You discover that grandma knows, well that's the person you go to. She was that person. She actually had a copy machine in her home that she leased so that she could make copies of genealogical information and books and census records and all that. And she told me that; and she married a Dollahite, she married my grandfather's brother, my father's father's brother. And she was Mormon and he was not and they divorced later but she kept doing—because she's a Mormon—she kept doing genealogy.

And so she gave me a lot more information about my ancestors in America and I didn't realize how many of my ancestors were from the South. I had no clue about that. I knew that my father had lived in Oklahoma before he moved out to California but I had no idea that my ancestors fought in the Civil War for the South. So when I learned that, that was shocking. You know, "What?! My ancestors were on the wrong side?" and I learned that my ancestors were the Dollahites who first moved to America, that they were slave owners and tobacco plantation owners and frankly that was a little bit troubling and, I don't know about shaming, but I wasn't thrilled to learn that my ancestors had slaves. And as an upright Mormon who didn't smoke, that my ancestors sold tobacco, so then I kept kind of pushing back and got back to where they came from. Turns out they came from Ireland not Germany or Denmark. I thought . . . I found that interesting. And turns out they were . . . Anglo-Norman Irish, do you know what that is? British people that were kind of put up into Ireland to, like, conquer the Irish. They lived in Dublin there, and they had a castle—the Delahyde castle—and they were, you know, from what I've learned, they were pretty prominent British kind of *lordlings* over the Irish people. Then I learned, going back on my mother's side that they were from, well, my mother's father was from Norway. He was first-generation immigrant; he immigrated from Norway to America when he was seventeen or eighteen, stowed away on a ship. And so I learned kind of more about that Norwegian branch and then my mother's mother was from Ireland but the kind of true Irish you know County Cork the kind of rural potato farming Irish folks that would have hated the ancestors on my dad's side that were kind of the British conquering types.

DH: So you're like my student who wrote, "My ancestors were slaves and people who owned them." [This from a previous conversation, referring to an article the author wrote about his students' perceptions of their ancestries.]

DD: Yeah, well and it depends on how far back you want. And if we're going just you know within a generation or two, I know more the farther back we go. In the U.S. I know more but then once it gets over to the old country then—it's obviously there's more speculation, there's more you know—there's actually a professional genealogist named Bill Dollarhide who's a distant cousin of mine. He's descended from the first Delahyde who came over and Dollahite is . . . let me show you how that's spelled so you can spell that. It's Delahyde, means "of the land," and that's the Latin thing, and *hide* is from an old English word that means [something like] 160 acres. That means enough land to take care of a freeman and his family, or something like that. So the name—you know the first guy that came was Delahyde and the name now has probably ten different spellings in the U.S. . . .

DH: With an o? Is that Dollar?

DD: Dollarhide. D-O-L-L-A-R-H-I-D-E is the way that his family spells it although there may only be one [letter *l*]. It's spelled lots of different ways. . . . The first one that came was probably a second son of one of these, you know kind of prominent Dublin

Delahyde families and because of primogeniture they would give the land to the oldest son and then the other sons would become priests or merchants or they would go try to make their fortune somewhere else. This guy came to America, Francis Delahyde, and he likely came as an indentured servant . . . and looking back in the history there were Delahydes that were on both sides during the fifteen, sixteen hundreds you know with all the stuff going on between the Catholics and the Protestants in Great Britain. I had found members, I don't know if they are my direct ancestors or just that they were, what's the right word . . . relatives of my direct ancestors, on both sides of the conflict. So this guy that came to America probably came as an indentured servant, he was definitely anti-Catholic. He got in, he was the high sheriff of Baltimore County for a while then he spent I think three or four terms in the legislature, in the Maryland legislature, and he sponsored bills to keep papists from immigrating there. So he kind of had some of this fervor that he brought to America and implemented some policies to try to keep Catholics from coming, which I just found really . . . I just thought America—it's the land of religious freedom—you know, everyone comes here and says, "Hey, whatever you are that's fine." No, turns out in the early—and this would have been the early seventeen hundreds—and they were still fighting some religious wars. And I was back up at Salt Lake City at the Family History Library and read in the Encyclopedia of Oxford University, there was a guy named David Delahyde, when Queen Elizabeth became the queen he would not do the oath of loyalty that they required [of] Oxford professors, loyalty to the king or the queen and he wouldn't do it because she was Protestant, he was Catholic so he went back to Ireland because he refused to support the queen. So I just found that interesting; I grew up in the Episcopal church, became a Mormon, I just have found it interesting to learn about my ancestors, how much religious stuff was going on.

DH: And when you're talking about these people, you're referring to direct line ancestors and also ancestors who are not direct line.

DD: Yes.

DH: Do you consider those people also your ancestors, the second sons and cousins?

DD: Well I mean the clan, yeah the Dollahides and you know, my direct line ancestors I know seven generations going back to France. The guy who came from Ireland to here, from him we know his son, his son, his son, his son, his son, his son, who is my dad, and then me. So I know those people, I know pretty much where they lived and when they lived. But then back in the old country, it becomes less clear whether it was a direct line ancestor or whatever they call non–direct line ancestors.

DH: You know you could extend ancestry to include not just people, but all living things. And Carl Jung says that ancient societies and cultures that have honored or . . .

DD: . . . respected . . .

DH: . . . respected ancestors . . . and ancient societies often included animals as ancestors. How far would you extend ancestry?

DD: I mean the ancestors that I knew best. The only one of my four grandparents that I knew—the others died, either before I was born or when I was young—he was the one from Norway and so I kind of have a more visceral connection with Norway and with him. In terms of back to animals? No, I don't. I'm a pretty orthodox Latter-day Saint, I believe that God—my interpretation of creation, evolution you know those kinds of issues—I believe the Lord created the earth in billions of years and allowed life to evolve to a point where when the earth was ready, then He placed Adam and Eve on the Earth, and I believe I'm a descendant of Adam. I don't believe I'm a descendant of apes or protozoa or anything like that. I'm pretty fundamentalist, you might say.

DH: But you also define these things very broadly. I mean, if you're descended from Adam and Eve, you're related to everybody.

DD: Everyone, yeah absolutely.

DH: Would you include everyone when you say "my ancestors"? You referred mostly to people by name.

DD: Oh yeah. And mostly for spiritual reasons. I mean, Mormon doctrine teaches that we're all children of God and so I would see every human being that's ever lived, no matter what tribe or race or language or whatever, as a literal spiritual brother and sister. So my family is very big in terms of that. But in terms of ancestry yeah I'm talking about a little bit of the more literalist kind of direct line ancestors.

DH: You use it in two ways.

DD: Yes, from a spiritual humanity kind of a perspective I think . . . everyone's related, everyone's family.

Dr. David Dollahite with family. Courtesy of David Dollahite.

DH: Can you say something about your relationship to ancestors today? What is your relationship to ancestors who are no longer with us? Do they have a continuing influence on you?

DD: Yes.

DH: Can you say something about your relationship today to your ancestors? Do they have a continuing influence on you?

[Dr. Dollahite relates several stories to explain that he grew up in an average household but in neighborhoods of wealth and privilege. He married into a family of "very successful kind of successful Mormon nobility," while his own family had more humble roots. When he began to study his ancestry, he learned that his Delahyde ancestors "were lords and ladies in Ireland," with a title, a coat of arms, and even a castle. This knowledge of his ancestry left him feeling "a little better" about his family's identity. "Something about that made me feel—okay, there is some nobility in my past. That was very meaningful to me and powerful."]

DH: Are ancestors models for you?

DD: No, it's more about identity and probably status. Identity was the issue. But so that's one way in which some aspect of my ancestry has had some effect on me. But a much more important, immediate deep way is my grandfather. You asked if any of these people still influence me. Kind of. I still think about them and they affect my life.

Now my grandfather Iver Stenen, he's the one who left the farm in Norway when he was seventeen, went to England, worked in the shipyards . . . there's lots of interesting stories about him. He cheated death many, many times. The first way was that he came to Southampton, which is the place where the *Titanic* sailed from. He arrived in Southampton and got work as a merchant marine about two weeks after the *Titanic* left. So he could of, had he been there two weeks earlier he would have likely been hired on, likely would have died and I wouldn't be here in this way. But then many other times he would come out and visit us, he lived in Boca Raton, Florida. He would come out most summers and spend anywhere from a couple of weeks to the whole summer with us. And he is a very strong, tall, dynamic, charismatic guy who had this very strong Norwegian accent. He was a lumberjack; he worked on the big towers that hold up the big power lines. He was a man's man. He drove a tugboat in the shipyards. He would just sort of tell these stories about kind of these, to my little boy mind he was this larger than life kind of Paul Bunyan kind of a heroic guy.

DH: But he is still the grandfather you know from your own experience. He's not just related as stories or family myths.

DD: It's both.

DH: His own stories?

DD: Yeah it's his stories and then stories that my mother told me about him and that my mother's sister told me about him.

DH: And you retell them now?

DD: I tell them a lot. My kids know more about their Grandpa Iver than any of the others, at least on my side. On my wife's side—because they're Mormons for five generations, they've kept family history. My wife's father has written two biographies about his father President Kimball, that were best sellers in the Mormon market. And so they have done the whole family history genealogy thing to the tee. My family, you know is new to this.

DH: Do you think that those historical, more historically well researched and documented stories and narratives of that family are more true or more authentic than your family's stories?

DD: Yes, in some ways.

DH: Than those of your grandfather?

DD: I mean, they have so many of them with five generations of Mormons all keeping detailed journals and because Mormon people believe in writing and family history. And my wife's father is a historian. I mean he was a law professor here but he's an amateur historian. He's written and published several histories; he just published one recently about his grandfather Andrew Kimball who lived down in Arizona. He is a meticulous, thorough historian. He belongs to the Mormon History Society; he's a true scholar. So in terms of facts, figures, dates, you know, accurate details, no question.

DH: But to the children who have descended from both of those groups, from both of those communities; is identifying with one more valuable than identifying with the other because of the contrasting authenticity of the stories?

DD: That's a good question.

DH: One is very scientific and methodical and the other is . . .

DD: That's actually a very good question and I've never thought of it this way but it's probably true that as in many things I feel like a second-class citizen. We have seven kids. What does my wife bring to our seven kids? Books, I mean literally published best-selling books that have earned hundreds of thousands of dollars that actually get given to the grandkids. About you know, heroic Mormon leaders with detailed, meticulous history, with footnotes. I mean pages and pages of footnotes. So, real history versus what do they get from me? They get stories that I tell but I of course, I tell the stories—I'm a storyteller, I've actually told stories at storytime festivals and it's one of the things that

I love to do. So when I tell stories about my Grandpa Iver, Iver Stenen . . . I am very animated and these are very heroic and exciting stories. I could tell you several of them; they're really fun. And so my kids love them, they know them, they tell them. My oldest daughter put together—you know these days you can do books online, you can submit, there's a book like Heritage Makers, companies that will make your family history into a book. She actually did a book on Irish family where she had my seven kids—her siblings—all drew pictures of their images as dad told stories about the time that Iver almost died but, you know . . . for example, he's driving a tugboat and two huge tankers came together and flipped the tugboat over and he went into the water and these two tankers kind of crushed, just destroyed this tugboat. There's a bunch of people looking over the side and they thought surely he was dead. Well he swam underneath one of the tankers and climbed up the ladder and came walking up behind, everyone looking over, seeing this horrible accident and sure this guy was dead. He came up behind them and said, "What are you looking at?" They said, "We're looking at this guy that just died. Dead!"
"That's me!" [Laughing]
"A dead man."
"That was me!"

DH: Even if he hadn't gotten crushed should he have gotten sucked through the propellers?

DD: Yeah, exactly. But that story, I know that story has a lot of impact—they'll remember that story for years. So anyway I wonder if this isn't just a choice that people who come after you will make and . . . one may be a documented heroism, the other may be a narrated heroism but I don't know that one is necessarily even more reliable in a certain sense. They're both reliable in different ways. One's reliable in a sense it's scholarly, it's written. The other is reliable in the sense that when you hear your father tell with enthusiasm enough times the story about the only grandparent that he knew and loved—and I worship my grandpa, he was an incredible person—and so it's reliable in the heart and in the life and in the mind and I don't know that they're going to have to read for themselves those stories that are about their other side because my wife isn't really a storyteller. She's a quiet kind; she writes [but] she doesn't talk. Although I write for a living, when I'm with my family I mostly talk and tell stories. So they're going to have the benefit of both the mythological, more informal narrative oral storytelling and they're also going to have the benefit of some pretty, really well done family history from their mom's side. And I think both are going to be a benefit to them, I hope. I would think.

DH: There is a third way ancestors might continue to influence their descendants. Many people believe their ancestors visit them in dreams or other ways, to comfort or guide them. What do you think of that? Might those occurrences really be ancestors visiting, or are they necessarily reconstructions of memories?

DD: I'll tell you two dreams . . . two experiences. I was a freshman at BYU. I had been a Mormon for seven or eight months. My mother called and told me that my grandfather

Iver Stenen had died and I had no idea that he was sick. He had a heart attack, he was eighty-two. I had no idea that this was imminent; it totally came out of the blue. And then she said, "And I didn't want to disrupt"—this was probably a month or two from the end of the semester my first semester in college—she said, "I didn't want to disrupt your college studies by having you come to the funeral so I need to tell you that we've already had a service. And he wished to be cremated and have his ashes strewn at sea and we did that. So that's all been done." And you know, I understood. At the time it was horrifically shocking that he was gone, that I wouldn't . . . at the time I didn't know the power and the blessing, the benefit for grief of funerals. I've later learned that, but I didn't have a chance to go hear people talk about him and not only that but there was no place where I could go . . . a grave, even an urn in a bank full of ashes there's no place I could go. He was gone.

DH: At sea?

DD: At sea. She described how they poured his ashes out from a little boat.

DH: Which sea was that?

DD: Well, in the Atlantic Ocean. And so this was, and this was the first person who I loved and who had died. I had an uncle who had died but you know, he wasn't that close to me he was one of my dad's brothers. I mean I knew him but my grandpa was really a hero and a beloved person to me. So it was devastating for me and I was reeling from that and I was a Mormon—I think it was eight months, so I had a newfound belief in resurrection and life after death, in the idea that the spirit lives on after death but this was all new and fresh to me. I was not a believer before that and so this was sort of the first test of my newfound beliefs. But that night, God blessed me with an incredibly powerful dream and it's one of those dreams, you might ask, "Was this all inside of my head?" I feel like this was more than that. So in my dream I saw kind of a mountain and went toward it and there was a cave and I walked toward it and out from the darkness of the cave walked the spirit of my grandfather. And I knew who it was, and I knew that I was dreaming but I knew that this was my grandfather not just random firing of synapses. I knew that I was having an experience beyond, um, just inside of my own head . . . And so I saw my grandfather and I came up to him and he said to me, "I love you. I'm still alive. What you've been taught about the life after death is true. I am, I am still who I am and we will see each other again and I'll be fine." I woke up from that dream feeling awash in love and spiritual power and alive and really on fire in kind of a spiritual way, the way Christians talk about the Holy Spirit . . . the scriptures talk about it in different ways but in Mormonism you're baptized by water then you're baptized by fire from the Holy Spirit. I felt alive and embraced in love in an incredibly deep and profound way. So that experience with my grandfather immediately after his death was for me . . . I feel a closeness to him in that way.

DH: In what way is it significant that you two are related? In other words, might that same opportunity have been offered to you if this man had not been your grandfather but had been your best friend, if he had been your mentor and you were only related in the way any two humans are related?

DD: That's a really good question.

DH: I mean, because you mentioned Adam and Eve and God creating family, which seems to suggest that God has some special acknowledgment or recognition of a family unit . . .

DD: Right, yeah.

DH: . . . As a spiritual entity. In this case is that somehow, is that coming through in this opportunity? *Opportunity* is the wrong word—this *gift*?

DD: Yeah, that's a good question. Yeah, would it have mattered that we're biologically related?

DH: Right, and closely related. And maybe it's awkward to separate out you know deep, personal senses in all of this. Have you known your other grandparents?

DD: Yes. Well I didn't know my grandmother on my mother's side. I wish I had but I didn't. I mean so I only knew one of my grandparents and he offered the kind of unconditional love and support that grandparents can offer the parents.

So I never had a grandmother. Both of my grandmothers died before I was born and he was a very warm, open, kindly, supportive person so yeah I received—and he's actually a lot like my father. He's my mother's father and my mother was very demanding and strict and tense. My dad's easygoing, low-key. My grandpa was a lot like that. Kind of easygoing and low-key. . . . So my grandpa was pretty important to me as a kid and so yeah, for me the fact that my grandpa—that God—allowed me to sort of have this interaction with my grandfather. Which I know that . . . I mean I don't know how spiritual things work. I've had experiences like that in other situations and the way Mormons think about it is that the spirit world is right here, that the people who have died are right here. People that are yet unborn are right here.

DH: Do you also think that way?

DD: I do, yes. So you know a different dimension. We can't see them with our natural eyes. They're very much alive in the spirit.

DH: Are they hearing us as we're speaking? Or is that not important?

DD: It doesn't matter and sometimes yes, and I think probably the Mormon sense is that on occasion they're sent to come and give some information or remind or warn or sort of interact in some way with us, but typically they're probably doing their own thing and we're kind of doing our own thing but there are times when there's kind of an intersection of the spirit world and this life that we're now living. But let me tell you about another person—about my grandfather's wife, my grandmother who I never knew.

DH: Was she Irish-American?

DD: She was Irish and she . . . let's see what's the best order to tell you this in . . . I'll tell you in the order that I learned it. So my mother never talked about her mother, ever. Never talked about her. But as a kid growing up I didn't think to myself, "How come my mom never talks about her mother?" Because her dad, my grandpa was this big guy in my life and I didn't know to think, "So why is my mom never talking about her mom?" But she never did so I knew nothing about her. And so . . . when I joined the Mormon church I did a ton of research about my father's side trying to get it back to the old country to figure out where Dollahite came from. Well I discovered . . .

DH: It doesn't seem like the Dollahites are more important to you. I mean the most important person . . .

DD: . . . is my mom's dad.

DH: Right. But this was a decision that was sort of determined by cultural norm and opportunity.

DD: That and probably . . . you walk around with your last name.

DH: Right.

DD: So interpersonally my mother's side is very important but as a lineage identity. And there's no question I spent tons of time trying to discover where the Dollahite name came from and I finally figured it out. Well, I didn't figure it out. I finally discovered it; other people had put some pieces together and figured it out so I finally got that knowledge. So one night I'm asleep in North Carolina, I was a professor at University of North Carolina Greensboro, and I'm asleep and my—at that time my wife and I had two kids, our oldest daughter Rachel was probably six or seven, maybe eight and our daughter Erica was a couple of years younger than that. So I was kind of excited that I had discovered and that I could now tell people you know, "Dollahite comes from Delahyde and it's an Anglo-Norman and the first Delahyde, Rogerus Delahyde, came with William the Conqueror in 1066." I mean wow, that was cool. So I'm asleep.

I'm asleep and whether he is a direct, a lineal descendent or ancestor of mine I don't care. I just know that the name was you know back there, it's in history books. Okay, so I wake up in the night and standing next to my bed is an older woman in a flower dress who I did not know. I didn't recognize who it was. In other words I didn't see her and then, "Oh that's . . ." No, but as I looked at her it was communicated to me clearly that she is my mother's mother. And she never spoke, I just knew and I knew that this was my grandmother and I was three when she died. I never knew her. My only memory of anything to do with her is when my mom put me on an airplane to go back for the funeral for her mom. . . . So that's my only memory of anything to do with my grandma and the question that my grandmother asked me was, "What about me? What about my family?" In other words, she knew that I had been focused wholly on my father's father's father's father, all the way back and I had ignored. . . . I had been a Mormon at this point maybe seven or eight years something and you know so there was time that I could have done some research on her line but I hadn't and so the question was, "What about me?" And it was very powerfully and indelibly imprinted in me and then my little daughter Rachel came running into our bedroom—this was in the middle of the night—and she came around my side—normally she would have gone to her mother, my wife is the most loving, marvelous mother and all the kids they go see their mom when they're scared—but she happened to come around my side of the bed where I was sleeping.

DH: You were still awake?

DD: I was . . . my grandmother was still there and my daughter ran through the spirit of my grandmother and as she did so, my grandmother disappeared or was beamed up or however you want to think about it. My daughter ran through the spirit of my grandmother and she ran and she hugged me and she said, "Daddy, I'm scared," and I said, "Why?" She said, "Because there was a woman in my room looking at me and I didn't know who it is." I said, "It's okay, honey. That's your great-grandma."

DH: Did your wife hear you say that?

DD: No, she was asleep.

DH: She was still asleep.

DD: And so that was a powerful thing.

DH: Why does your grandmother have an interest in you pursuing her family line?

DD: And that's a religious question.

DH: Did you learn these things from religious teaching or did you kind of find them and then say, "Oh yeah, that's what I believed," or how? This doesn't sound like an experience that comes out of Mormon teaching.

DD: No this doesn't.

DH: But you're using Mormon teaching in some ways to interpret it.

DD: I am, yeah. The reason why is because I had been baptized for my grandfather at that point and that's a Mormon doctrine of baptism. I'm not sure how much you're aware of that but the idea that people on the other side, people who have died, are still able to learn and make choices and make commitments and learn truth and the idea is that if they on the other side accept the Gospel, then we can be baptized in our temples for them to help them progress. It's kind of like the Catholic idea of purgatory. . . . Similar notion that as we do ancestry, as we do genealogy and we find out people's names and the dates that they lived and died and so forth, we can go to our temples, be baptized and then married for them and that allows them to progress in the next life.

DH: And they are apparently aware of this as well?

DD: Exactly.

DH: And this is hereditary . . .

DD: There's thousands of stories with Mormons having interactions with their grand-parents, with ancestors about this whole issue. The kind of classic Mormon story is they're trying to find a missing link you know between a great-great-great-grandma and a great-great-great-great-grandma and you can't figure out how they're connected, or when they died or whatever and so you're studying census records or you're in the library or you're at a cemetery looking at records jotting down things and you either hear some "go down this aisle" or "walk down that path" or "go get that book." I mean you either hear or kind of just have an idea and you know it's not from you and so you go grab that book or you go walk down that path and then you find the tombstone. Or you're checking through microfiche records and you have this idea you're supposed to go grab that one, so you go grab that one and then you find that person. It's like they wanted you to find them because they're ready to have you do the baptism or the mar-riage for them. So there were a lot of stories like that.

DH: And in your case I assume you would think that some of these are real occurrences?

DD: Absolutely!

DH: And some are not.

DD: In any faith community, in any community, in any group experiences happen and then they get told and then they get embellished.

DH: Sure.

DD: But the ones I've heard from people that have had those experiences themselves I trust them, unless I know that they're not entirely sane, then I assume that those . . . are true.

DH: It seems like there's also some room here to maneuver between the influence of hereditary connections and the influence of adopted relationships. Would you say so?

DD: Absolutely. For Mormons, I've heard of a lot of Latter-day Saints who have ad-opted kids talk about how they recognize that the child isn't biologically genetically theirs, but they believe that the spiritual connection between them and their adopted child or their adopted child and the parent is if not equally even sometimes more strong. People have had amazing spiritual experiences. Because Mormons tend to like big families and if a couple can't have children, let's say, or maybe they've had one or two kids and they'd like to have six or seven kids, then they will do almost anything to get more kids. And I've heard these stories about people going to Russia, to China, all over the world on kinds of spiritual journeys where they felt led by God and led by the spirit to this child in this orphanage and they feel very powerfully, spiritually, and *familialy* connected to that person.

DH: And in the sense that we've been discussing family and ancestry, would you say that people who don't have direct line descendants can still become ancestors?

DD: Oh sure. You know fictive kin, I mean our African American families very much adopt people in to their family and I think that's probably the norm.

DH: Whatever recognition there is of a family organization being divine or sacred, would that also apply to adopted members?

DD: Oh, absolutely. Absolutely. And so for Mormons and for me as a person, you know blood ancestry is obviously very important but there's a spiritual idea of being adopted into Abraham's family. I'm thinking of a Jewish community that I attended three or four times and one of the times they had a visiting cantor there who, an African American guy with a voice like James Earl Jones and he chanted in Hebrew these incredibly beautiful, powerful Psalms. It was interesting to see, this was a Jewish community-—everyone's white except for the cantor—and he's chanted ancient Hebrew hymns in Hebrew and there was no sense that this guy is black. He can't really be a descendant of Abraham like we, there was none of that. There was total acceptance of, "This person is of Israel, he's been adopted in." And in fact, this person because of his gift, because of his voice wherever he went, he packed them in. It was like the high holy day.

DH: The way you describe it is as a positive thing, that this person is accepted into the community as a legitimate member. Do you think that DNA research is going to have some destructive impact on those kinds of open-minded, welcoming . . . ?

DD: Yeah, you remind me of this: one of the classes I teach we talk about Jewish families and Muslim families and Catholic families and Orthodox Christian families and Evangelical Christian families and Mormon families and so on. We talk about Jewish families; we talk about the Jewish priesthood, the kohanim—the kohens—and there's now this kohen modal Haplotype, I don't know whether you've heard of this.

. . . It's fascinating, it's like 90 percent of the people who are kohen retain that marker on the Y-chromosome. . . .

. . . Actually my mother's best friend was Jewish so I have kind of a Jewish grand-mother, actually she's my godmother; this is an interesting story. I can show you the picture when I was baptized in the Episcopal church as an infant my godfather was my father's brother who is now an Episcopal priest, has been an Episcopal priest for all of my life. My godmother is mother's best friend Anne Scinski at the time, she was Rosenbaum I think and so she's my Jewish godmother and when Father Ewald said to my mother, "So Elizabeth, who's David's godfather going to be?" And she said, "Oh, his Uncle Gene, my wife's brother," and he said, "That's a great choice." He was a deacon in the Episcopal Church at that time so that was a great choice.

"And who will be his godmother?"

"Oh, my best friend Anne Scinski."

"Tell me about Anne."

"Oh, we've been best friends for our whole life."

CHAPTER 5

"And what faith is Anne?"

"Well she's a non-practicing Jew."

"Well Elizabeth we can't have a Jewish godmother for a Christian baptism, she has to be a baptized Christian."

"Well no she's agreed that she will make sure he gets raised in the Christian faith if something happens to me."

"No you don't understand, you can't have a Jewish godmother for a Christian baptism." And my mom said, "Well then he won't be baptized." And Father Ewald backed off and said, "I guess we can make an exception." So a part of me, I mean, part of me is Jewish in the sense that my mother has always talked about this dear friend of hers and so the idea of DNA and blood and all that, I actually feel closer to the Jewish people than I feel to the Norwegian people or the Irish people. I mean, I feel a connection to my Jewish brothers and sisters meaning spiritual. I feel a much deeper spiritual connection to them than I do to my blood ancestors and let me actually tell you the rest of the story on my grandmother because I learned this after my mother died. My mother died of cancer when she was only fifty-eight and so I went out and I was with her for the few days before she died and it was not until after she died that her best friend, my Jewish godmother Anne, told me this: that my grandmother was an alcoholic. Again, my mother never talked about her mother. I had no idea my grandmother was an alcoholic.

DH: Iver's wife?

DD: Iver's wife. Catherine. Catherine Tevlin was her name and she comes from the O'Malley clan, a very prominent clan in Ireland. And so my grandmother was an alcoholic and she was a sweet woman when she wasn't drunk but when she was drunk she was a violent person. You know how some people get very different when they're drunk? Once when my grandmother was drunk she would chase my mother around the house with a knife threatening to kill her. Okay so this grandmother who appeared to me and kind of asked me, "What about my family?" (By the way, when I described to my mother this experience and I described this flower dress that my mother was wearing she began crying. She said, "She always wore that. It was red. What you described was what she always wore.") Anyways, so I learned from my Jewish godmother that my grandmother was an alcoholic and went into you know violent rages against my mother. That was very hard to hear because you know grandmothers aren't supposed to threaten to kill your mother, right? But at this point when I learned this I was in my late twenties, I had a degree in marriage and family therapy, I had a doctorate in family studies. I knew what substance abuse could do to people. I knew what having an alcoholic in a family could do to people's psyche and their identity and their sense of well-being. And it actually was very helpful for me to hear that from Anne because it completely explained to me why my mother was such a powerful personality, why she had to be right, why she had to be in control, why she was so intense and such a dominating force in my life. I always pictured her as this very large, powerful—she was very tall, powerful woman who would not suffer fools. Who would not be bossed around by anybody.

136

DH: Not even a priest . . . Does it alter the composition of your ancestry when one person does bad things?

DD: Well, I had learned about the concept of a transitional character and that's a marriage and family therapy term. For someone who is the person that kind of is in a lineage of let's say alcoholism, you know three, four generations of alcoholism or abuse and most physical abuse takes place when people are under the influence of alcohol, research shows it. Anywhere from I think it's 50–70 percent of family abuse takes place when a person is under the influence. And so I learned some of these facts and a transitional character is someone who, even though their lineage, the patterns of the ancestors, are negative let's say poor or abusive or substance abuse or whatever it is, this person somehow stops that pattern when every indication is that if you were abused or your parents were alcoholic, the chances of you being that are higher than for someone who's not. I mean, there's lots of psychological reasons and physical and DNA reasons why. The susceptibility to alcoholism is carried on. And so I, my respect for my mother as a person who yeah she wasn't perfect, yeah she was a kind of dominating person but she did not drink, she never beat me, she worked hard to kind of stop any of that.

DH: But it doesn't sound like you are going to rewrite your ancestral narrative because there's bad things in there. You're acknowledging the bad things. You're acknowledging the alcohol or the violence or the erratic behavior and you're integrating that into the picture.

DD: It is what it is.

DH: It's not idealized.

DD: Yeah, people under the influence of substances can become very bad.

DH: Do you have any thoughts on why people are so interested in their own ancestries? I think of the mystic Rabbi Kook's comment that people and other creatures naturally long for their origins. For Kook, those origins lead back to God. For others it might lead elsewhere. Do you have any sense of why it is that people seek their origins and look to their families for that?

DD: I think you're asking a really hugely important question and a good question in that there's not a simple answer and I agree with Rabbi Kook; the way I would say it from a Mormon perspective we're all children of God but the story goes a little deeper. Mormon theology is that every human being is what we call "intelligence" like pure truth, pure intelligence and we are eternal, we are coexisting with God so that we all have an eternal, infinite identity as an individual and then God, our heavenly father and heavenly mother—Mormons believe in heavenly parents—at some point in our eons of development as light and truth kind of as an entity, at some point they adopt (may not be the right word) or they formed us as their spiritual children and then we lived with them for eons of time and then we were placed on this Earth in families with fathers and mother ideally. Of course we all genetically come from a father and mother. But ideally, we have both a father and a mother who kind of represent God the father and god the mother to us and we have this very deep, very profound eternal longing for home that is longing for God, longing for unity, perfection, longing for union with our father and mother and that gets projected onto our earthly father and mother. The anthropological, kind of secular anthropological idea is that human beings create God in the image of themselves or in the image of their parents; they kind of project earthly parents up into heaven. What Mormons would say is it's the other way around. It's that we all do have both infinite identity as an individual, so we recognize that every human being has infinite worth, infinite potential to become like heavenly father and heavenly mother, infinite—we are infinite beings, we are eternal beings. But we also are connected to heavenly parents and our earthly parents are kind of an echo of that, a shadow of that, a type of that and so we sort of because we don't know God in this life you know we have our eyes and our hands and our bodily senses that mask a lot of the sort of infinite, eternal, spiritual truth. If our eyes were open to all things we would see that there's reality beyond just the things of this flesh, this material world but we have sort of our bodies put a veil over our minds and over our ability to perceive things as they really are. So I would say, I mean Rabbi Kook's point I think is I would say it similarly, all human beings yearn in a profoundly deep and eternal way, yearn for origins and yes it is—who is my father, who is my mother, who is my grandpa, who is my grandmother. For Jews, it's all the way back to Abraham as sort of the founding member of their clan as it is for Muslims actually, back to Abraham at least Arab Muslims. And then back to Adam and Eve and then back to God and so I believe that there is a . . . my wife actually says this now and then. She's a deeply humble, spiritual, loving, marvelous person and now and then she'll just say something like, and sometimes I can tell that she's just sort of this sad, just a little bit just not fully engaged in the here and now and she'll say that she just misses home, she misses God, she misses heaven, she misses that sort of perfection. Because on this earth we're dealing with our moral, fallen, sinful selves and others and this earth can be pretty crummy, it can be pretty evil and so the sense of yearning for a connection to what's infinite and eternal and good and true that's deep in us and I think it's normal; I think it's universal. It can get masked, it can get depending on how people are treated it can get snuffed out for a while but I think ultimately all human beings come back to: Who am I? Where am I from? Why am I here?

DH: It sounds like you're saying "Who I am" runs through a family identity because that's the nature of God.

DD: That's my belief.

DH: What then do you do with the larger family organization that goes beyond a man and a woman to a tribal organization for example? Because, people often look to tribal groups not just to fathers and mothers.

DD: Yeah, it's interesting from Mormon theology, the house of Israel you know God chose Abraham and he chose Isaac and Jacob and he made a covenant with Abraham and he renewed that covenant with Isaac, he renewed that covenant with Jacob who became Israel and the twelve tribes of Israel sort of spread throughout the world and so what we would say is yeah, the Lord does place us into tribes, family at large and we do feel a sense of kinship identity with that.

[Some people] see themselves as not simply individuals and not simply little nuclear families but that there's kind of an identity with maybe thousands, maybe millions of other people like them and that's kind of being a people.

DH: Is that consistent with the pursuit of family?

DD: Absolutely.

DH: Even though it's a larger number.

DD: It is, because most of these clans or tribes at some point in some way trace themselves back to a founder.

DH: Right.

DD: For Jews, it's Abraham, for Muslims Abraham.

DH: Interesting.

DD: Yeah and so I think that there is that sense, and I look at my own wife's family, I look at my kids—-their great-great-grandfather was this prominent religious leader who was widely respected, widely loved. I mean really profoundly loved and there's a picture of him on our wall. There's no pictures of my grandparents or my wife's other grandparents but there's a picture of him on our wall and we have pictures of Jesus and of you know temples and kind of like big things to us and he's sort of the clan father and there are reunions. Mormons do a lot of family reunions. We have reunions every year with descendants of especially of Kimball, with Heber C. Kimball who was his grandfather who was one of Joseph's best friends and apostles. So yeah there's something about kind of connecting a whole group of people. And I've been to these Mormon family reunions that my wife's family has. Never once has there ever been a family reunion with the Dollahite clan, it has never happened. But with Mormons it's huge in their kind of psyche that you should honor and respect and kind of revere these founder ancestor people, the pioneers or people who did good things. And I see them, I mean they have on T-shirts you know "Heber C. Kimball Reunion." They'll eat food that he ate, they'll sing songs that he sang, they'll hear stories about his life and it creates this sense of solidarity beyond just drawn nuclear family. There are hundreds of people at these reunions and there's this sort of sense of okay, I'm a part of something that's bigger than me, that's bigger than even the people that live in the house I live in. I'm part of something bigger and greater and that's cool. So I think that that's part of it, that's probably the psychological thing. For me, probably the deeper thing is the spiritual reality that every human being is connected; every human being is a child of God. And so it's hard to connect with everybody in the world and your own family you see them every day and you fight over the last piece of cake with them and you fight over what you're going to watch on TV so your own immediate family isn't always transcendent, right? Your own immediate family is pretty earthy, it's pretty kind of in your face but the extended family—people you see once a year and you're all descended from this kind of prominent guy or gal and you all feel like God placed me in this family, in this extended family and I can be proud of my heritage.

NARRATIVES OF SUFFERING AND SACRIFICE

All but one or two interviewees describe in their interviews their ancestors' great suffering and sacrifices. Persecutions, injustices, and other indignities of ancestors are described in interviews as part of political, racial, or gender conflicts. So prominent and so frequently do themes of suffering occur in the narratives, they appear to serve a primary function in ancestral identities. Suffering and sacrifice signal hard work, resilience, and hope and are offered as moral lessons for descendants.

Descendants more than simply relate stories of suffering; they share the burdens of ancestors' pain. Through telling and honoring ancestors' resilience, sacrifices, and strength, descendants present ancestors as positive ideals, and give ancestors' suffering lasting meaning. Through rituals and celebrations, descendants remember and honor the ancestors' noble examples. Suffering is commonly narrated as sacrifice for the sake of descendants and interviewees often describe how they work hard in their own lives out of respect for ancestors' examples. Descendants try to live up to the stature of those before them and to carry on their courage and strength. Loubert Trahan says,

> The culture that's been passed down here is a result of the deportation out of Nova Scotia in 1755 and the struggles and the hardships that those deportees had to suffer either in Liverpool or in France as outcasts, paupers, and trying to make a better life for themselves. So they learned how to really struggle and that, I guess, that gene, that lifestyle, that desire to amount to something was more or less inbred into the ones that came here in the 1780, '85, '90s on the seven Spanish ships which the crown of Spain furnished to them to bring them to New Orleans and spread over the Acadian countryside.

Suffering and persecution define the background to Trahan's "Acadian Oasis," pitched defensively against the outside world. Trahan's ancestors suffered at the hands of bigoted outsiders and their descendants will not betray that legacy by submitting to or joining in with outsiders.

Artifacts and pictures confirm the authenticity of stories of suffering and serve as kinds of relics of the dead. But descendants know the stories by heart. In her interview, Henrietta Mann describes her ancestors who suffered attacks from the U.S. Cavalry. "My mother's grandmother too was at Sand Creek who too was at the Washita; I never knew. Her name was Vister, V-I-S-T-E-R. . . . I don't necessarily pray to them but I acknowledge them in all that I do, that I acknowledge the past talks to me." Dr. Mann honors ancestral sacrifices by preserving the culture for which they were persecuted. "The culture, the way of seeing, a way of being," was passed down from grandmothers and grandfathers who survived genocide. Promoting Cheyenne ways and identity is Dr. Mann's way of joining their battle and continuing their fight. It is incumbent on the people of the present to sustain the past just as it was incumbent on the people of the past to prepare the way for the people of the future.

June York shows persecution and suffering as essential themes of her family's ancestral narrative.

> We are of Japanese ancestry, and our families did survive the World War Two. That had a lot of effect on our lives and culture. So, I would like my children to understand the hardships that my ancestors went through to be here, and the privilege to be here, and what they went through and fought for to be an American.

The lessons of the suffering of ancestors are told for children to understand and to show the ancestors respect. In some cases, the descendants' successes as American citizens might even be a triumph for the ancestors, their battle for respect finally won.

Interviewees describe ancestors as having suffered not only for their cultures and ways but for the sake of their descendants. Father Tran believes his grandmother suffered martyrdom for her faith but also for the sake of her family and eventually for her grandson Christopher, whom she would never meet. As he performs daily Mass, Father Tran remembers Grandmother's horrible death, and honors her with ceremony and prayer.

> See I never knew my grandmother. But when I look back . . . and know . . . why that woman suffered . . . and then because whatever they sacrifice, it's for you, then you're willing to do that . . . for your grandmother, for whatever they did for you. And then, "Grandmother, I do this for you."

Grandmother's sacrifice also contributes to a family identification with piety and religious convictions. When asked if he might feel similar responsibility toward other martyrs who were not related so closely to him, or if he had adoptive grandparents who had suffered for him, Father Tran replied, "Sure. If they had done good to you."

Father Tran sees his Grandmother's death as an act of supreme good—surrendering her life for God and for her loved ones, including her eventual descendants. Grandmother's sacrifice produced good things for those who followed her. "What I'm saying is, 'Good trees bear good fruit,'" says Father Tran, while he connects his own vocation as a priest to his grandmother's faith and martyrdom. In a beautiful spiritual-ancestral form, Grandmother died never knowing Grandson Christopher, but through the family narrative and love, grandmother and grandson now bless each other, somehow.

INTERVIEW WITH TERRI OMORI, STANLEY ARAI, JUNE YORK, AND FORD OMORI

"When the Wave Hits the Shore"

DH: Can each of you please tell me your names, your first language, and your occupation?

June York: My first language was Japanese growing up, but once we entered school, my language was English. School art teacher.

Stanley Arai: My first language is Japanese, aerospace engineer.

Terri Omori: My first language is English, office administrator at Vista Buddhist Temple.

Ford Omori: My first language is English, public works.

DH [to all]: Can you tell me who are your ancestors?

TO: My ancestors are from a small town near Hiroshima, Japan, called Kaita. They are on my grandmother's side, the Matsumotos and my grandfather's side the Hananos. My grandparents came to America originally 1920. My grandmother was born in 1900 and my grandfather was older than her by five years or so. So my grandparents are considered first generation, and my parents were born here so they are considered second generation, and I was born here so I'm considered third generation Japanese-American.

DH: So when you describe your ancestors you're describing them by family, and also as individuals.

TO: Yes, partly family. I don't know them very well individually beyond my grandparents.

DH: What about outside of your direct line? Are you thinking of uncles, cousins, aunts, also as your ancestors?

TO: Yes, but probably mostly my direct paternal and maternal lines. When I think ancestors I think many generations away, like, almost evolution.

DH: You think of ancestors as extending how far back?

TO: Oh, generations and generations and generations; more than I know.

DH: More than ten? A hundred?

TO: Probably not more than a hundred, probably ten-ish. . . . I think of the word *ancestry* as so far back beyond what I know. So, people. So like ancestry I guess would be Asians descended from the Mongolian race is what I understand.

DH: Would there be a first ancestor?

TO: I don't know. I've never considered that.

DH: What about people outside of Asia?

TO: I never thought about it that way, but what I'm understanding now, [is] all man came from the African countries. . . .

DH: Would you think of other animals, or other forms of life as your ancestors?

TO: No. I would just think of ancestors as being human. But you're getting me deep into ancestry but on a day-to-day basis my ancestors would just be from family ancestors.

DH: Would you think of ancestry as more of a cultural or a genealogical thing?

TO: Probably both, cultural and genealogical.

DH: Stanley, who are your ancestors?

SA: It's a similar definition. I descended from various people and my parents are in Japan and all my generation before me are in Hiroshima. But I'm considered fourth generation because my grandpa was born in Hawaii and so was my dad. . . . My dad married my mom who was from Hiroshima, Japan, then they moved back to Hiroshima.

DH: And along the way, there are a lot of people coming and going within your family group. Would you consider those people to be ancestors as well?

SA: From a Buddhist point of view, we all come from the same ocean so to speak. So we're all in the same group, including animals.

DH: Is that how you think of ancestry?

SA: Yea, that's a little different concept from the ocean, versus ancestor. The way I define ancestors is where I'm descended from.

DH: Is the ocean a spiritual relationship?

SA: We're all part of this big vast ocean, and the waves above it are our individual selves. I am a part of the ocean.

DH: So, you're not descended from the ocean, you're . . .

SA: Part of it. Part of it.

DH: Would you think of cousins and aunts as part of your ancestry?

SA: I wouldn't consider them part of my ancestors. I would consider them as my relatives.

DH: Is there a difference between ancestors and relatives?

SA: Yes.

DH: Could a person be adopted into your genealogical family?

SA: [Indicates yes] Yes. I guess so.

DH: June, can you tell me who are your ancestors?

JY: When I hear the term *ancestry*, I just think of all those who have come before us, before me. That's the term ancestry. But my personal ancestry or ancestors is basically all my relatives and all my family before me.

DH: When you say "all people" do you mean all people, however many billion people there are . . . in the way that Stanley says all people are related?

JY: When I say "ancestors" I mean all my family before me. And even though I may not know who they are, it's that link.

DH: How do you define family?

JY: From my family, into my parents to my grandparents to their grandparents, and all their brothers and sisters, and all the extended family . . .

DH: Cousins?

JY: Yes.

DH: Second cousins?

JY: Yea.

DH: Third cousins?

JY: We're all related. Family, extended family.

DH: Is there a cultural limit to that?

JY: Cultural limit?

DH: Such as, they would be people of Japan, or people of Asia, or people of America, or some kind of cultural limit?

JY: Hmmm. I guess when I keep thinking about it . . . I've only thought of it as in Japan, but I'm sure it goes further. I guess I would.

DH: Are animals or prehumans also ancestors?

JY: No animals or other nonhuman things are included. . . . Adopted members are included.

DH: If a child was adopted into your family, could the child claim your family as her own or his own?

JY: Yes, sure. Because within my family there are adopted.

DH: Ford, can you tell me who are your ancestors?

FO: My parents and grandparents—we had the opportunity to visit my father's side of the family in Japan. I would consider them family even though I don't know them well or personally but consider them as family. I'm a third generation, born and raised in this area, same as my parents, my father's side of the family. I guess an appreciation for all others and living things, as far as acknowledging that, but as far as immediate family, as far as your ancestral connection, it's my parents and grandparents.

DH: Would you include your uncles and aunts? And cousins also?

FO: Yes.

DH: Do you have any sense of how broadly you would take that?

FO: We're all interconnected so I accept that and appreciate that.

DH: Do you ever think of people coming out of Africa as your ancestors?

FO: No, not specifically but it's about acknowledging and respecting everyone and everything.

DH: Do you have any idea of an ancestral beginning, a first person?

FO: No. I never thought back further than my grandparents really. But it's appreciating everybody and everything for the opportunity to experience that.

DH: Why is that important?

FO: I think it gives you a broader perspective of not thinking it's just you, it's all of these causes and conditions.

DH: Why is that important?

FO: So you don't take things for granted, we have kids and we want to make sure things are possible for them.

DH: When you think of an ancestral community or group, do you include your community's children?

FO: Yes.

DH: June, is that part of the importance of remembering ancestors?

JY: Definitely, having it being passed on to the children and their children.

DH: Is remembering genealogical ancestors different from remembering cultural ancestors?

JY: I think it's important for me, and probably everyone here because we are of Japanese ancestry, and our families did survive the World War Two, that had a lot of affect on our lives and culture. So, I would like my children to understand the hardships that my ancestors went through to be here, and the privilege to be here, and what they went through and fought for to be an American. I think that's important to pass on. And the culture, because we are Japanese is important. I married a Caucasian, so it's important for me to pass on the Japanese culture to my children, who are half Caucasian and half Japanese. So, it gets lost. If you look at the other Americans, we are all immigrants, but most of them have lost their roots or belongings. And I think it's something that we understand and keep, so that we're tolerant of each other; and I would like my children to understand that also.

DH: Why is it important to understand that they come from those people rather than just to hold those people up as good examples?

JY: They need to relate that that's part of their ancestors or relatives, and that they were able to make it, and that there's a standard. Culturally, I think we as Japanese-Americans—it's a little bit different for us, because we are a culture that has assimilated into the United States, where a lot of other cultures don't completely assimilate. Like, most of us don't speak Japanese anymore, we don't generally speak it in public—not that we're ashamed of it, but we find it—I find it, my family finds it—rude to speak a language amongst other people who don't understand your language. And we don't live in towns, Koreatown, Chinatown, Thai-town, we assimilated out into the culture. That's why the Obon is so important to us, because it's one of the few things we strongly and culturally identify with.

So, when the war broke out, the Japanese came here, and were dedicated to making a go of it in America and become Americans, they didn't speak Japanese in public, because Americans didn't speak Japanese, they moved into neighborhoods and tried to blend in with the American people. That's the way we were brought up. I spoke Japanese at home, but once we entered school it was lost. We grew up with a prejudice, I didn't tell anyone in elementary school I was Buddhist, and very few people I knew did, because we were, I don't want to say ridiculed, but there was definitely a non-understanding of that. So, as time goes on, we are now at a state where America is more tolerant of other religions, and it's just something I think is important to see where our ancestry, relatives came from, and how hard they worked to be here.

DH: Does a personal association between the young people who are learning those lessons and the ancestors who experienced these things change the lesson? Is it different from just reading a lesson in a history book?

JY: Oh yes, because what happened to our ancestors affected us. Our parents are not college educated most of them, because of the war they didn't graduate high school, they couldn't afford college. By the time they'd get out they were put into camps.* Therefore their importance was pushed upon us to get an education and graduate college. Everything was for education, to better themselves that and they couldn't do that. Their opportunities didn't allow for them to. And I don't believe that there is anger, but it's just the way it is. So my generation has the opportunity, so you're going to make the best of it. And my parents could have been doctors, lawyers, professionals making a lot of money, giving us even more opportunities however due to the circumstances of the war, my parents were gardeners and farmers and worked hard to get us into college, and I think that is being lost in newer generations.

DH: Did you grow up in California?

JY: Yes, I was born in Los Angeles and I grew up in Orange County.

DH: Stanley, do you agree it's important to transmit lessons and examples from ancestors to children?

SA: Well it gives them a sense of belonging to some cultural race or whatever, just to feel like they're part of something.

DH: Part of what?

SA: That their ancestors—like my grandparents and everybody had growing up.

DH: You agree with June that it's a little bit different to say, "This is what your ancestors did," than to say, "This is what a group of people did"? How would it be different for other American children to read Japanese American experiences, than for the descendants of Japanese Americans to read about it or hear about it?

SA: It gives them a sense that, "Oh, that was part of me." That's the way I envision it. Every time there's something, like a toy, or video game that's based from Japan I always say, "Oh you're culturally related to that."

DH: So it's a psychological, economic, and social connection. Is it a spiritual connection?

SA: I wouldn't say spiritual.

DH: Terri do you agree with that? There are many connections but not really a spiritual connection?

---

*Internment camps set up by the US government to isolate Japanese American families during the Second World War.

147

TO: Yeah, I agree with that. I think it's important, like you said, the difference from reading it in a book, which is still important because I think there's still a lot of people who don't even know about what happened in World War Two, and so it is important. But I think it's important for our children to understand that Grandma and Grandpa and their great-grandma and -grandpa, they were all put into these camps; and Grandpa he went ahead and he enlisted in the army, even though the U.S. government put them in the camp, and fought in the 442 infantry and he did all that.* I think it's important that children know what their relatives or their family did, because I totally agree with June, everything that they did is the life that we're living today, basically. It is important. And then for myself, growing up I was very close to my grandparents, and then luckily my children's great-grandmas were still living when they were younger, so they got to know them also. But I had the opportunity to go to Japan for a year when I was in college, and that's when it really hit me; I mean I knew about culturally I guess, the Japanese way that I had learned from my grandparents and I was learning the language and everything, but once I lived in Japan I personally knew I was an American. Because socially and just their way of thinking and everything is totally different from my way of thinking and my way of doing things, being raised in America. But I got to meet all the relatives in Japan and I want my children to know that whole connection, because it is—it's all a part of them, that's what makes them. And they can pass it on to their children.

DH: Ford, do you agree it's who they are psychologically, socially, culturally, but it's not a spiritual relationship?

FO: I don't know if it's actually spiritual but it's an acknowledgment and appreciation for that. For myself, it's an appreciation and acknowledgment of everyone, so I don't know if you'd call that spiritual, it's recognizing it and, I mean it's that everybody is as Stanley said, "in the same ocean." [And whoever our kids want to meet and marry, it doesn't have to be Japanese.]

DH: Ford, can you tell me what is your relationship to your ancestors today, to those who have passed?

FO: I guess an appreciation for what they endured, giving a real sense of gratitude. Even when we had the opportunity to meet some of the relatives, the distances they traveled just so we could meet that one time! It's appreciating all the sacrifices that everyone's done.

DH: Do you have a continuing dialogue with ancestors?

FO: Just the immediate aunts, uncles, cousins, like that.

DH: Do you consider ancestors before you make a decision?

---

*The 442 was a U.S. Army regiment comprised almost entirely of Americans of Japanese descent, formed during the Second World War. It became one of the most decorated fighting units in the history of the United States.

FO: I think all of those—not consciously but it's all the influences that everyone has, so, in that aspect, all the influences have effect.

DH: What kind of influences?

FO: I think I'm a lot more tolerant than what I used to be. I recognize things more and am not so judgmental. At times it kind of makes me slow in doing things because I analyze things more.

DH: Is it just an intellectual process?

FO: I think emotional.

DH: Are your ancestors in any way a living influence on you? It could be through DNA or something, but many people in the world believe the spirits of their ancestors are still alive in some fashion and continue to have an influence on them, through talking, coming to them in dreams or something.

FO: I wouldn't call it spiritually, but I can envision my grandfather saying something or grandmother.

DH: If you do, would it be your grandfather really saying that, or just constructed from a memory?

FO: [Indicates it would be from a memory]

DH: Terri, can you tell me what is your relationship to your ancestors who have passed?

TO: Who have passed? Funny you asked Ford those questions and then mention about the dreams? I don't know if it was just a coincidence or what but with both my father and my maternal grandfather—in our Buddhist tradition we have what's called a "forty-ninth day memorial service" and so on the forty-ninth day of their passing, we have a memorial service. It doesn't necessarily mean the service is on that day but with my father and my grandfather on that forty-ninth day of passing, they were in my dreams. And it was, for my grandfather, I never got to say goodbye to him so it was almost like—I kind of felt he was coming back so I had that opportunity to say goodbye. And then my father, I was at his bedside, but it was almost like he came back to say goodbye to me too.

DH: And do you feel like this is really something from both directions, from them to you as well as you to them?

TO: I think so, yes. But it was only the two of them. It was never any other, of my grandparents but it just so happened it was on that day, the forty-ninth day.

DH: Would you believe then that they continue to care about you?

TO: Yes.

DH: Why would they visit to give you a chance to say goodbye?

TO: Maybe it was just for me, myself. To have that opportunity.

DH: They would do that for you?

TO: Yea, maybe. For them maybe?

DH: Do you feel that the coincidence of the forty-ninth day indicates some initiative on your part as well?

TO: Maybe, subconsciously. But I wasn't even thinking about it, but it just so happened.

DH: Do you think there might be other occasions when they might be interested in your actions, or your life, or your people who are still alive?

TO: I think so, yes. I know for my mom, she always tells me that whenever she's having a frustrated or difficult time, she talks to my father. There's been times when she's misplaced something really, really important, right? And she can't find it and she needs to find it, and at times she'll just start talking to my dad and then the next day, Boom! there it is, or something. I think, perhaps they are helping guide us.

DH: Do you get the sense that this is what your mother believes is what happens?

TO: I think so.

DH: You know the Bon Odori. Is it not a celebration for ancestors?

TO: [Terri indicates yes.]

DH: What is the purpose of the celebration?

TO: It's a time for us the living to express our gratitude and appreciation for all those who have come before us and all their sacrifices that they made. It's also to remind us that what we do is going to affect future generations. That's what Bon Odori means to me. But while I'm participating in Bon Odori, I feel like . . . I'm doing it out of appreciation and gratitude, but for me personally too . . . I love dancing. My father, he really enjoyed dancing. He participated in all the Bon Odoris and so growing up, whether we danced together or not, it didn't matter but he was in the dance circle and he would be just enjoying himself. So as I'm dancing each year, it's like he's there, like he is still there, dancing along with us.

I can almost see him in the dance circle, enjoying it. I mean, I'm enjoying it so much . . . my father. I watched my father enjoy it so much.

DH: Would you say he's there? Sometimes when people say that, they mean it. Are ancestors visiting the festival?

TO: I don't know that. I just know that I can feel my father, I mean I can vividly feel him out in the circle and everything.

DH: In the origin story of the festival, is the presumption about the story that the disciple did really see his mother, and that she was really released from the place? Do you think this is possible?

TO: That's the story. Do I believe that? That that happened?

DH: More or less.

TO: Do I believe that that is how the Bon Odori originated? [Laughing around the table]

DH: Well, that's historical.

TO: Yes, that's historical. But that he actually had the powers to see? I'm not sure that he actually had the power to see, to really actually see his mother in that terrible state, but maybe he could sense it, I'm not sure.

DH: But maybe he did?

TO: Maybe he did, yeah.

DH: And if he did, is it the same power that you have when you sense your father at the dancing?

TO: It's more emotional maybe, more an emotional feeling and a memory, for me. Not so much that sense . . . of . . . I don't compare it the same I think.

DH: Stanley, can you tell me what is your relationship to your ancestors today?

SA: Well, I don't dream about my ancestors but culturally my parents tell me about my great-grandfather—he would be a drummer during the dance and that's what I do now. But I think about my parents and grandparents occasionally.

DH: Do you think about them as a continuing influence?

SA: Well, yes, but not from Obon point of view, because my parents never danced, my grandfather never danced. When I was growing up, my parents just kind of dropped me off at dance practice, I just grew into it. [General laughter]

DH: What kind of relationship would you say you have with your ancestors?

SA: I talk to my mom and dad occasionally on the phone. They're in Japan.

DH: And ancestors who have passed on, do you have any relationship to them?

SA: I think about it, but I don't have any dreams or. . . I don't have communications. I don't talk with ancestors that passed on.

DH: And when you hear stories . . . [examples from some of the other interviewees] say their ancestors visit them to give encouragement. Would you think things like that are possible?

SA: Oh yes, yes, but it's from their own perspective. Their memories, and so-called dreams, they may have occurred, but they are constructed.

DH: So, when you do the drumming, are you doing this for your ancestors?

SA: Not really. It's just something I grew into.

DH: And what do you make of the story of the origin of the celebration?

SA: Well, most part, I don't know if you know about, but the reason why that disciple, he saw his mother in hell and he went to the . . . guide, the Buddha. And he told him, if you find any house that has no death in it, I will save your mother or something like that. And from that realization, he released his mother. He was suffering from the loss of his mother.

DH: Did he possibly really release his mother?

SA: I think he released in his own mind, he released his mother.

DH: June, can you tell me about your relationship to your ancestors?

JY: My ancestors that passed before me? I don't speak to them or have any way of communicating with them. Obon Odori is something I grew up as Shinzi Buddhist, as Japanese American Buddhism. Obon Odori is something I have danced since I was able to walk. It's more important to me now as an adult and having experienced death and having people die. It's like Terri said, you have the memories, the vision of those who passed away. My parents passed away, my mother unexpectedly, and no matter how much I want to see her there, I never see her but I have the memory of her dancing. She was always dancing, she danced regularly; she enjoyed it.

SA: She was a dance instructor.

JY: Yeah. And so when I dance, I feel like I am honoring her, remembering her, closer to her, but not in the sense that physically she is dancing right there. My father never danced but I still feel like it is remembering him. I had my . . . I encourage my two boys to dance for the same reason. I just feel like it is acknowledging our culture, our gratitude to our parents, our ancestors who passed before us and what they went through. It is a celebration of . . . more for me their memory than anything, and continuing that. And it makes me . . . it makes me happy. It makes me feel closer to them. I don't believe . . . there have been some times I want to communicate with my mother. And no matter how hard I try, I never saw a sign of her . . . and I figured when she passed if there was afterlife, if there were any of those things that we all grew up reading about, because of her dedication to her family, we would see something of her. It wouldn't be scary, it wouldn't be a ghost per se, it wouldn't be harmful, but . . . she would want to come back to make sure her family, her brother, her sister, were okay. And I never saw that. So, it has confirmed my belief that they don't—there's nothing that comes back because if anything, my mother would come back to make sure my brother was okay. And so Obon is important because, I know she's not coming back but mentally, it's my way of communicating with her, even though I'm not communicating with her.

DH: Just communicating with the "her" that is still with you?

JY: Right, right.

DH: Would you say it's possible that she's aware of that?

JY: I guess it is possible . . . you know, it's hard to say because to say it's possible acknowledges that there is a life after death. I think it is possible that she knows beforehand . . . that that would happen, that we would continue that.

DH: What do you mean by "beforehand"?

JY: That before she passed away, she knew beforehand that we would do this, because she was brought up in this tradition. So it's difficult to say. I . . . you know, I think Obon Odori is similar to Day of the Dead but in Day of the Dead the people come back and it's all celebratory. This is more of an honor; it's more I don't know if you want to say emotional, you know every person is different and so everybody, they dance for different reasons, but the ultimate reason is for the memories of the ones who passed.

DH: More for the living than for the dead?

JY: Yes.

DH: But are there celebrations that can actually benefit the dead? Or influence the dead?

JY: I'm sure there are cultures that do that. Like you talk about the Native Americans, but it could be they were brought up with the cultural knowledge of spirits and dreams and whatnot and the belief in that. We weren't, so we're not as open to that, where they're more open to it. I've had dreams of my loved ones who passed away, my parents or whatever but it didn't . . . I don't . . . that's a hard question. Maybe in our own way, we want them to communicate to us so we take certain things as a way of communication with them. So a lot of it is emotional and it's just how you see it, you know your point of perspective. For some people like the Native Americans, it's easier for them to see it, because their culture believes in that. I won't necessarily say my culture, my ancestors believed in seeing things so maybe I'm not as open minded to see it. And I'm more of a person who, I want proof. And I so wanted to see anything of my mother and I never saw it. To this day, and I still, you know, look for it.

DH: Maybe they don't have a choice.

JY: Right, yes. So, I more, like honor their memory, you know, my memories of them. And I encourage . . . since my kids didn't know her, I probably pass on my memories of her to them. But they have no standard to which . . . to base those memories, they just take what I said as truth. Do you get what I'm saying? They're just taking the story . . .

DH: As it's passed on?

JY: Right, as truth.

DH: But as people get older, they have experiences of their own, to shape those stories, or to rewrite those experiences of their own. And some of those experiences maybe come out of the stories, maybe they don't. . . . What do you make of the cultures that celebrate funerals for the sake of the dead, to help the dead along, so to speak? Some are not very different from the same principles of the disciple of Buddha and his mother.

JY: I believe that any story and memory or anything that is positive and we learn from, benefits the dead and the living.

DH: Then is there a continuing relationship between them?

JY: That's a hard one because . . .

DH: They're all hard! [Laughter] That's why I'm asking wise people. [More laughter] It's kind of true though. If not you, then who?

JY: As you get older, you experience more. Ask me these questions thirty years ago, I would not give you the same answer.

DH: And your answer is today likely richer and better considered.

JY: . . . Right. And understanding and having children, raising children changes your total point of view. It's like karma, in a sense like karma, because everything you do affects something. Buddhism is very much that way, you know whatever your action is you have to be prepared to accept the consequence. You know, no one's going to forgive you, no one's going to give you a pass, you deal with it. And I believe that Obon helps us with the memory. Maybe there is an afterlife. I don't personally believe it because I feel like my mother would have shown some sort of sign. You know you always have some sort of hope, you always think that, you know there is something there and maybe it's disappointment, or the reality of "we have to move on and I can't expect her to show up." Yea, I do dream about her but it's just . . . you dream about her during more difficult times, so I think about her more and dream about her more. So that helps me so maybe there is some connection in the psyche inside your head. You know my family's gone through some stuff so I think about it, "What would mom have said? What would mom have done?" So I think Obon is important for that.

DH: Last question. Would you say—and the word *God* is subjective as much as any other—but would you say your ancestors are closer to God?

FO: I don't associate that. For myself I don't . . . I think it's just what they've influenced with me and what we try to influence with our kids.

DH: Would you think of God as your ancestor?

TO: I never thought of that at all. No . . . I never thought of it. So, for me, in Buddhist system, and . . . when one passes away, we say they go to the pure land, or they're in a better place. Then when it's our time, that's where we'll go also. And we might see one another again. But that's as far as the thinking goes, they go to a better place. They're no longer suffering, they're no longer here. But with God, I never thought of that.

DH: Stanley?

SA: Technically, Buddhists, we don't have a soul so there's nothing to go to God or whatever so what I've been taught is we're part of this big vast ocean where we're this little wave, but when the wave hits the shore, it disappears and we're back to part of the ocean again.

DH: Is the ocean a creating force?

SA: Some ministers call it the Buddha nature, some "the energy," but there's no personality or ego or anything there. But the memory of the ancestors is still there, but not a soul or anything.

DH: Is there any way you could make that a metaphor for DNA?

SA: DNA?

DH: That people share DNA, a parallel to the ocean?

SA: You know, DNA after we pass, it's gone. It doesn't survive. But we're all created from that. It's a tricky question.

DH: June, do you think your ancestors are closer to God, or God could be an ancestor to humanity in any way?

JY: No, I don't. Like Terri said, I never thought of seeing it that way. I don't believe in a God in any way. I don't worship a God and if there was a God I believe this world would be a better place. But only we can deal with it and fix it. I don't think my ancestors are closer to a god.

DH: Anything one would like to add?

JY: I just found it difficult, the terminology of ancestors and relatives, and cultural and religious. It's difficult . . . the difference between culture and religion. . . . Relatives to me are people I knew.

DH: One is intimate and the other is not?

JY: I think for us is a little different because we're Japanese Americans, which is a different experience from Japanese-Japanese. So when you see Japanese nationals come here who are from Japan, they are . . . like Terri said when she was in Japan, their ethic and belief are totally different from ours. They didn't face discrimination, so they speak Japanese, in public. They were never shown prejudice.

TO: Well they come from . . . their society they are all the same. We're here in America and it's a very diverse society, with so many cultural influences we were brought up in, and they were only brought up in one. And you can see the difference right away.

JY: I don't know if the Japanese in Japan would see Obon Odori as serious as we see it. I see it that they see it as a celebration. I've only been to Japan once. We go to temple on Sundays; they don't have that in Japan, they don't go to temple so our vision of

Obon Odori is based on our experiences in America, where theirs is different. And not everyone is [the same] Buddhist in Japan. So, they're whole view of Buddhism is different from ours.

TO: Their practice is different. Their tradition is different.

SA: Yea . . . I visited Japan during Obon time and they have Obon dancing but it's more of a cultural dance. They have it almost every night throughout the whole week.

DH: Did you drum with them?

SA: Yea, a little bit. They only play one song over and over and over again. . . . [Laughter]

TO: And Obon is almost seen almost like a holiday in Japan. They take their vacation time, when Obon is observed, so they can go back home, to the gravesite to pay their respects and all that.

FO: Here too we invite the community to participate in our Obon, in the dancing and everything. And part of that too is to help extend the appreciation for everyone . . . we kind of give a description of what the festival is at the beginning but it's really nice to see everyone participate and all enjoying themselves, and even for that moment for people to reflect. And that's it!

TO: And part of the dancing is also part of what we're practicing in Buddhism is letting go of ego. You don't have to be a master dancer, you don't have to know the stuff, just letting that go, just being in the moment, just enjoying it.

FO: Just appreciating everybody participating or engaging in it. It's acknowledging that. Taking the moment to be in the moment.

6

ANCESTORS IN
SPACE AND TIME

O nly a few of the thirty-four interviewees identify a historical point in time
or a specific person that might represent an ancestral "beginning." Most
interviewees see origins as vague, fading into history, or dissolving into the
misty uncertainties of evolutionary time, beyond the reach of collective memories. Some interviewees, such as Jean Neal and Daniel Essim, suggest that God,
as creator of all things, is an original ancestor. Essim reports that his ancestry
began with Abraham (of the Torah) but "God is our number one Father." Sri
Acharya Srinivasa Vedala says his Hindu ancestors began with the Rootman,
but Rootman is not a figure associated with a historical time. His mythical
power lies in his identity, and while he stands outside of time and above the con-
straints of space, his time is specifically unspecific, while his authority in space
can be measured: it lies where the Hindu nations thrive. On the other hand,
interviewees are generally familiar with family stories that tell "where we come
from," such as Muatasem Ubeidat's three brothers coming from the desert. The
place is identified, the time frame for the brothers is vague, "maybe ten generations, maybe more. I don't know." In general, interviewees are more confident
to identify original ancestral places than original times.

PLACE

Geography plays an important role in many narratives, and *place* makes up
a significant part of most ancestral identities. Place is less abstract than time,
it can be visited and touched, tasted, heard, and breathed. Place has color,

sound, landscape, words, and the individual descendant can interact intimately with the air, food, and scenery of a place, a homeland, or a country. Place sensually embodies concepts of land and climate, which provide tactile materials for tools and homes, and people become organically connected to their places through hunting, gathering, cooking, clothing, and burying. Places hold ancestors' physical remains.

Some interviewees, including Henrietta Mann and Stanley Fuke, describe place as more than the location of the material culture of ancestors; they describe place as itself one of the ancestors. It is not unusual for people in general to say they are "related" to the land, for culture celebrates and bemoans its natural environment; sustenance comes from the land, water, and air, people bury the placentas of their newborns in the ground, and in death people are returned to the natural elements. But naming place as an ancestor gives relatedness a literal meaning, and places acquire sacred status because of their communion with ancestors. Stanley Fuke says he adopts the character of the places of his ancestors because his family holds deep roots in Kumamoto, the district of Japan that gave his ancestors a name, a language, and personality.

While some interviewees name places among their relations and ancestors, others acknowledge more practical ways in which place is important to ancestral identity. Loubert Trahan uses geography as one element in determining his family associations. Trahan considers every one of the 120,000 names he has registered in his genealogical database to be part of his ancestry, but he identifies most closely with those who live nearby and those with whom he more frequently socializes and visits.

DH: With which do you most closely identify?

LT: Well anyone living . . . [within a] one hundred mile radius of my town. We get together fairly regularly and recognize that we have common ancestry.

Trahan's framing of his ancestral community is geographically rational and pragmatic; the social circumstances of his community are contingent on his locale.

Daniel Essim also uses geography as a focus in narrating his ancestry; in his case the place is an ancestral village in West Africa.

Let me start from my village, my maternal village. If you go [there] and you want to go through our ancestral tree, almost before you get to the second generation, third generation, you realize that there has been some intermarriage amongst us. . . . The whole village is almost all your family. . . . When our great-great-grandfather moved to that village and started having kids and kids having kids and that ancestral tree is lost, people go to Europe, go to the city and get married to each other and you realize that you've been married to your fourth cousin. So, that's how broad we are.

The geography of Essim's modern relatives is expansive—spanning three continents. But the heart and source of the kinship identity can still be found in the African village of his grandfathers.

TIME

Ancestry precedes a descendant, and it also survives him. Ancestry branches outward in time, reaching back before the life of a descendant who in turn projects the ancestors into the future. Honoring one's ancestors is for many interviewees a process of securing one's own people and ways for the future, to keep alive an identity and values apparently built a long time before. Loubert Trahan says, "The biggest push is to get young people involved, our kids, grandkids, etcetera, to become part of this Acadian movement and I guess, to sustain it indefinitely." Trahan and others can project an ancestral ethos from the past into the future because their ancestral construct represents a constant, that transcends time. An ancestral narrative exists across time, with the present a mere moment, an incidental marker at which ancestor, descendant, and future descendants meet and negotiate values and culture. Together, they construct and reconstruct identity through a narrative that exists in an undefined temporal context.

Narratives describe ancestors as if they ride down the centuries, generations following generations, unchanged in their essential significance and meaning, facing new and different challenges with an ethic that spans history. Ancestors of course existed in the past and descendants will exist in the future but the identities of the narrated past and future only differ superficially, or at least this is the common presentation of narratives: the ancestry and its people are timeless. Death does not destroy ancestry, neither does time significantly alter the ancestors' character. To the contrary, geographical, generational, and even technological changes typically serve to reinforce an ancestry's perpetual identity. Simon Jacobson observes ancestry:

It's almost like existential coordinates to find our bearings. In a sense, spiritual GPS. Trying to find "Where am I?" I'm here in New York. When I look at where my father came from, okay that's where I came from. Where did his father come from? Where did his mother come from? But then, there is definitely a spiritual-religious side to it, which is "Where does it all come from?" "How did we get here?" And, "Who are we really, what is my true identity?"

The principal cultural markers of ancestral identity occur and reoccur into perpetuity. Jacobson continues,

> I see it also very much like my own life. I have little grandchildren now. And I look at them as I say, "I was once a baby like that" . . . but I don't remember myself . . . Past generations? I can't even figure out my own history!

Ancestors arrive from their own times, in the form of memories, narratives, and spiritual visits, cloaked in myth and mysticism. Individual ancestors stand as symbols of the whole—and like Rootman, acquire meaning far greater than their own lives. Ancestral ethos are created over time in the past, applied in the present, and will be delivered to the future. David Gelsenliter refers to German Americans as "my father's people" and when he identifies the values his father's Germans and German Americans share he says, "They had the same kind of ideas my father had." His father is a prototype for the ancestral model, which has been occurring for centuries and will occur far into the future. It is incumbent on Gelsenliter's generation to ensure the model survives.

Historical details within narrated ancestries commonly conform to philosophy and myth rather than the more scientific reverse. History provides the scaffolding for the construction of the ancestral home, but it is the finished building that is more important than the temporary frame. History and timelessness function cooperatively, each one serving the ancestral ethic. Jason Felihkatubbe says learning Choctaw, the language of his ancestors, connects him to something deep in spirit and time, establishing profound connections far beyond the one or two generations of people he knows in life. Learning his ancestral ways carries him into the realms of an ancient identity, even to an original Choctaw people.

> Well, it was my grandparents who taught me my first words in our language and I'm learning from a cousin and you know for me that's one of the ways that we do connect with our ancestors, with our past, because this language . . . is older than we are and it goes all the way back to the very beginning so to speak. For me language is one of the ways we do connect with our ancestors and with the past.

Through language and stories, Felihkatubbe joins his ancestors across time. "There's stories that are passed down between families over the generations that haven't changed," he says, and through their maintenance he and his people perpetuate a Choctaw ethos; though he will die, his people will not.

Interviewees' ancestral identities grow out of mythical pasts and project towards mystical futures, following cycles of life. An individual descendant holds a secure position in the circle of life and death, as he or she participates in the creation and perpetuation of an ancestral cosmology, extending the individual into the family and into the tribe. An individual descendant shares identity timelessly with ancestors and the mystical places from whence they came.

INTERVIEW WITH CHIEF CHARLES SLEEPER

"You Can't Separate Them and Us"

CS: My name is Charles Sleeper.

DH: Traditional chief of the Arapaho?

CS: Yes, that's right.

Charles Sleeper Explains *Traditional Chief*

Each tribe has its own definitions of what a chief is and is not. Ours is basically a moral and wise individual that has a family and takes cares of a family. He has the ability and knowledge of what and how a community of people should act according to specific requirements of how our ancestors took care of us. That is a chief in a traditional sense.

DH: Is English your first language?

CS: I teach Arapaho and I was brought up in the Cheyenne and Arapaho. When I was little I could really understand Cheyenne and Arapaho.

Charles Sleeper Explains *Arapaho*

Arapaho is a Pawnee word for "traders." We were traders with other tribes and later white men.

DH: Both languages?

CS: Yes. But when I got into school, well I kind of lost it. Now I'm going back to it a little bit.

DH: Can you tell me who are your ancestors?

CS: On one side, I'm more Arapaho. I got a little bit of Cheyenne in me. My father's father and mother were full-blooded Arapaho but you never know [laughs]. Well they were recognized by the federal government as Arapaho, well [actually] as four-fourths Cheyenne-Arapaho but they were full-blood Arapahos, my father's mother and father. The government gave my grandfather the last name Kendricks and my grandmother was a Wolfrobe, she came out of the Wolfrobe family of Arapahos. And my father went to Haskell [where they] made him change it back to what his original name was, Sleeping Under the Water. . . . My father, they wanted his Indian name so it was Sleeping Under the Water, he said it in Arapaho.* Well in English it meant you know, the name was too like so [they] cut it down to Sleeper.

Charles Sleeper Explains *Four-fourths*

Four-fourths refers to a full-blood Cheyenne and Arapaho tribal member. Many tribes have different blood quantum requirements to be a tribal member.

DH: So you've kind of done two things when you identify your ancestors, you identify some specific people, like the Kendricks, the Wolfrobes, your mother. But you also identify groups of people, Cheyenne and mostly Arapaho people. So when you think of your ancestors, do you think of them as collections of people or as . . .

CS: They're extended families on the lineage and my mother was a Lumpmouth and when the soldiers were given a ration, a bee stung my grandfather in the mouth and he had big lumps so they gave him that name. So his real name was you know, I can't really recall right now but he just quoted the Lumpmouth. My mother's mother was a Cheyenne . . . it's kind of like an extended family. That all seven brothers and my mother's father, and they were all brothers but they had different names by the federal government.

DH: And you're not directly descended from all seven brothers yet you're including them as part of your ancestry, is that right?

CS: Well they were all brothers. . . . They're all blood brothers.

DH: They're brothers, but they wouldn't be in your direct line of ancestry.

CS: Yeah, they are. [Laughs]

DH: You could only be descended direct line from one of them.

CS: Well, I was a direct line from my grandfather but he had, his brothers were all blood brothers.

---

*Haskell is an "Indian school" in Lawrence, Kansas. It had an early-twentieth-century history of severe oppression and punishment of Indian children. It is in operation today as Haskell Indian Nations University and is an institution that is oriented towards Native people and activities.

DH: Are you saying that you're descended from all of them?

CS: Well, yeah, you could say that . . . they were all my relations.

DH: Yeah. And how far, how far out would you extend that? Would you include any person that could say he or she was Arapaho in the past was a part of your ancestors?

CS: Yeah, yeah.

DH: I'm trying to get an idea of where you might draw a boundary.

CS: Well you could try and draw the boundaries but we're all related.

Traditional Chief Charles Sleeper.
Courtesy of Mr. Charles Sleeper Jr.

DH: Eventually we're all related. Would you include everybody?

CS: Yeah, I would have to.

DH: All humanity?

CS: Oh yeah.

DH: So your—when you say ancestry, you're thinking of the world of human beings?

CS: Yeah, the human being race.

DH: And what about other things beyond human beings? Animals?

CS: Well we're all interrelated or you know, just . . . we need to have each other in order for us to survive. We can't just say, you know, you look at that circle of life, you're going to see the red, the black, the white, and the yellow.

DH: Are those people?

CS: The sacred wheel, like . . . and that we're all from one body eventually.* People like to say, "Well, the Bible says one way." Yeah, that's true but in the traditional legends of the Arapaho, we came from the, you're going to see the water, the turtle, the pipe, the duck in the story of creation. And it's almost similar. . . . Here's one of my relatives right now [laughs] [Talking to relative] . . . Where was I now?

DH: You were describing how your ancestry includes more than people.

CS: Yes . . . people call it animistic or whatever you want to call it, it's just that we're all needed in this one form or another in the ecosystem or we're just a microcosm of the whole system.

---

*Charles Sleeper later wrote in a message to the author, "The Sacred wheel is a (Sundance). It brings blessings to our tribe."

DH: And do you include in that also other living things beyond animals?

CS: Oh yeah. Yeah you have to include them because, if you dichotomize things—making it that kind of philosophy—that's why we have all the problems in the world. Them and they and those, instead of saying "we."

DH: So when you say ancestors, this is the "we," is that right?

CS: We relations.

DH: Right. So ancestors, you're using this, you're thinking of this as all your relations?

CS: All my relations.

DH: . . . are your ancestors?

CS: All my relations are the ancestors.

DH: Are you also a part of your ancestral community?

CS: Mmhmm [yes]. We have our differences; I mean yeah we're just like a family. We have our ideas of how things should go but we're all related.

DH: And you said that all of these relatives lead back to one body?

CS: Yeah.

DH: All of the living things. Are ancestors in the past closer to like a creator than you are? Are they a route or a path to a creator?

CS: No. [Laughs]

DH: Well the reason I ask is, when you said that they lead back to one body, I'm trying to think . . .

CS: Yeah, yeah I know what you're saying. It's just a holistic way of viewing it—what we do, how we think, how we operate.

DH: When you say "we" do you mean all?

CS: Nature and people, well we're part of that nature. Or they may say the human race, well we're part of that. Or that they were part of the earth, wind and fire and water, we're part of that.

DH: When you say "ancestry," does it only refer to the past?

CS: No, no. Those are coming, those are you know not reincarnation kind of stuff it's just, the new human beings. . . . We work in a holistic way, physical and spiritual.

DH: Are you saying that the body of ancestors, the community of ancestors is more than physical, more than a physical ecosystem; it's also something spiritual?

CS: Yeah it has to be because, if you understood the way they, the way they did things let's say, communication, well they always had . . . well you see the Jews, they always wore their cap because they're honoring their spirit and good spirit/bad spirit. That was the way, we didn't call it a bad spirit; it was just a trickster. It was, you know positive and negative . . . in our spirituality, and how they didn't have that kind of fear that the white spirituality has. They had a respect for the spirituality . . .

DH: And do you also try to have that kind of respect for the spirituality of your ancestry?

CS: Yeah, because . . . the way they taught us, you know in our spirituality, you'll see it in the empires of this "New World" as you call it, it has something to do with something called . . . how would you say . . . it has something to do with the way we look at ourselves and how we are a part of the larger body.

DH: And when you say, "We look at ourselves," can I ask who you mean by "We"?

CS: Yeah. The whole group of people.

. . .

DH: Do you talk to them? Do you have a relationship with them that's a daily relationship?

CS: Well you can go in any ceremony and they hear a lot of the words, the frogs, the four-legged, the two-legged.

DH: And biologists also talk about frogs . . .

CS: But that's just one group of people. We're all biologists and some of us are sociologists, some are lawyers and so forth but we always recognize the importance of these things around us.

DH: How do you do that? How does one go about recognizing the importance of those things?

CS: When you wake up in the morning, you know.

DH: What do you do when you wake up in the morning?

CS: Yeah, I just start praying. . . . I say, "Thank you for another day, a good day. Thank you for my hard days." Yeah.

DH: Is it a prayer *to* that group or are you praying *with* that group or are you praying *about* that group?

CS: I'm with the group. . . . I mean you can't separate about them and us and those. I mean they try that but that's just an old . . . western way of thinking I guess.

DH: My grandmother taught me to pray for her dead brother, but I always thought she was praying *with* Tommy.

CS: Yeah, that's the way we pray.

DH: And this is what I'm asking, and so that's something you do, but not only with your uncle but also with everything within that ecosystem?

CS: Yeah, we have to recognize it.

DH: And you recognize it by praying with it?

CS: Yeah. Pray with it and, otherwise you become psychotic [laughs].

DH: Psychotic in the sense that . . . ?

CS: It makes us something that's not real. . . I've seen a bunch of those.

DH: What do you— ?

CS: I used to tease my professor when I went to theology school. He said, we went to see that movie *Exorcist*. . . . I said, "Man, white man can sell anything! He has sold that devil." That was you know, my way of. . . but he said, "Yeah, we can even sell you." It's cowboys and Indians and that's what he was meaning. But you see what was his name, Billy Graham? He's a . . . what do you call those guys? An evangelist? Yeah, I got a big kick out of them, how they make people think through that process and I said, "Well, this would never work in like the Native American church, Peyote meetings." . . . They tried that but it's not working.

DH: Well when you say that people who are separated from that group or people who don't pray with that group are psychotic, what do you mean by psychotic?

CS: Well, they become more . . . addicted to the religion rather than spirituality.

DH: Where have you learned this about the nature of your ancestry?

CS: I practice my tradition and culture spirituality.

DH: It comes from practice?

CS: Yes it has to. No school around here could teach what I learned in those things.

DH: Because it's not people who taught you or because there aren't people who know that?

CS: You have to teach yourself.

DH: How can you teach yourself?

CS: You learn by what the spirit tells you. . . . Oh there's a lot of ways in the Indian world to make changes.

DH: And to make changes with an individual, could this come from a specific ancestral individual?

CS: No . . . there are a lot of spirits just . . . well, they come and give you I don't know what you call it, what do they call those things, doctrines?

DH: Usually by "doctrine," people mean a teaching of some kind.

CS: Yeah, well these spirits come to you and give you the medicines or the teachings.

DH: And can you say that those spirits that come to you are ancestral spirits?

CS: Yes, they have to be. They wouldn't come from the other one.

DH: And so, oh wait a minute, there's another one?

CS: [Laughs] You know, the white man.

DH: Oh, okay. So with the ancestral spirits, can you distinguish one from another or is it . . .

CS: Oh there are many differences. There are many different groups, collections of them.

DH: And are the groups . . . ?

CS: They can either give you life or they can take your life. . . .

DH: Is there a spirit who is your grandmother?

CS: That's a good spirit.

DH: Is that spirit the same person that grandmother was when grandmother had a body and walked on the earth?

CS: Right grandfather, grandmother.

DH: Does the person have the same voice that the person had when he or she had a body?

CS: Well they come in many forms, yeah, but usually they tell you why they're there and what you need to do.

DH: So a lot of the people I've talked to have had experiences where they have had vivid, sometimes dreams sometimes visions, where they encounter an ancestor. Sometimes somebody they met, sometimes somebody they hadn't met.

CS: Oh that happens quite a bit.

DH: And if that happens, would you suppose that that really was your great-grandmother or would you suppose that it is something you created to look like your great-grandmother? . . .

CS: I take them as real, as my real father or my real grandfather.

DH: Can they communicate with you verbally?

CS: Oh yeah, we sing together in Peyote meetings somewhere.

DH: May I ask in what language?

CS: Just the language that's whatever we're talking.

DH: Could they speak one language and you speak another and you communicate?

CS: Yeah, we do that. It's just . . . you become, when I was growing up, I was born in Lawton [Oklahoma], okay?

DH: Mmhmm.

CS: And I was raised around Comanches and I was very immersed in that language. . . . And then I learned Kiowa, then I learned Apache. And I came up here, I didn't even you know, I just started talking Arapaho with my grandma and grandpa and Cheyenne. But you . . . it can be done, immersed in it. And you understand what all of them are saying.

DH: And what are they saying?

CS: When a person's under pressure, they will come. And that's one of the reasons why I think we have a lot of problems with alcoholism because they can't handle the pressure. They're afraid of something that may happen.

DH: Are the ancestors somehow involved in that?

CS: No, it just . . . the reality today, something may occur. The challenges, maybe obstacles or some kind of controversy. And it puts them under a lot of stress or pressure and they have . . . what do you call it, a nightmare to release the stress and pressure and sometimes they dream about them and the spirits come and comfort them.

DH: And are there ways that society could break down those connections to ancestors and ancestral groups? In other words, might some of these people you're talking about who have stress and sort of give in to the stress, is there some way that they're not listening to the ancestors?

CS: Oh yeah, a lot of times I won't listen to them [laughs]. And they get mad at me, I mean just like anything else.

DH: Can you misunderstand them?

CS: Oh yeah you can misunderstand, you think that you've got . . . it's just that you have doubts and you're skeptical if that's the correct way or the wrong way.

DH: So might they tell you something you might imagine you're acting on when really you're not?

CS: Yeah, nature plays tricks. Dreams play tricks. Spirits play tricks.

DH: Spirits play tricks in the same way that people would?

CS: Yeah. . . .

DH: You talked about being related to and including in an ancestral group water and turtles and things like that. So you also include the land in a sense? Or rocks?

CS: The earth didn't come until later. Everything was water and you know what water is in Christian thinking?

DH: What?

CS: Death.

DH: And what is it in your thinking?

CS: Life.

DH: Is this part of the break in the understanding of the group?

CS: Yeah, it is. It has to be. It's like . . . the Bible talks about why there's snow, you know. It's supposed to be pure, whatever. And then white man is pure because he's white. And in my culture black is the good luck sign.

DH: Do you have any sense of obligation to ancestors? Like personal obligation?

CS: Yeah, I remember them.

DH: By remembering them? What does that do?

CS: Yeah, let me put it to you like this: My son asked me one morning when we were out in the country, when we lived out in the country, "Daddy." What did he say? But anyway he said something and I started thinking about it. If it wasn't for my ancestors back when they did the Medicine Lodge Treaty,* I wouldn't have a house, I wouldn't have any place to live. I would probably be like those gypsies in Europe, roaming around. If it wasn't for my ancestors, planning this, making a way for me, I probably wouldn't have what I've got. I have land, I have a house, I have a full stomach. I know eventually it comes from the creator but they had planned it in their treaty-making with the government that I was to have something. They thought about me. I wasn't even around.

DH: Is this a reciprocal remembrance that continues today?

CS: Oh yeah, that's why we fight so hard. The BIA wants to destroy it but we fight so hard.† The BIA, by keeping us from really becoming you know, our people are undeveloped, but the undeveloped, somebody has to take care of them. By being undeveloped, we're being taken care of. If we were developed we would be just like any other competitive society, dog eat dog, you know.

DH: So what you're saying is that in a certain sense your ancestors are still taking care of you because you said you have a full belly and you live on the land and so on, that they prepared that way for you.

CS: Yeah they made a way for us.

DH: And by making a way for you, do you somehow in turn make a way for them still?

*Charles Sleeper explains that the Medicine Lodge Treaty was "an event held at Medicine Lodge, Kansas, in making a treaty to allow the Arapaho people to live in Oklahoma."
†BIA is the federal Bureau of Indian Affairs.

CS: My ancestors?

DH: Yes.

CS: Yes, I recognize them and I pray homage.

DH: How does that . . .

CS: I honor them.

DH: How does that help them or make a way for them?

CS: We remember them then, we have a heart.

DH: Why are they interested in you remembering them?

CS: Why are they interested in me remembering them?

DH: Yes, and I'm not sure about the verb if it's right. I mean interested might not be exactly right but why is it, why is it important to them that you remember them?

CS: Because if you don't, what did you come from? What are you here for? Your existence is you know by what they did. If you say well you're here because the white man allowed you to be here, well yeah that's true but they're the ones that sacrificed and died in the Trail of Tears or. . . fought in the battles.

DH: And those are people that you're talking about, but you could also include in that . . . some of the animals that you mentioned earlier could also be a part of that.

CS: Yeah, animals are gifts to us to use for . . . to survive. And that's the basic thing; that's the bottom line.

DH: I'm trying to get at the idea that those ancestors that prepared the way for you are pleased if you remember them.

CS: Yeah.

DH: I'm trying to figure out what you mean by that. Why. . .

CS: By remembering what they did for us?

DH: No. Why does that please them?

CS: Huh?

DH: Why does that please them?

CS: A lot of tribes have been extinct, okay? . . . What, twelve million when the white man landed. Now we're down to a couple million. And they made it possible for us to keep going and have a place in this world, rather than just becoming extinct. And so . . . becoming nothing!

DH: And becoming nothing would make them also become less?

CS: Yes, they would be less important.

DH: And is this . . . idea of reparations of human remains as part of cultural artifacts, is this part of this idea?

CS: Well, like I told Alden [a mutual friend], I said, "there's people that do that, I don't do it because I don't have enough knowledge about it." And they repatriate those things because they respect them and they were a part of the tribe or they're a part of the family or they were just unknown . . . to get them in a place of home, the home area of the center of the tribal nation.

DH: Do ancestors and homes change over time? In other words, do you have the same ancestors and home that your ancestors had when they had bodies and were alive?

CS: We'll see when they buried them, like out in the prairie—it could be in a cave with a rock over it or it could be in a tree or it could be a bill and a rafter with a burial ground. Or sometimes they maybe even . . . burned them up.

DH: So you're saying their practices changed?

CS: Yeah. They just. . . they were nomadic in the prairie area. But they were very sedentary when my people lived in the northeastern part of the country. They were farmers.

DH: Is there a cultural ancestry that you're identifying?

CS: Well, we're . . . we came out of one of the bands out of the Algonquians, northeast part of the country . . . we came from the eastern part of the country and we split up. There were seven different bands up and down Oklahoma to Montana.

DH: Bands of what?

CS: Arapaho.

DH: At some point you have made a choice about which "we" you're referring to.

CS: You see they're the ones that the . . . made it where the . . . American Indians' tradition and culture and spirituality was pagan and all that. And when we respect others, the way they believed, they [white people] didn't. They want to dominate it.

DH: You say "we" to refer to kind of a cultural descent or ancestry. And you're saying, "We came out of Algonquin and then we were seven bands stretching in this geographical area." Well during those thousand years of time or however many years it might have been, you have a lot of different ancestors who come and go and some of them were Comanche and some were white people and some were French and some were Iroquois and so on. But you're selecting this one set of bands of Arapaho.

CS: Yeah.

DH: How have you selected that one over the others or instead of the others? Why not choose one of the others?

CS: I was born into it. . . . That's what everybody recognizes me as.

DH: So it's that people have told you and taught you that that's who you are?

CS: Yeah, that's the way it is.

DH: Could they have taught you were something different?

CS: If I was born into the . . . Comanches. They had many different bands.

DH: Sure.

CS: And the Apaches and the Kiowa, they had many different bands.

DH: Then you're likely related to a number of them.

CS: Yeah, I am. They're my relatives down there; I go down there and visit them.

DH: But you've chosen the one, the Arapaho as sort of your . . . I mean how would you describe it? How have you chosen it?

CS: I didn't make myself an Arapaho. Who made me an Arapaho? The BIA made me an Arapaho! They got me a card and I said I was from this area. That's how you know they interpret my lineage.

DH: That's incredible. So you're saying that not only another person but an institution could choose for a person what that person's ancestry is?

CS: Yes. You get labeled that way.

DH: And if it's . . . but surely it's more than a label. Because the way you've been describing . . .

CS: Well yeah, but they don't realize that. They just see he's a number I guess.

DH: Is it just a lucky coincidence for you that the label coincided with the reality, with the spiritual reality?

CS: We used to all worship together at Greenfield. . . . We had a big old group at Greenfield. . . . Those people could say, "No, I don't care what the BIA says, I'm a different," but then the Christian church came in, "That's pagan, you do that you're going hell" and all that junk . . . they take everything and you just say "Okay!" You know, it's paradoxical.

DH: You are saying that those are the same people that have identified you as Arapaho and you've accepted that.

CS: I had no choice. I go around you know, my relatives around here, they see me and they know, "Who's your folks?" And I tell them. "Oh, you're my relation," and I said, "Alright, I am."

DH: So people inform you about who . . .

CS: Yeah. They say, "Yeah you're on my Cheyenne side," and I say, "Oh, okay."

DH: Then let me ask you, if you don't mind, a hypothetical question. If a person had been informed his entire life, say the person is in his thirties or forties or something, an adult, and had been informed that he was something really his DNA was not. Is it . . . completely unimportant?

CS: That's not really important, if that's what he wants to be, that's what he wants to be.

DH: And so that person could honor his . . . his Sioux ancestors or his Irish ancestors even though they weren't physically his genetic[s]?

CS: On my mother's side, okay, there was a lady named Woods and she was a captured Omaha by the Sioux. The Sioux brought her here to the Cheyenne in this area, on my mother's side and she stayed here and that's where that family started out there west of Geary (Oklahoma). Woods, old lady Ella Woods, she was Omaha and through this system of my body I have Omaha in me.

DH: Sure.

CS: And maybe Sioux too, I guess.

DH: It sounds like you're saying that you honor the ancestors you can.

CS: Yeah . . . the ones we know about. The ones that we don't know about, you know, maybe someday I will know, I mean good or bad.

DH: And that brings me to another question, the good and the bad. . . .What do you do with bad ancestors? I mean, clearly you have people who have done bad things in your ancestry.

CS: Well, every culture has its good and bad.

DH: How do you deal with that? I mean do you acknowledge them, do you atone for them?

CS: Well, being a traditional leader here, they come to me [to say], "We want to ban this person." And the only way you can do that is if this person took another person's life. If you just ban them because you don't like them because of their beliefs or political ideas or anything of that nature, family, you can't do it. I remember a long time ago my grandpa told my dad, that [when] just lied that was a very hideous crime and they killed them right there. I mean, that was a taboo. If you lied, you got killed [laughs]. . . . That's why you really had to straighten up. No, the lie nowadays, that's not a real hideous crime. It's changed. . . . Everybody has to lie nowadays in this society.

DH: Do you continue to ban those, I mean you personally continue to ban those people who have been banned?

CS: Most people know, I mean people know people. If you sleep with another woman, you're going to be tainted. Or if you sleep with another man you're going to be tainted. Or if you lie you're going to be tainted. People know.

DH: And are you in any way responsible for the crimes or the sins of ancestors?

CS: No, they have to live with it. They have to make atones themselves. If they can't and they don't, well there you know they're just lost. . . . They're just more isolated and shunned.

DH: If they're lost and shunned is there not something that should be done to help them be found and not be shunned?

CS: They have to go through it on their own.

DH: Is the spirit of the person who has been shunned, can that . . .

CS: Nobody can take on anybody's burdens. But you go, like a healing process, you may take on that person's burdens.

DH: So there is something that you could do?

CS: Yeah.

DH: After the person's death?

CS: Yes. Like me and my wife right now, we're taking care of her, her father just passed away Thanksgiving. And we're taking care of her mother. She's still in her home but we go over there and keep her clean, clean the house, do what we can. That's the way we respect our ancestors.

DH: And you're respecting her father at the same time?

CS: Yeah. My father-in-law. See when I lost my home out there, I couldn't cry. I was sitting on a hill, that tornado took it and . . . and I had all kinds of ideas why, I was thinking Christian I guess. I said, "You know that's just a fluke. Why am I sitting here? I've got work to do!" And my father-in-law came up to me and he started crying. Everybody came up to me crying, I said, "Why are we crying? Let's just clean up and we'll get it back. We'll be okay." I was thinking more Indian then, because things come and go in this world and there's nothing you can do about it.

DH: You said that you can atone for the crimes of ancestors and then you've also said that you can't. I'm a little bit lost. Is it not that clear, one way or the other?

CS: Well, really . . . it's how you look at it, how it's done, you go into a ceremony and ask for purification rites or healing rites or strength or courage or whatever because eventually that person's going to have to deal with it.

DH: So can you ask for that person?

CS: Yeah, you can ask for it.

DH: I see. Even if that person's dead?

CS: Yeah. You hope and pray that you know when I'm, when I went into the hospital to see my father-in-law. He was laying there, he was gone for a few minutes and I started praying that you know he's on his journey now, he's crossed to the spirit world and I told the Creator just, for better or worse, good or bad, just help him because he did his best he could here. He loved his family, he loved his community, and he loved this nation.

DH: And do you suppose that he also heard you pray that?

CS: Oh yeah, he heard.

DH: Is the Creator also your ancestor?

CS: Yeah. Or better be. [Laughs] Because . . . have you ever noticed how, this is my own theory, how people say, "I'm bored, there's nothing to do." Maybe it's just a haphazard thing they say while they're sitting around and if you have a spirit, if you have that spirituality, you become creative. You have visions, you have dreams, you have entities, ideas and you see them more busy. So they say, "I don't have nothing to do," it just seems like they're not really in contact with the spirit.

DH: That seems kind of spoiled.

CS: [Laughs] Yeah. I like to be bored, I mean just sit around enjoying being bored but I worked all my life. I mean, I tell my wife, I said, "I've got five more years and I retire and we're going to Guatemala and retire."

DH: Oh, which reminds me. May I ask how old you are?

CS: Sixty-one. I'll be sixty-one the fourteenth.

DH: Okay, thank you.

CS: I hope it helps you, I don't know what you're really looking for. We have a place we came from and we're going on to another place. . . . Well it was, like my mother used to tell me when she was walking with her mother. She was Cheyenne and my grandmother told me when she was a little girl, my grandmother told her, "You know, things change in this world." And she was telling that to my mother, "Things change in this world. You're going to have to walk two roads." And she didn't know what that meant and she said, "Well you're going to go this road, one road, you're going to have to follow this other road, the Indian road. Red road, two trails; you're going to learn how to do. It can be done," she said. Because she married an Arapaho, my grandfather. . . . So she, well she really never did like white culture.

. . . She descended from the Frenchmen Lewis and Clark. The Lewis and Clark expedition, that Frenchman was named Treaton . . . my grandmother had gray eyes and gray hair. And she descended from that. But she never did like the way that culture treated this culture and so she, kind of left it alone because of that treatment. But she did tell the kids, her children, "You have to walk two roads in order to survive." . . . When my father, he went off. . . he didn't really have any kind of idea about white people, he just thought of them as another group of crazies. [Laughs]

And when he went off, when he got drafted in World War Two and he went off to Europe and he came back, he said, "You know what? They really are crazy."

ANCESTORS RETURNING

Interviewees report that they stay in contact with ancestors in a great variety of ways. Physically, people inherit traits that daily remind descendants of genetic connections between the generations. Culturally, interviewees commune with their ancestors through manifold remembrances, rituals, telling stories, conducting genealogical research, and carrying on the identifiers of their ancestors, such as language, names, and places. Interviewees—like people everywhere, no doubt—also stay emotionally close to ancestors, not losing love and anger and recalling ancestors not only on special occasions, but also on ordinary days. Some interviewees also say that through dreaming, visions, or just through quiet meditation, they are sometimes also in spiritual contact with their ancestors.

Around half of interviewees believe they maintain connections to their ancestors, not only reconstructed from memories and emotions, but reflecting a spiritual reality of communion between the living and dead. Another smaller group of interviewees say spiritual communion seems possible or even likely, but they have not personally had such experiences. The remaining interviewees say whether or not humans persist in an afterlife, there is no crossing over between the living and the dead.

Janna Thompson and Sheryl Siddiqui argue that any perceived "interaction" from the dead to the living can only occur when the living reconstruct memories, or have normal dreams of the dead. Stanley Arai agrees, and offers his own explanation.

DH: What kind of relationship would you say you have with your ancestors?

SA: I talk to my mom and dad occasionally on the phone.

DH: And ancestors who have passed on, do you have any relationship to them?

SA: I think about it, but I don't have any dreams or . . . I don't have communications. I don't talk with ancestors that passed on.

DH: And when you hear stories . . . [examples are discussed from some of the interviewees] that people say their ancestors visit them to give encouragement; would you think things like that are possible?

SA: Oh yes, yes, but it's from their own perspective. Their memories, and so-called dreams, they may have occurred, but they are deconstructed.

Thomas Hertzel, Simon Jacobson, Christopher Tran, and Glenda Mattoon say communication from ancestors after their deaths is possible or even likely, but it is not something they have personally experienced. Kiyoko Messenger,

Stanley Fuke, Jason Felihkatubbe, Charles Sleeper, David Dollahite, Dr. Sri Srinivasa Vedala, Grandmother Oh, Lee Guem Ok, Terri Omori, and others on the other hand, describe visits from ancestors they feel confident were the actual return of an ancestor to deliver a message, a feeling, or a farewell.

Some of those who report visits from ancestors also report visits from other relatives, particularly deceased spouses. Kiyoko Messenger describes a dream she had after her husband died.

> When he died I felt like I don't know what to do. I don't have to have fixed breakfast . . . I always talk to him, his spirit. Not memory I am talking to him! You know the Dead Sea in Europe? I have a dream, there was salt so I was floating like this and all the sky and the water were all the same I was nobody but Kiyoko by herself I don't sink, I just hold like a pedestal, like an umbrella, I hold like this, so enjoying, nice, sky blue, water blue, nobody I just me. So then suddenly I saw it and the water was clear and a big concrete slab and so I just stand up, I stand up touched my concrete slab somehow thought that's a funny dream so when I stand up I saw it way far away kind of water coming this way like it's HATCHA! [Kiyoko makes a frightened yell] like dark sky and storm is coming and I thought, "Oh no I was right there enjoying it but now oh my goodness, oh that is too dark too strong!" I said. I heard it in my ear then I saw right beside big tall man, white, so white so like bear, so he was watching me. "Too dark! Too strong for me!" I just repeated twice then I saw just the profile, calm, breathe. So suddenly I woke up I remember my voice screamed so to wake up the next room. . . . I believe. I don't know what. People say after you die, something . . . something . . . I believe it.

Kiyoko Messenger makes it clear her experience was not a normal dreaming event; it had a unique feel, a special quality her ordinary dreaming does not possess. She does not claim to know who was the man standing next to her but she believes the experience was connected to her family, possibly her husband, or possibly ancestors.

Dr. Sri Srinivasa Vedala recalls an episode from his childhood that made a deep impression on him and on his understanding of ancestors, particularly his Grandmother.

> When I was young, my grandmother, my paternal Grandmother, when I was nine years old, she died. And I used to be all the time on her lap. She told stories, so many stories, God stories and so on, you know I was so fond of her. And then she died and then after one month, they used to do ceremony after death you know, they used to do funeral services. And so the first month I was sleeping with my mother, I was young boy, I was sleeping at her side and my father was there and

so suddenly I woke up, and she liked the mango fruits and so my Father bought so many mango fruits to do that ceremony to distribute to all the people. So they put it bunches of so many hundreds of mango fruits in so many big basket and close to my bedside in a big cart. And then I was sleeping and suddenly something sounds! I woke up and looked up. MY GRANDMOTHER! She came and sitting on the chair and she's picking and smelling that. You believe or not, I have seen probably forty seconds. Then, AAAAHHHH! I say it! AAAAHHHHH! Then she put up from there, she stood up from there and then she walked in the front door, she closed the front door, and then she went out. Out of the room! "Mom! Mom! Mom! I have seen Grandmother here." So she said, in a year it's possible for you because she likes you very much. You were the baby boy in the house, even nighttime also you used to go, you used to sleep with her, you know when you were young, three years old, even two years old. And she said it. Sometimes the connection is going to be there even in Hindu or even in German or even in Chinese, anybody! Anybody! If the connection is good personally, the connection is going to be there.

Dr. Vedala's experience shows some specific details similar to accounts from other interviewees. First, ancestral visits commonly coincide with a celebration of remembrance or holiday. Several interviewees report ancestors visiting during holidays, even when the descendant was not aware of the timing. The visits of Terri Omori's father and grandfather follow this pattern. The Parks also report that ancestors visit around the times of festivals of remembrance.

Second, many visits occur within a month or two after an ancestor's passing, or close to the times of anniversaries of passing. Jason Felihkatubbe reports ancestors visit on important dates or celebrations, not only those performed for ancestors but those performed for the living as well. Felihkatubbe says that his ancestors "celebrate with us."

Third, interviewees describe a peculiar physical sensation associated with ancestral visits, a special touch, or a unique sound. Some report feelings of caressing, the sensation of a hand on a shoulder, or unusual feelings of warmth and comfort. Kiyoko Messenger, Christopher Tran, and David Dollahite all describe such feelings.

Fourth, there is among those visited a sense that the experience even when visitors appeared during a dream, was not an ordinary daydream or other dream event but was qualitatively different from their usual dreaming. Kiyoko Messenger relates her Dead Sea dream in response to a question about whether visits are different from normal dreams or the same as dreams. Grandmother Kim says that when her ancestors visit, she might be sleeping but she is not dreaming. Although they usually come to her during sleep, "I do not dream about them," she says. Stanley Fuke's experience following his grandmother's death was dream-like but Fuke says it was not a dream.

> Another time I was at college in Iowa, my father's mother passed away. I didn't know. But that night I just lay there staring, and all of a sudden I was just talking to her and I was telling her about the college in Iowa and for some reason I had in my mind taken her all through campus and showed her . . . and the next day when my father called and told me she had passed away, I said, "I know."

Stanley Fuke's grandmother's visit felt strange, vivid, and very real. It was something he never forgot. And of course the timing of his grandmother's visit was also significant, coming within a day of her death.

Jason Felihkatubbe also perceives visits from ancestors as more than dreams or memories.

> I mean, I can relate because my father has been dead for twenty years now and I had similar dreams and for me that was really him. It wasn't an image, it wasn't you know a remembrance so to speak, it was happening now and in the present in this dream.

Ancestors "visit" for many reasons but usually during times of important transitions, celebrations, or stress. Some ancestors come to descendants apparently to say "goodbye." Other times, interviewees understand ancestors as attending to emotional suffering, and grieving. Sometimes ancestors visit to complete an unfinished act. When her mother-in-law visited Lee Guem Park it was not only to comfort her, it was also to guide her young daughter-in-law through difficult times. "After the dream," she reports, "I accepted my status knowing how to overcome hardship and so I tried to live my life to the fullest." The visit changed Lee Guem's attitude towards life in general and incidentally towards her understanding of ancestors. It was to be the first of many visits for her.

It cannot be ignored that ancestors visit, as Vedala reports, out of love for their descendants. This factor is tricky to consider because not all ancestors who loved visit and not all descendants who deeply miss their loved ones are visited. No interviewee felt comfortable trying to decipher that mystery. June York says,

> There have been some times I want to communicate with my mother. And no matter how hard I try, I never saw a sign of her . . . and I figured when she passed if there was afterlife, if there was any of those things that we all grew up reading about, because of her dedication to her family, we would see something of her.

The Park family in prayer to their ancestors. Courtesy of Seonghwan Jack Park.

It wouldn't be scary, it wouldn't be a ghost per se, it wouldn't be harmful, but . . . she would want to come back to make sure her family, her brother, her sister, were ok. And I never saw that.

Nevertheless, the unifying element of ancestors returning appears to be love. Daniel Essim agrees. "Absolutely! Absolutely, it has to do with love." But, he adds, "And even my tenet that it may have to do with hate! Or is that a different topic?"

INTERVIEW WITH DR. DANIEL ESSIM

"Start from My Village"

DE: My name is Daniel Essim. I work with Walmart, I'm the district director for Health and Wellness on Market 54 which is out of Lumberton, Texas.

DH: Can you tell me what is your first language?

DE: My first language is actually English. And then my native language is Bayang. Actually Bayangi is our cultural heritage. When the British colonized us, and they came to the village, the people being a little bit primitive they were hiding from them. And when the British found them, they said, "Bayangi" "they found us." So, that's how they call them Bayangi. . . . I grew up in Cameroon, West Africa.

DH: Can you tell me who are your ancestors?

DE: I can go as far as my grandfather and my great-grandmother.

DH: Those are people in your direct line. Would you include people outside of your direct line as part of your ancestors? Uncles, aunts, cousins?

DE: Absolutely! Absolutely! Yes, sir.

DH: How broadly would you think of your ancestry?

DE: We are quite broad, quite broad. For instance . . . Let me start from my village, Nseinchang, my maternal village. If you go to the village and you want to go through our ancestral tree, before you get to the second generation, third generation, you realize there has been some intermarriage amongst us. Fifth-sixth generation cousins. What I'm trying to get to is that, the whole village is almost your family. Because . . . you should know, when our great-great-grandfather moved that village and started having kids and down the road, kids having kids and that ancestral tree is lost, people go to Europe or go to the city and get married to each other, and after a while you realize you've been married to your fourth cousin. So, that's how broad we are.

DH: Do a lot of the people have the name Essim?

DE: No. They come up like for instance, I'm Essim, my kids wanted to bear my middle name, Egbe. Because my mother-in-law (their grandmother) said she liked Egbe. So you find people who come up with their surname or their last name and end up giving their last name to their kids, or they will give their middle name to their kids. To answer your question, most people speak with their last names, some do not. So, you'll find a whole village, the majority of them, even brothers—like my Uncle is Mr. Edbair but my other Uncle is Mr. Enow, and then you have the Essims. These are brothers, but they decided to go with [those names]. For instance, if I'm growing up and my parents don't have money, they decide to send me to go to my uncle. Automatically, since my uncle is sponsoring me, helping me go through elementary school, under my uncle's name. Saumbe Essim Egbe. And you end up growing up known as such, Mr. Egbe. So that's literally what happened to most of my nephews and nieces that went and lived with their uncles and aunts in the city.

DH: If they go and live with an uncle or a person with a different name, do they adopt that person's ancestors? Does it change their ancestry?

DE: Just the name.

DH: So, there is no real close connection between the name and the ancestry?

DE: No. (There is no connection.) The way I see it, in the States here, when they are trying to look for ancestral roots, where you put one name and before you know what's happening, you can trace who your great-grandfather was. In Africa, people would have a very hard time doing that.

DH: So, do you think of your ancestry as being that fluid? That there are people you cannot name, people who migrated . . .

DE: Absolutely. Yes, sir. That's the way I look at it.

DH: It sounds like you think of ancestry as a larger group that is vaguely defined?

DE: No, I think I look at ancestry by the Oxford Dictionary definition, people from the same roots. You know again, it's not like a group of people, it's just people from the same heritage, you know, the same—that have the same genetic link. That's how I look at it.

DH: What role do you think culture plays in your definition of ancestry?

DE: Wow. A whole lot! Because if we were to apply the Western culture in our place, I think the whole idea where you go and live with somebody, with probably a minimum of years, you have to adopt his family name. Just because he's helping you go to school. I think culture has a lot to do with it. And to us it's ok. To us, it's absolutely fine.

DH: Do you think of your ancestors then as a group that shares your culture?

DE: That is the way it is but that is not the way I think it should be. I think I look at ancestry as people who have the same genotype.

DH: Do you believe that ultimately all people have the same genotype? That all people are ultimately related?

DE: Well [laughing] absolutely! Being a Christian, I believe everybody is related. We have the one father, Abraham, and Isaac, and Jacob.

DH: Yet you don't think of everybody as part of your ancestry? Or do you?

DE: You mean my belief? What I would say is I do not believe that we should all be considered from the same ancestral tree if we are just a bunch of people that came together because of culture or other things.

DH: What about things outside of human beings? Would you include animals or plants or other forms of life as part of your ancestors?

DE: No. No. I look at ancestral tree and ancestry in terms of human beings.

DH: Do you think of your ancestral tree as having a beginning?

DE: Oh, absolutely! From the Bible, our beginning is from our father Abraham.

DH: And God? Do you think of God as an ancestor?

DE: Absolutely! He is our number one Father.

DH: All people are ultimately children from God?

DE: That's what I think.

DH: It sounds like you are more connected to more recent ancestors, or those from Cameroon, or . . .

DE: That's what I believe that my ancestry goes through Cameroon.

DH: Going back a few generations?

DE: A few generations.

DH: Can you tell me what is your present personal relationship to those ancestors?

DE: That is a very good question because that is what we're trying to do here. Again, I just had a conference call with all of my third and fourth and fifth cousins (I know their parents) and one of them just died in Maryland so we tried to manage to put some things together to send the corpse back home. So, the first thing I did was—I didn't know everybody, so I asked everybody to introduce themselves, to tell a little bit about their parents, their grandparents, and if they remember, their great-grandparents. And if they knew about the village. That is how we now are trying to put these things together. To answer your question directly, I can only talk to probably the second generation of mine, to my grandparents that I saw, I lived with. Beyond that, most of them died prematurely, so you cannot do the connection.

DH: Do you have any active connection to ancestors who have died?

DE: No.

DH: Do you have any funerals or other ways of honoring those who have died?

DE: Absolutely, yes sir! Particularly, my mom died about a year ago. We were supposed to honor her this January. So, yes, we honor them, we go back to the village. We are Christians; we just go to the church and give thanks and offer a church service for them.

DH: Do you offer it for her now, or for her former life, or what is the context of the honoring after she's past?

DE: We just want to keep her memories alive, so we honor her for the past, for the life she had lived . . . we constantly celebrate her life. That's what we do. That's what we do. In some cases, we do that every year.

DH: What is the purpose of that?

DE: To keep her memory alive.

DH: For her or for you?

DE: For all the children. To remind her that, hey, we're still thinking of her. Because we have this belief that the dead still listen to us. So, there are times when you are having hardship, you pray to the Lord and you also pray to your late mom to guide you through the hardship. Whether she's listening or not, whether she's actually guiding you or not, you believe in it, that she is guiding you. So, to answer your question, we have those things just to remind them that we're just thinking about them and for them to guide us as we go through difficulties in life.

DH: Do you have any personal experience to support that she can actually hear you or is listening?

DE: Mmmm, no, no, no. But I think I have a gift of dream. I have a gift to dream. And it would not exactly be the same . . . it would not exactly come what was going to happen, it gives me . . . if I calm down and pray, it gives me something close but from a different angle. You know, I mean for instance . . .

DH: You mean a spiritual angle?

DE: Yes, let me put it that way. Spiritual angle. Because again, like the plane crash happened, the plane crash from Paris. Two days ago I dreamed I was on a bus and I was involved in an accident, and I found myself inside a valley. So I did not drive my company car because I was afraid that if something was going to happen to me it only happened to my personal car, not the car that I use to work every day and I park it in my garage. So I woke up the morning of the plane crash. That's how I see things. A few months before that, I dreamt how somebody had a stroke but it was my mom who responded to that person, even though it was my mom who was going to have the stroke. So, you probably help me out here, I've asked people to tell me why I see those things. When I was in pharmacy school, about eighteen years ago, I was really very very poor and there were times I didn't even have twenty-five cents to buy something.

DH: In the United States at this time?

DE: Yes, I was in Maryland. . . . So, a check came from IRS, even though I was owing the IRS for the previous tax season, three hundred dollars or something and the check came for four thousand and something and I had to pay my tuition and fees. I used that money and I prayed about using the money and I [decided] this is a loan without interest. I knew it was the wrong thing but I said the Lord sent that money to me, so I used that money to pay my tuition and fees and said to myself, I need to go to school [and will use the credit] and I called the IRS and said, "You sent me the check." They said, "Oh send it back" I said I had already used it. They asked me to make payment arrangement. We can pay it back, with ease! You know, and that's not the first time that has happened to me. So the Lord always does those things. I don't know if it's my ancestors who are doing that, if it's the Lord, so you probably might help me just tell me these dreams and these things that happen to me, why do they happen to me?

DH: Do you feel like your ancestors are involved in this?

DE: I feel it is the Lord. . . . I wouldn't say the Lord is one of my ancestors in particular because I don't believe in that. But then again I cannot dispute that, that they are not looking over me.

DH: You did say you feel like they are looking over you in a way.

DE: Yes, absolutely because there are times . . . I flew in to Cameroon, I was supposed to go to a funeral . . . my mom was alive and had gotten me involved to help one of my relatives with tuition and fees. . . . This person prevented me from going to that bereavement of a friend's mother and there were some attacks on the road so if I had gone that night, I don't know what would have happened. So these kind of things happen to me. When things happen . . . to answer your question, was this tied to my late mother? I think so! She sent this person to intercept, to prevent me from going to that place at night, to drive to that city at night, where they were ambushing people.

DH: If your ancestors do that, why do they?

DE: Just to protect you, to try to make sure nothing bad happens to you.

DH: What is their interest in the living?

DE: It's a difficult question and at the same time it's also not a difficult question. If you are a father or a parent and you are dying, in your dying breath, all you are hoping for is that your kids will live a better life. You wish them all the best. So, everything in death . . . I'm not one of those theorists to think that they are watching over us, but kind of! When we pray we pray for the dead, I kind of want to believe that they are looking over us and they want to do good, and they want to protect us that no bad things should happen to us! Why I would say that is because they are with God. And even as I believe in God I will believe in them because they are with Him and everything they're telling me is what the Lord is telling me or the guidance they give me is what God would give me because they are with Him. That is the angle I would argue. But again, it could be a difficult question in the sense that I don't know . . . if they're actually watching over us.

DH: If they are and they are with God, does it have something to do with love?

DE: Absolutely! Absolutely! It has to do with love. And even my tenet that it may have to do with hate. Or is that a different topic?

DH: I think it's the same.

DE: I know of hate—but I believe it because my niece—we grew up together in the school, we grew up in a home that did not have electricity. So, when we were in school we used to use lanterns. When we would walk back to her house, the streets were pitch dark! When we were growing up in our town—no electricity! Only lanterns, with crickets making noise [he makes cricket noises]. So I did not see any spirits, any devil—something so you understand, anybody who had died would walk the streets! I did not see any of them but somebody has told me recently, a lady who had a husband who had died and was mad at the wife came later and killed the wife. . . . So, I don't know . . . that's why I say it could be love and it could be hatred. But again, do I believe that? I don't have any reason to believe or not to believe. But it sounded funny to me.

DH: But it sounds like from your own experience, it has more to do with love?

DE: That is correct.

DH: And when you pray for your ancestors who have passed . . . what is the intent or the purpose of the prayer for ancestors?

DE: Oh boy. [Pauses] I pray for them . . . I'm getting emotional. I pray for them to rest in peace, and I also pray for them for their guidance. This is the theme of my prayer constantly.

DH: For their guidance or for them to help guide you?

DE: For them to help guide me. And the rest of the family that they left behind.

DH: And do you find any correlation between those prayers and events you know will happen?

DE: I think so. Yes, I think so. But more importantly, when I really pray . . . I become a prayer warrior ask the Lord for something, it always happens. The Lord particularly, not my late ancestors. Now, when I ask the Lord for something, He always—He always!— the only problem is I don't do it frequently, I don't ask Him as much as I should have loved. I believe that all of us do that.

DH: It must fit with your understanding of God and the universe that you can do this with your ancestors.

DE: True.

DH: When you pray for your ancestors, do you ever pray *to* them or more *for* them?

DE: I pray for them and I pray to them.

DH: Do you ever feel like you pray with them also?

DE: No, I don't pray with them.

DH: Do you feel in a sense like they pray for you?

DE: I would say pray for me . . . the intent . . . I don't know if they pray for me, it's like the guidance that is guiding me is kind of like prayer. Yeah, but I would say directly, they don't pray for me. I say they look over me.

DH: Do they visit you? Do you see them in dreams? Do you more than just "feel their presence"?

DE: No, I see them in dreams.

DH: And when you see them, do you say that is really them, you are really seeing them? Or just memories?

DE: No, it's not just a memory, it's not a memory. Sometimes I am frightened and I wake up and I say, "Oh my God." Sometimes I say, "Why is it in a dream? Why wasn't it true?" Like when my sister died, I didn't know I was going to go to China, but I found myself among so many people and then she just surfaced. She didn't get back to me, you know, we talk and talk but she did not respond, I would have wanted to tell her everything and . . . she would help me with my trip to China to be more successful . . . because I would be going to China without knowing anybody and I was going to buy some business things for my pharmacy business in Africa.

DH: Do you think you could be visited or helped by ancestors who you didn't know in life?

DE: Yes. When my sister (who is now in Norway) was in Gabon, she told us that our great-great Uncle who died when she didn't even know—she only saw pictures—she said he came and asked, "Are you not this person's daughter of my sister? I want you to go back to Cameroon, from Gabon." I don't know if she saw it in a dream or something but honestly I've not sat down to ask her definitely. But she said our uncle—our great-great-uncle came to her in person. This is somebody who died more than fifty years ago! They are helping us.

DH: Do you feel like there are things that you can do for your ancestors who have died? It sounds like this ancestor was asking for help.

DE: No, they are helping us. Not us helping them.

DH: What about the cousin who has died and you are trying to send his body back to Cameroon?

DE: He died in Maryland at University Hospital. They discovered he has cancer of the pancreas.

DH: Why is it important that he be buried in Cameroon?

DE: That is a good question that will be debated and not only in Cameroon but in the village close to my uncle's. . . . If he's buried by the side of his father, they can become conversant.

DH: Would you also think that's possible?

DE: [Laughs] How can I say? I don't know. But it seems that spirits talk among themselves. I don't know.

DH: It seems like they can travel farther than that sometimes.

DE: I believe so because people who are buried in Africa, and you see them, you are dreaming about them; they are probably around you, protecting you.

DH: Do you think that you have a special connection to ancestors who are not in your direct line, uncles, cousins?

DE: Yes, yes.

DH: So, the bloodline is not critical, or maybe the bloodline is less important than the relationship to an individual.

DE: Give me a definition of "bloodline." Because bloodline to me my uncle is my bloodline because he is the child of my grandfather. So I don't know. It depends on bloodline. . . . In direct line of ancestors, like your father, your grandfather—no I think it's broad because you know my cousins, nieces and things like that, I can think about them being around me and helping me.

DH: What about an adopted family member? If a person were adopted from another village or even another country, could that person be part of your ancestors?

DE: I'm happy you brought that up. Can it be an ancestor? So, like I've dreamed about my neighbors, my neighborhood who died. So, I am from Maryland, you are from Oklahoma; that's how distant we are in terms of where we come from. But we lived together, I was born in their house . . . we grew up together knowing each other. Yes, I dream about them too.

DH: So, in a way can you make ancestors or make relatives?

DE: If dreaming about people, or dreaming or praying about guidance from people who died, or praying about them resting in peace, means you can make ancestors out of that, then I will go with that. Define to me, let me know where my boundaries are. What is your definition of *ancestors*?

DH: You're asking me personally?

DE: Yes. As a specialist in this field, what's your definition of *ancestors*?

DH: You know, almost everybody I've interviewed has been a little older, self-confident, most of them elders in some community, like grandmothers, tribal elders, and they all—almost all—agree that people have choices with ancestors. There are enough accidents and enough misinformation in anybody's ancestry so there are people who you think are your ancestors but who are not really in your direct line and there are some in your direct line you don't know about. So, what I'm coming to believe is that people really create much of their own ancestry. But they don't do it alone, they do it together with all the elements of their ancestries. Each person is part of his own ancestry and works to help create it, and the ancestries all intersect and so I don't think it necessarily has a boundary except in what it has to do with your own experience, or what you're able to carry.

DE: Good words spoken! But what is your definition—just to help me down the road in my own life, what would you understand as ancestral tree? Not about people creating their own ancestral tree, but what do you understand for ancestor tree?

DH: "Ancestor" includes things that are not just people. It is also things that are cultural. So, I think people descend from people, they descend from music, they descend from food, they descend from land, from language, from songs, from ideas.

DE: Wow.

DH: And all of those things together is what in my mind creates a person's identity. . . . And when people say, "I come from these people," "I come from the Cherokee people," or "I come from the Mexican people of Texas," they don't mean just people, they mean all of the things, the horses, the land, the food, the music. So, to me, ancestry is coming to mean something much broader than just genetic ancestors. And if I look at my own family, I can see there are people in my family, maybe cousins, maybe second cousins, third cousins, who kind of move out of the family and disappear from my experience. But then there are people who are not even cousins who move in to the family, like they marry in to the family, or they are adopted in to the family, or they are very close friends, and they become my family. So I have a pretty fluid definition. Does that help?

DE: Absolutely, absolutely! Because you know, when you talk [about] people believe in their village, they go and worship a stone and they believe that they came from that stone or whatever. You are right in that concept.

DH: Do you agree with that part of it?

DE: I agree with that and I could be wrong but to me ancestral tree means just your bloodline. Who makes the ancestor tree of my ancestors?

DH: I think it sometimes does but . . . three or four of the people I've interviewed are pretty strict genealogists and even those people said, "Yeah, we do make ancestors. We create ancestors." In the same way that you create family. If someone marries in, they're not really your relatives, but they become part of your family. Not that it's random—I don't just get the choice, I can't say I'm Cameroonian just because I like Cameroon. That's artificial. There has to be something that joins together in a real way, like your dreams and your mother and so on, that's not fake, that's real. So you can't just make things up, but on the other hand, you can participate in the creation of or of the building of your own ancestry. Do you think people without children can still be ancestors?

DE: Absolutely, yes! Because not everybody could have children it does not mean they are not part of the bloodline.

LOVE TRANSCENDING DEATH

Interviewee Thomas Hertzel tells a story about an ancestral uncle, a farmer in Argentina three generations back. The uncle told his children, "You must plant cashew trees so your grandchildren have cashews." Now, Hertzel says, that uncle's grandchildren have cashew trees producing plenty of nuts and the uncle is celebrated in his family as a wise and loving ancestor. Hertzel feels most closely connected to those ancestors who during their lifetimes worked for the well-being of their eventual descendants, including those they would never meet. But Hertzel conversely feels "severed" from those ancestors "who did not care," who were not considerate of their eventual heirs. He muses that his genealogical work might be part of an effort to reconcile with those ancestors who were less than thoughtful. "Maybe I'm trying to re-create [a spiritual connection] with my genealogy work."

In general, in the context of interview conversations, a "good ancestor" is one who, like the Argentine grandfather in Hertzel's story, honors his descendants. Jason Felihkatubbe, Henri Mann, Jeff Livingston, and others describe "good" ancestors as those who were concerned during their lives for the provision of those who would follow them. Most interviewees say such actions are primarily motivated by love.

The story of exchange, caring, and love between ancestor and descendant requires trust in two directions, ancestors looking forward to their descendants' respect for the ancestors' efforts, and descendants looking back to interpret ancestors' work in a positive light. Henrietta Mann says her grandmother instilled something good in her, not only "by talking to me, but [by] what must have been her prayers, her thoughts for me, her teaching that she passed on to her son and grandson." Dr. Mann believes in her grandmother's good intentions and she has faith that her grandmother trusted her granddaughter to listen, even in grandmother's absence.

Though he never met her, Father Christopher Tran loves his grandmother. Tran knows his mother and understands how dearly his mother loved her mother. Father Tran recalls his grandmother every day, in every Mass he leads, because of the love between mother and grandmother. He trusts that his grandmother's love passes to him and he returns it as best he can.

Interviewees commonly relate a lesson for both an ancestor and a descendant: Influence and love function in two directions, from the living to the dead and from the dead to the living. Love reaches across death to affect, motivate, and move the lives of relatives one, two, three, or more generations removed. And though genetics are important, love is usually described as a greater influence than genealogy on both memories and narratives. Genetics and genealogical charts provide information, ancestral raw data. But love ties the generations together and enriches a narrative with emotion, intimacy, and meaning. Love listens, trusts, and justifies the efforts of the past into the lives of the present, and the efforts of the present into the lives of the past and the future as well.

When Jason Felihkatubbe's father lay in his coffin, Jason touched his father's hands.

> Seeing him in the coffin, feeling his hands, how torn and rough, you know, it was worse than sandpaper. But it was so that we could have a good life, so we could have a roof over our heads, food on our table, you know so that we could attend better schools. And those are the things that you remember.

The affection Felihkatubbe holds for his father he extends to other ancestors and to the whole of his ancestry. His father represents in an intimate way the sacrifices and legacies of the larger community of ancestors. As his father worked, so also did the tribal and ancestral community work. As his father sacrificed, so also did the tribe and ancestors sacrifice. And those who had not led good lives like father, are absorbed into the general well-being of the larger group, because Felihkatubbe emphasizes the good.

Charles Sleeper says, "You need to learn what the spirit tells you. A lot of spirits, they come and give you . . . medicine or the teachings." Sleeper says the ancestral spirits "can either give you life or take your life. They come in many forms—they tell you they're there, what you need to do. When a person's under stress they come." Genealogy, says Sleeper, is important, but the love that connects and identifies a family is more important. He distinguishes between behavior and genetics and explains, "It is more important how they were than what they were!"

When interviewee David Dollahite was in college, his grandfather died and Dollahite did not learn of the death of his most beloved relative until several days after it happened. By the time the young student heard the tragic news, the family had already strewn Grandfather's ashes into the Atlantic Ocean. But the night he learned of his hero's death, he had "one of those dreams."

> You might ask "Was this all inside my head?" I feel like this was more than that. In my dream, I saw kind of a mountain and went toward it, and there was a cave and I walked toward it and out from the darkness of the cave walked the spirit of my grandfather, and I knew who it was, I knew that I was dreaming but I knew that this was my grandfather, not just random firing of synapses. I knew that I was having an experience beyond just inside my head. . . . I woke up from that dream feeling awash in love and spiritual power and alive and really on fire in kind of a spiritual way, the way Christians talk about the Holy Spirit as—alive

and embraced in love in an incredibly deep and profound way. So that experience with my grandfather immediately after his death was for me . . . I feel a closeness to him in that way.

Grandfather came to comfort his grandson and, reminiscent of the childhood experiences of Vedala, Fuke, and others, to complete a spiritual act. Dollahite explains the overwhelming sense of his experience of love that transcended death, moving in both directions, from the living towards the dead, and from the dead towards the living.

Jeff Livingston tells a story secondhand, of his father being visited by the spirit of Livingston's grandfather.

> My dad was at a real low spot in his life and he was ministering to people up in . . . Alberta. He was doing a suicide workshop and all of the feelings of how bad it was with the Natives in terms of all the suicides, he got real down and he was walking along the road and . . . it was the middle of the winter and it was real real cold and he just had a T-shirt on or a light shirt and he just was so down and he didn't care whether he died or not. . . . And he said that his grandfather came and told him to take the next ride that came along because he was declining rides on the road. And his love for his grandfather snapped him, made him realize, "Whoa, what am I doing?" And so he took the next ride and got over it. But that's the story he tells and the spirit of his grandfather came to him and told him, "Take the next ride!" So I think that people that have passed on are aware of what we're doing and I think they can have some kind of influence like that. I don't know exactly how.

A grandfather's love motivated the son to do good work, to persevere, and to have courage.

Ancestors bequeath to their descendants so many things. Interviewees identify names, languages, values, ethics, religion, community, psychological states, and spiritual "culture" all descending from ancestors. What type of legacy a person leaves is a complicated question, the answers to which place responsibilities at the feet of both ancestors-to-be, and descendants, groups that share responsibilities. In order for the ancestor-descendant-descendant relationship to be active and healthy, descendants must respect inherited values, sort the good from the bad, and pass ancestors' positive values on to future generations. In order to do these things, descendants must listen to voices of the past. A person's work and life becomes another child's inherited identity, and people of the present must act cautiously to defend and preserve the good they inherit and reject that which was not good.

INTERVIEW WITH PARK SIN JOO*

"My Descendants Will Do What I Have Done"

DH: May I ask your name?

PSJ: Park Sin Joo

DH: And your profession?

PSJ: I work in a construction company called Busan Industry.

DH: May I ask your age?

PSJ: I was born in 1961. In Korean age, I am fifty-three.

DH: What is your first language?

PSJ: Korean.

DH: Can you tell us who are your ancestors?

PSJ: I think that ancestry is all about descending from the very beginning of the Park's family. I consider ancestors going back to great-great-grandparents. In other words, I really only consider four generations of ancestors.

DH: Does ancestors include only direct lines?

PSJ: All those whose last name is Park are [our] ancestors, regardless of direct line or indirect line.

DH: What about a wife's relatives, such as uncles?

PSJ: No, they are not my ancestors. From my position, I consider them only relatives because they have different last names.

DH: What if a Park is not Korean? Is that still an ancestor? Or, are Parks only Koreans?

PSJ: Yes. All Parks are Koreans.

DH: How far back in time would you carry this? Do you have a first ancestor?

PSJ: The first ancestor of Parks was Park Hyuk Gu Se. Parks descend from him, and I am the fifty-sixth.[†]

DH: Before that person, are they not ancestors?

PSJ: There is a creation myth in my country. Han-Ung who came from the sky married a bear who turned into a girl and founded a country called Go Jo Sun, which is the first

---

*Seonghwan Jack Park, translator.
†Mr. Park counts fifty-six generations from Park Hyuk Gu Se to himself. His family is essentially fifty-six generations old. He only ritually remembers more recent generations.

Three members of the Park family: [from left to right] Father, Son, Mother. Courtesy of Seonghwan Jack Park.

nation of Korea. As time went by, one of his descendants, Park Huk gu se, went to a city called Mil Yang where he spread his descendants who became the Parks, named after him.

DH: Are we descended from things other than people? Are we also relatives of animals?

PSJ: No, we are not. That is a myth, which cannot be verified.

DH: In the Park family, when people who are not born as Park become Parks, like people who are adopted or who marry in, do they also become part of the Park ancestors? Or do they have to be born Park? In other words, is the ancestry carried on by blood or by name?

PSJ: [He paraphrases the question.] We think that they are also parts of Parks. So the answer would be both [blood and name].

DH: Is the significance of ancestry more cultural or genealogical?

PSJ: Yes. Both of those.

DH: What is your relationship to your ancestors these days?

PSJ: Ancestry is a broad concept, like I said. Ancestors are recognized up to a relative in the eighth degree from my side, and to the fourth degree on my wife's side.*

---

*Mr. Park serves both his wife's side and his own side, though he serves more generations and ancestors on his own side than on his wife's.

DH: Active relationship? Do you have any experiences with ancestors who have passed on?

PSJ: The reason why we are doing ancestral rites is that we always think about our ancestors. They help and take care of us. They help us do well in every way. I remember them by having a state of mind to worship them every day. I feel more comfortable by doing that. I think this is the relationship between them and me.

DH: Do you consider ancestors before doing simple normal daily things like eating, walking, or working?

PSJ: In my heart, we appreciate the help of ancestors. Since we perform a memorial ceremony once a year at the time when they passed away, we can think about them once again on that day. Basically, we have only a general appreciation in our minds on ordinary days.

DH: Are the ancestors aware of your remembering?

PSJ: Yes, if they died, they look down at us from the sky. They know of the day when the descendants get together to perform the ceremony with food. They know we are sincere and that we do this for them. By doing [these rituals], we can be unified and think about them once again. This creates good harmony with relatives and gives us an excuse to take the time, even when we are very busy. We can get a peace of mind.

DH: Are ancestors grateful when people get together?

PSJ: Yes, they feel grateful, so they can take care of the descendants.

DH: When you bow* [during ceremonies], do you talk to ancestors?

PSJ: Yes, while I'm bowing, I think about them again with the mind of what I hope is them taking care of us. But I don't speak out.

DH: Is this different from praying?

PSJ: It is similar to praying. By bowing and thinking of them, we can feel comfortable. Because we do this for a better life. In that way what we do is the same as praying.

DH: What do you mean by "taking care of us"?

PSJ: It is based on faith, supposing that the ancestors are alive. We believe that they will help us in everything we do.

DH: Does the faith come from experience or have you been taught by somebody?

---

*The Korean word is 제사 (*Jesa*), which means much more than its usual English translation "to bow." *Jesa* is a word that delivers the whole sense of the ceremony for ancestors. *Jesa* refers to honoring with food, preparation, bowing, incense, and a moment of silence for remembrance. It is a traditional ritual revering, symbolized by bowing.

PSJ: It is a connection between my ancestors and me. If I respect my mother, my children will later respect me as well, by watching what I'm doing now. I also feel comfortable about that. It's hereditary.

DH: Do you have any personal experiences you can tell us about?

PSJ: My father was sick when I was little. I took him to the hospital and looked after him. When my ancestors have any problem like that, we deal with it together. After I get old, my descendants will also do what I've done. This is our family background. If the ancestors do well, then the descendants will also follow them well. The environment is really important.

DH: Do ancestors visit their descendants?

PSJ: Yes, the ancestors who have died sometimes visit me in dreams. The ancestors who are alive can also meet with me when we have a big event, and then give us some advice.

DH: Why after death do the ancestors visit the descendants?

PSJ: The reason is that the ancestors want to see their descendants, or because I think about them. If something bad happens, they will give us a hint to be cautious.

DH: Have ancestors who you have never met visited you?

PSJ: Ancestors that I don't know sometimes show up in my dreams. They introduce themselves in advance, and give us a foreshadowing. Then, I try to be more cautious on that day.

DH: Do they speak with you in words or do you just understand them?

PSJ: We speak with words regardless of whether I know them or not.

DH: Have they ever told you something you did not understand?

PSJ: I always fully understood. They spoke more about things I already knew, so I just consider it a little more carefully.

DH: Do they ever give you new information?

PSJ: They also tell us what I don't know, maybe ten percent of the time. The rest of the time it is things I already knew.

DH: When this happens, were you always sleeping?

PSJ: Yes, I was sleeping. The thing is that they give us a hint. For example, my company got sunk under water due to a flood, in my dream. After that day, something bad happened to my company when I went to work.

DH: Are visitors to dreams always Parks, or might they be ancestors of friends?

PSJ: Only Parks.

DH: Are the ancestors closer to God than you are?

PSJ: There are good and bad ancestors. Even though they are bad, they are still my ancestors. Since they exist, therefore I exist. I don't particularly believe in God.

DH: Why do ancestors care about you?

PSJ: They have the same mind of parents and of parenting. They want their descendants to be happy like I love my children.

DH: Can we do anything for the ancestors?

PSJ: They are dead, so we don't need to do something special. Just on the day of ritual ceremonies, we should show them that we are doing well, and prepare good food for them.

DH: Do you have favorite rituals?

PSJ: The one we perform for my father and my grandparents.

DH: How do you know all about this? From your personal experience or by being taught?

PSJ: Since I was little, I observed what my parents were doing. When people get together during the ceremony, they talk about the ancestors and genealogy. I learned this naturally both by myself and from my ancestors. Basically, I was taught.

DH: How did you learn to interpret the dreams when they speak to you?

PSJ: They just started showing up!

INTERVIEW WITH LEE GUEM OK PARK (GRANDMOTHER PARK)*

"Thanks to Them We Are Born and Make Family"

DH: Can you please tell me your name?

LGP: Lee Guem Ok

DH: And your occupation?

LGP: I am a housewife.

DH: Please tell me your first language?

LGP: Korean.

DH: Where did you grow up?

LGP: Ham-Ahn, in Korea.†

---

*Seonghwan Jack Park, translator.
†Ham-Ahn is a town of around seventy thousand people, located in Haman County, Korea.

DH: Can you tell me who are your ancestors?

LGP: I take care of my ancestors and do the ancestral rituals. When we do that, we are doing well in every way. I feel really thankful to my ancestors.

DH: Do you feel thankful to any particular ancestor, or in general?

LGP: I feel thankful to my son and his wife and also to my grandsons. I'm really happy these days, because they're doing very well. I'm alright to die because of that. In addition, I feel especially happy to have the chance to get to know my grandson like Jack.

DH: Do you include your grandsons as your ancestors?

LGP: Yes.

DH: Who is the very first ancestor?

LGP: I don't know.

DH: Do you include among ancestors cousins who are outside of your direct line?

LGP: Yes, they are also my ancestors. All people who died are my ancestors.

DH: Are your ancestors all Korean?

LGP: Yes. There are no foreigners.

DH: Do ancestors know that you feel grateful to them?

LGP: They know.

DH: How do they know?

LGP: They know because we're performing the ritual sincerely. It is really up to us whether to prepare a lot of food and to spend a lot of money on the rituals. But they help us stay healthy and they are helping everything.

Lee Guem Ok Park. Courtesy of Seonghwan Jack Park.

DH: Do you have obligations towards them?

LGP: Yes, the obligation is the ancestral ritual. After I die, my son has to do it. After he dies, my grandson has to do it. It's like after marriage, we have a responsibility to our children as well as our ancestors.

DH: Where did you learn how to do this?

LGP: I just thought and spoke. I didn't learn anything from others. I'm illiterate. All of these things I say are from my own head.

DH: Do you have a specific experience that led you to know your obligations?

LGP: I didn't learn anything, so I just told you what I know from myself. I'm sorry that I'm not smart.

DH: Do you have experience with the ancestors, that leads you to believe them?

LGP: Yes, performing the ancestral ritual. It's like when you feel thankful to your parents when they give you something to eat. So my ancestors feel thankful when we give them food during the ritual.

DH: Do you communicate with your ancestors in any way?

LGP: No. They are dead, so they can't talk to me. They just come to my dreams. When they do, I feel that a shadow is hovering, a shadow like living people. One day, my husband came to me in a dream.

DH: Who else appears?

LGP: My mother-in-law, father-in-law, and husband, especially a few days after their ancestral rituals. They never speak, because they're dead. They just pass by.

DH: Is it your parents or your memory of parents?

LGP: Actual ancestors.

DH: Do ancestors who you don't know also come to your dreams?

LGP: No, only Park family members. Other ancestors don't need to visit other people's dreams. The purpose of visit to my dream is to help me.

DH: Why do the ancestors care for their descendants?

LGP: That's because we are one family.

DH: Do they visit you more often around the time of the ritual than other times?

LGP: No, only on that date when we perform the ritual. Once a year or once several years. We don't know when they're coming. If I think about them and take care of them with my best heart, they help us to do well in everything.*

---

*Lee Guem Ok later clarified to Seonghwan Jack that her ancestors visit her around four or five times per year, usually around the times of festivals in February, July, and September.

DH: Do they bring messages?

LGP: No. After a dream, something bad or something especially good happens. I might get sick, hurt, or harmed myself. If I dream something bad, I try to be more cautious.

DH: Do they ever give you a specific hint for those things?

LGP: No, they don't give me those things. I can just feel something. Yesterday, I picked up a wallet on the way to a market, and I handed it in to the police. They said thank you, and the owner of the wallet called me several times to show his gratitude.

DH: Do the ancestors cause those things, or do they know that those things will happen?

LGP: It's almost like that they made it happen. That's why I was very lucky. Actually, I could get cash from the wallet, but I decided to do the good thing, considering also that I have lived a hard life. Considering that, I took it to the police.

DH: When something good happens, do you feel thankful to your ancestors for that?

LGP: Definitely, I feel thankful.

DH: Do you say thank you aloud in daily life or at the temple?

LGP: If I pass by the temple, I bow for them. I say thank you inwardly, not loudly. If I get something to eat, I say thank you to them. If I get hurt when I work out, I say please help me get better.

DH: Do they hear that?

LGP: I don't know, because I say it in my heart. If people die, they are only spirits.

DH: If you have bad ancestors, do you perform the ancestral ritual for them as well as those who were good?

LGP: We should not think of them as bad ancestors. When I perform rituals, it is for all of my ancestors. There is a no exception, though only for my ancestors, not for other family's ancestors.

DH: If your ancestors adopted a child, do you think that the adopted child also can be your ancestor?

LGP: Yes. One of my relatives had seven daughters and no son, so they picked up a guy on the street and adopted him. That's because people want to keep their clan alive into the future. There was no concept of formal adoptions at that time. He (the son of the boy who was adopted) also comes to tidy up his ancestors' graves exactly like other descendants.

DH: Is he a Park?

LGP: Yes.

DH: Do you include among the ancestors only humans or do you include animals as well?

LGP: Neither of them. They turn to the soil after death and are buried. If they are cremated, they turn to the ash. Those are merely traces. So there are only wandering spirits as if we have good flies and bad flies.

DH: Do animals also have spirits?

LGP: I haven't experienced that, so I don't know. I think we change to the animals after death. I think they are also like humans.

DH: Are ancestors closer to God than we are?

LGP: Yes, they are closer to God in every way.

DH: In what way?

LGP: I don't know. I just think that they are closer to God.

DH: Are there spirits around us right now?

LGP: Yes, they are hanging around.

DH: When did the ancestors visit you in your dream?

LGP: When I got Jack's father in Junra province, my mother-in-law visited my dream. At that time, something bad had happened to my husband, and I cried over and over, staying up all night. After I finally fell asleep, she patted me on my head to console me. After the dream, I went to the market to do business, and I made lots of money. It was a very lucky day.

DH: Do ancestors cause the living to fall in love?

LGP: Yes. Thanks to them, we are born, and make family. We live as we think. If I think that they help me, I live my life with this value. If I think they are the reason I am doing well, everything works better. It really depends on how I think and accept them.

DH: Do you believe more strongly now than when you were young, or before you got married?

LGP: Yes, I do.

DH: Is that from experience or teaching?

LGP: It comes from my experience. I established my own thoughts about them during my lifetime.

DH: If they don't speak, how do you know who the ancestors are when they visit you?

LGP: I just understand. My ancestors come to my dream, because they are my ancestors.

DH: Do you have responsibility to bad ancestors?

LGP: Sure, we are their descendants. No matter how bad or good it was, we have to accept and understand it.

DH: Do you have a favorite ritual?

LGP: Not one in particular. I consider all of them equal.

DH: Is there anything important that I haven't asked you, but you think I should know?

LGP: No, you just think that every ancestor from the top to the bottom is equally great. We are one family. I can't explain one by one specifically to someone. [But] only the Park family.

DH: Do you have a specific experience with your ancestors you would like to relate?

LGP: No, they are dead, and they don't talk. They are like nothing (nonexisting) but still traces.

DH: What about your mother-in-law?

LGP: They just come and go. She was a spirit.

DH: But she comforted you?

LGP: I meant that I fell asleep after I had cried it out, because I felt so pitiful and miserable to myself.

DH: Did she visit you because she knew the situation?

LGP: Yes, she came to comfort me. After the dream, I accepted my status and to overcome the hardships and I tried to live my life to the fullest.

DH: Do you know of anyone who has experienced ancestors firsthand apart from in dreams?

LGP: No one.

DH: If someone says that he or she meets ancestors in person, would you believe it?

LGP: I don't believe it unless it was in a dream. They are dead.

7

GOOD ANCESTORS,
BAD ANCESTORS:
PRUNING BRANCHES

S anctifying ancestors does not necessarily assign to them inherent goodness, neither in their spiritual nor in their previous, worldly states. Just as there are people who behave badly in any family or community, there are also ancestors whose lives do not serve as positive examples and whose behavior is best not repeated. Interviewees offer various ways of confronting bad behaviors in their ancestral pasts and narratives.

Some interviewees set aside issues of "good" and "bad" altogether, recognizing ancestors simply as ancestors, deserving respect. Lee Guem Ok takes this position, as does Kiyoko Messenger.

KM: I respect them. I don't know who they are, I never saw them, I never spoke to them, but if they are not there, Kiyoko is not here!

DH: Why do you respect them?

KM: Because they are ancestors.

Jeff Livingston agrees that ancestors need to be generally respected, but Livingston is more cautious than Messenger and applies the same principle to those in his family's past as he applies to living relatives.

They're still your ancestors whether they're good, bad, ugly, whatever. They're still your ancestors and that's part of life. [But] I have an uncle . . . I would consider one of those black sheep kind of the family . . . I don't have an overly amount of stuff to do with him because he's not the kind of person I want to be around. But he's still family and he still deserves that much respect.

Bad behavior should be challenged, whether it occurs in the past or present. Livingston continues,

> They pass on traits and those traits keep building and building. And some—you have . . . each person has a chance to weed out the bad traits.

Livingston adds that it is not always easy to "kick out" ancestors. "It's easier," he says, "to bring them in!" Narratives can accommodate this; they are fluid and flexible, they evolve and they are reformed. But artificially altering ancestral narratives by "removing" ancestors may deny the native identity of a group, even in subconscious ways. An authentic, healthy narrative best evolves organically.

Ancestral identities might remain intact when a "bad" ancestor is held up as an example of how not to be—a sacrifice of sorts to the family, for the welfare of descendants. "Bad" ancestors might themselves have hoped for (or hope for) as much. If their failures are passed down as morality tales, their own suffering might serve progress rather than ruin, benefitting their families. A life ruined by alcohol or violence might find new meaning in the lessons of future generations. Jason Felihkatubbe offers this possibility regarding an ancestor of his own.

> In that particular instance, it got to the point where I did not see him [an uncle] for about twelve, fifteen years. [He] and I finally came to terms, I did see him, when—I don't know why or what feeling I had—but I knew it would be the last time I saw him. And it did end up being that way before he was murdered. And I think you know, at that time when I did see him that last time he was different. And I think that if it were up to him, yes, he would be happy that we were not like that and that we were doing better.

Felihkatubbe believes his unfortunate uncle might have wished for his descendants to avoid the types of mistakes he made. Felihkatubbe adds, "Somebody, somewhere has to wake up and say, 'This isn't how we're supposed to live.' But [some people] just get caught up in that repetitive cycle . . . they just don't realize anything." For the health of the community, a descendant can rehabilitate the work and legacy of those who did not do well.

It is not unusual for interviewees to declare that "bad" ancestors need to be simply expunged from a family narrative, as it were, in a kind of retroactive banishment. Loubert Trahan relates a saying that tells how best to address less positive examples from a family's past. "When I do a family tree for somebody I say, 'When you want to do a good family tree you have to carry a good pruning shear!'" In his massive genealogical holdings, Trahan might not shear off the names of all undesirables from the records, but he and his family shun the stories of bad examples.

Some interviewees see themselves as part of an ancestral system so badly broken, cutting branches and holding up examples cannot address the damage that has been done to the community of descendants. More radical steps need to be taken. So terrible was the behavior of some ancestors during their lives, and so great their crimes, their descendants feel more cursed than blessed by their inherited names and identities. Still bearing the force of the sacred in the morally nuanced, Latin sense and in Durkheim's sense of "special," ancestors who perpetrated great crimes are as difficult to ignore as are positive ancestors difficult not to honor. An intuitive impulse to narrate the lives and ethos of bad ancestors might be no less than an impulse to honor good ancestors.

Alexandra Senfft's ancestor's betrayal of their descendants began with her grandfather Hanns Ludin. Ludin was executed in Czechoslovakia in 1947, convicted of war crimes committed on a massive scale. But the decay of Senfft's ancestral community that began with Ludin continued well into the lifetimes of his grandchildren. Still in the twenty-first century, there persists residual, painful remnants of the family's violent past, perpetuated by a family culture of denial.

Not comfortable to simply "hack" bad elements from her ancestry, and not willing to attend the family culture of denial, as she grew into adulthood, Senfft felt compelled to acknowledge and confront her family's past. Throughout her adult life, she has worked to establish a moral and political path different from those of her grandparents and other family members, to redefine—perhaps to rehabilitate—her ancestral identity and family culture. Senfft's family experience showed her that ignoring evil does not make it disappear and staying silent about evil creates more problems. The title of her 2009 book in which she describes the Ludin legacy translates to English as *Silence Hurts: A German Family Story.*

For many years following Ludin's execution, his descendants were mute about his crimes. Alexandra Senfft calls the complicity of silence with past crimes the Family Codex, essentially a family taboo against openly discussing Ludin's life and crimes. The acceptable family narrative described Grandfather as a diligent German officer who may not have been entirely innocent but whose real guilt was that he had been a loyal, obedient military man. Ludin was the product of a terrible time, they would say. A patriot caught up in war, he was nevertheless a good grandfather and a loving father and husband.

Living the lie of the family's whitewashed narrative caused Ludin's descendants to suffer, through denial, repressed guilt, and shame. Ludin was in fact a war criminal, a leader as much as a follower in atrocities, and this reality and the subsequent family silence was like a disease spread through the corpus of the family, perpetuated by a false narrative. Four generations after his death, the ancestor Hanns Ludin still divides his descent in sinister ways and his legacy sows discord between cousins. Family members punish or ostracize those who speak more honestly, and those who do not speak openly suffer the guilt and confusion of an accomplice to any lie.

Alexandra Senfft is not the only person to have ancestors who left to their descendants criminal legacies and broken connections, and she is not the only interviewee with ancestors who betrayed their responsibilities to their descendants. But Alexandra is unique among the thirty-four interviewees in that she is ashamed of her ancestry. Her relationship to her ancestors is a psychological and spiritual trauma, nothing less. She sees it as her familial, social, and human responsibility to break with her ancestors' unhealthy patterns, to speak the truth about the past, to redefine her family's identity and to build an authentic narrative for the sake of future generations.

Alexandra Senfft believes in principle that ancestry and family are important. "I am very ancestor-minded," she says, and she hopes to pass positive values on to her children and to their children. In particular, Senfft strives to reestablish within the ancestral narratives of her children respect for, "well, truth." But in the context of her family's struggle, rehabilitating a more honest narrative has its own consequences. In order to identify and develop a healthy familial identity and ethos, Alexandra must redefine herself, while still "integrating the influence of ancestors into my existence."

"Alexandra, do you have a positive sense of ancestry?"

"No, David. I don't."

Alexandra Senfft's efforts to reform the record of her ancestors plays out in both political and psychological spheres. She is now the descendant and holds the authority to reshape her narrative. If she is successful, she might begin to build a healthy ancestral community and narrative in all its richness, good and bad alike.

INTERVIEW WITH ALEXANDRA SENFFT

"A Family-Minded Person"

DH: Alexandra, who are your ancestors?

AS: I don't know very much about my ancestors to be true, to be honest. I basically know a lot about my immediate ancestors so to say, my grandparents on my mother's side. And when I started researching about them, especially my grandfather, I also went into researching a bit about my great-grandparents. It doesn't actually go much farther than that . . . because other than in my mother's family, a lot of material was lost, was also burned in the bombing in Berlin and I think my grandmother on my father's side she also made a point of not keeping records and documents. Also, she was an illegitimate . . . child so I don't even know exactly who her father was. So I know relatively little about my family on my father's side.

DH: So when you think of ancestors, it sounds like you're not thinking of a community, you're thinking of specific individuals. Is that right?

AS: I think that is precise, yes. I don't have, let's say a very strong sense of family although on my mother's side there was such strong sense. Therefore I also don't have those kinds of strong group feelings. If I look for ancestors, I would rather as you say look for individuals, and the chain of individuals through the generations rather than a family at the time.

DH: Would that chain have to include only direct-line ancestors? Only people from whom you are descended specifically? In other words, would you include uncles and aunts and cousins as a part of your ancestors or ancestry?

AS: I certainly would, yes, but it would I think only really interest me if these, these ancestors from the past were in some way involved in a dynamic that would be relevant to a topic I may be looking into. Else they would be like characters on the margins and would not be strong acting figures, let's say, in the family history.

DH: But then in that sense why choose family relations at all? If your interest is strictly political or social, why take a particular interest in a family member whose political or social influence is important to you today rather than a person down the street?

AS: I read a lot of biographies of people who are not related to me and historically speaking I go a lot into other people's life stories. However, I found it's relevant in certain cases to look into family histories when I suspected that the history basically has effects on us up till today in cases when I think that maybe the private is so political, that it is relevant to look into it.

DH: Can you tell me what you mean by private?

AS: The private is what happens apart from the public eye, within ourselves as individuals or within groups such as families. Let me be more concrete because in this interview it hasn't been raised yet. I gave you an example of my grandfather on my mother's side who was the envoy of the Third Reich to Slovakia. He was executed there in 1947 and I was born only—let me count—fourteen years later in 1961. I grew up with [a] specific image of that person which was transmitted through family narratives which I accepted when I was a young person—although I even then, through my father's side, had different political perspectives on him than the rest of my mother's family had. This image made my Nazi grandfather look like a victim, not like the perpetrator that he was. He was up till—up to a certain point he was somebody I didn't actually relate to except for the fact that I said, "Okay, my grandfather was a National Socialist and I can read about him in some history books but he is sort of a neutral person. He is somebody I don't really relate to, definitely not emotionally." That was the case, let's say, until ten years ago. I had a clear political position and said, "He shouldn't have been involved and it was a horrible thing." However, I did not relate to him as one would to a relative. The relationship did not exist in my thinking let alone my feelings. And I, only when I really started going into his history and respectively my mother's history—who was his eldest child of six children, did this person lose this kind of neutrality. I suddenly realized, "Oh my god, this was my grandfather. I'm actually very closely related to him." And just imagine he hadn't been executed in 1947 and I would have grown up with him, I would have sat on his lap as a young girl and related to him in in my teens, I would have maybe confronted him with the past and how would we have dealt with each other then? These were all questions that only arose when I started exposing myself to my family history and especially taking a contrary position to what was being said about this figure in my family. I clearly said my grandfather was a Nazi-perpetrator, which made me a whistleblower within my family. So in a sense, in a horrible way you could say this relative finally became a person, yeah. He wasn't anymore just a figure from the history books. He became a real person and I was forced to relate to him as my grandfather, as a very close relative. And when you do that and you have never met this person but you have a clear idea of history and a political opinion about it, it can have rather horrifying and shocking effects and it raises a lot of questions like, "What does it mean that I'm the grandchild of these grandparents?" And I wouldn't exclude my grandmother that I did grow up with; she was very important to me in my life because, other than my mother, she was a very stable-—and with me a very loving character and a person I would have never suspected to have supported her husband as a National Socialist. So I had to really redefine my relationship to my grandparents and to an extent, if you look at it from the psychological point of view, I had to integrate their existence and their doing in my own identity and the fact of having to come to terms with it and not to hack it off from my own biography saying, "Ah, he was a Nazi. That's all I want to know about him, forget about him." I had to really come to terms with this close family relationship and what it would mean to me.

DH: And when you say "my own biography," you're referring to your biography as part of the community of ancestors, is that not right? Because in order to clarify your own biography, you need to clarify your relations with these people.

AS: Well, in a sense yes. I'll give you another example as far as my biography is concerned. I studied Middle Eastern studies. Only when I started taking up those studies in Great Britain I found out that my grandfather on my father's side, who died very early from a kidney disease, was an enthusiastic traveler in the Middle East in the early twentieth century. And he collected all these books and he wrote diaries. That was one item . . .

Alexandra Senfft. Courtesy of Alexandra Senfft.

DH: Was he German?

AS: He was, yes. He was. The other was that I pretty soon started concentrating on the Palestinian-Israeli conflict and then I started working in the Palestinian territories and later in Israel. So I got to know both sides very closely and intimately, I got to know both societies well. And I was always a person who tried to dialogue and to have dialogue between those who were or are enemies and in the beginning, in my early years, I thought that was a coincidence that I happened to suddenly work in the Middle East. Nowadays I would say, "No, I don't think it was a coincidence." I feel that this is something that clearly has to do with my family history in the sense of me picking up that I'm somehow related to that region and its conflict and that it has something to do with my own family history. So basically, professionally I started doing things of which in the beginning I wasn't aware of psychologically. I did not yet understand my inner motivation.

DH: Are you saying that there is something beyond your own personal initiative that has led you to these things? Something . . .

AS: Well, I'm not . . .

DH: Something not so individual. In other words, are you suggesting that your ancestors are in some ways guiding you or leading you towards these studies or these ideas?

AS: I think—well they can't guide me but I believe that instinctively I sensed that there was something that—in the Middle East, that there was something hidden in my identity that was maybe passed down from the generations and it's very difficult to explain this, David. I think it's a psychological approach.

DH: When you say passed down, there's a number of different ways something could be passed down.

AS: Oh absolutely, yes.

DH: And so there's genetic, there's . . .

AS: That you raised the question so that there are no misunderstandings, I—for one, I'm speaking about the transgenerational transmissions. What do parents and grandparents pass down to the next generation in hidden agendas, verbally or nonverbally? What do they transmit, as far as, for example, guilt feelings and shame are concerned? And I feel that my conclusion from the past of my grandparents was to do the exact opposite of what they did. And that was to seek peace, to try and work in human rights, to try and support dialogue in conflicting situations. And in one of my latest books which is about dialogues between Palestinians and Israelis and Germans, I'm also introducing a few characters, for example from Israel, one of which is a friend of mine and he was the same generation and he comes from the completely different perspective because his mother is a survivor from the concentration camp and we sat together, both looking at history from such different ends, and we both said our conclusion was to fight for human rights, that's the conclusion we drew. I could have gone another way too in my biography. I could have done exactly the opposite and continue the patterns that were set in my mother's family. I could be provocative, I could try to politically be polarizing et cetera, et cetera. But I didn't, and I think there are many different factors that have fed into my biography to make me go that way and one of which also, again when we speak of ancestors, is my father and my father's influence who always taught me to fight for human rights and to protect the weak and to be historically aware.

DH: You said your ancestors couldn't guide you, or that any "guidance" is psychological. But there are people who believe that their ancestors influence them directly through other routes, including through DNA, for example.

AS: I don't believe in DNA or genetically passed on issues except maybe traumas that we know can genetically leave their footprints. If anything, I believe more in the psychological side of things. I don't think my grandfather would have guided me to go to Israel and to work for peace there, you know. It's more the reaction to what he did and maybe a reaction to the positions maybe taken in parts of my family that made me guide myself that way, you know. And the choices I took in my life and the risks I took, these were my decisions and they weren't guided by ancestors at all. It was basically being aware in my life today about what happened in the past and the more I worked on the past to try and understand it, the more aware I became of how important it is to look at the past in order to also work for the future. This is for me also a political decision.

DH: And putting and joining those two things together, the past to the future, is the work of the present. What is the relation to your—not just your grandfather, but maybe your grandfather, or to the other ancestors you have?

AS: I grew up with this family codex that, in my mother's family, that my grandfather—respectively their father did not know that the Jews were deported to the concentration and death camps. They still cling to the benefit of the doubt—from their point of view, the Jews were deported to work camps and that my grandfather didn't know they were being killed. And I know my mother had a lot of doubts about that, especially because my father kept on kind of pushing her nose into this and saying, "It's not like that." Of course my grandfather knew what fate was awaiting the deported, you know. And for me, I grew up in a family where it wasn't really allowed to ask too critical questions and that for a long time I was unconsciously . . . being a player in the family game. And not knowing that there were hidden agendas and that there were kind of secrets hidden away and kept away from me. But if my mother hadn't been so sick and suffering so much, maybe I wouldn't have properly asked up to this day, really because it was her psychological suffering that made me suffer as a child so I understood there was something wrong, or foul you could say. There was something odd, there was something strange going on and it took me a long time to be able to move out of this—what I would sometimes call nowadays "family prison." And I can see how my mother failed to do so. She tried, but she was unable to stand up with a different perspective and to go through the pain that this causes when you turn your back to your family, so to say.

DH: Or to create a lie about what the family is.

AS: Oh yes, yes.

DH: And why is that destructive, why is that hurtful? You say you turned your back on the family in a sense. Is that a bad thing? Does it shape your view of family so that you see family as kind of a sick thing or as a bad thing?

AS: I don't think—no I wouldn't generally say something like that. I mean I am very family-minded; I have children of my own. But if a family is used as a group and, as you mentioned early on, if it becomes a group that covers up for wrongdoings, for crimes, and the loyalty to family members is so strong that you become . . . what is *Komplize* in English, David? Accomplice?

DH: Yes, accomplice.

AS: Yes, that you unconsciously, unwillingly become an accomplice. Then I went against family in a sense, or because there's a lot of group pressure then suddenly and it has nothing to do with love. I consider love that you accept that somebody has a different perspective than you.

DH: And family should be constructed or built around love, is that what you say?

AS: Yes, I think these are the people closest to you in your life. And these are the people you grow up with and you have to deal with and however, I don't—you know, friends can replace family and colleagues or . . . you can find different support nets. And yet I feel that this relation is a love relation to friends or very close relation to colleagues or whatever. I would not argue that family is the last word. I have a lot of friends that I would consider a large family so to say.

DH: Alex, most interviewees in this research have been generally positive about their ancestors. Do you have a positive sense of ancestry in that way that sort of would be the other side to your family's negative ancestry?

AS: No David, I don't.

DH: Yet, are you trying to create one? You say you have children and you're trying—are you trying to correct the family errors and by doing that healing the family in a sense?

AS: Well, I certainly feel that, let's put it this way—I started early on, I had to learn to integrate the bad influence from my ancestors into my existence. I had to accept that this was part of the German history, part of the German society, and even worse part of my own family and that it indirectly had effects on even my life today. And I consciously did not chop off those parts of my ancestry, and I'm especially talking about my grandmother. I told you early on, she was a very positive figure in my youth although I certainly look at her with different eyes now. I decided I will not chop off the love that there was between her and me but I would certainly look at her very critically now in many ways. And I don't have any positive role models from the past and I have never sought them. It was more important that I had a role model, for example, in my father or in one or the other good teacher or in somebody like the Israeli psychologist Dan Bar-On whom I worked a lot together and from who I learned a lot. I think that meant much more to me than looking for a model in the past. However, after having integrated let's say these bad parts from the past in my present situation, it has certainly created—more often urged me to pass this knowledge about their great-grandparents on to my children. I want to teach them quite clearly how racism and anti-Semitism and Islamophobia patterns—how patterns of exclusion work. And in that sense I am yes, I am being very ancestor-minded because I might pass it on to them, well the truth, the facts. And I feel now today while we're all living, I can live what I want to pass on to them. Yeah.

DH: And if you do that successfully, they could look more openly at the whole family history and the community of ancestors in a more accepting light?

AS: I'm often being asked when I do my readings for my book, "So have you liberated yourself from the past?" And I always say, "I don't think you can liberate yourself from the past. You have to accept that it's there and you have to confront it openly." I say, "You can't liberate yourself," however I feel that I grew up with so many unknown factors in my life with so many dark, hidden issues with a depressive mother who destroyed herself, where I always felt there is an agenda behind what I actually see. There's something that is hidden from me and I don't know what it is. And I feel it had a very frightening effect on my early life. There was a frightening element to it and I feel that knowing what really happened in the past, that shedding light on this, one knows basically with what monsters you are fighting and what you're confronting and what you have to do. So I feel it lessened the fear and it makes you, it definitely made me stronger to stand up for my positions politically here in my society. And I hope to pass this on to my children in the sense of them not growing up with taboos and lies, and I strongly believe that this will make them more healthy individuals in their societies and I sincerely hope that they will stand up for the right issues and protect the weaker et cetera, et cetera. At least they will have more energy to work constructively and positively in a society than, for example, my mother did who spent most of her energy on fending—fending off what she wasn't supposed to know and putting up all her defenses which is costing a lot of energy and it's quite self-destructive.

DH: Do you talk with your ancestors?

AS: Well no, not really, but I certainly dialogue with my descendants, with my children and maybe it's just about a dialogue with my generation, which is my cousins. I try to establish a dialogue with the generation of my mother and that is very difficult. I can see the limitations of moving or changing anything there. I certainly dialogued in dealing with my family history. I went into a silent and sometimes very horrible dialogue with my grandparents or even my great-grandparents to some extent because I try to understand their thinking, their motivations. I try to grasp what psychologically happened at the time to make people act the way they did and why a whole society come to be so totally inhuman. And in that sense yes you could say I did dialogue with my ancestors because I try to understand the connections, to understand what really happened and how can I analyze that today. How can I make it tangible too in the sense of really seeing the signs on the wall? I mean, for me it is also very important nowadays to think how can one keep the memory alive. How can we make younger people understand what happened in the past? For them to become active, to emotionally feel that it is important to fight for human rights and not to exclude people in the society I mean . . . how do we do that? And I have learned from Dan Bar-On, my work with him, and through my books that the biographical approach is very powerful. Because when I read in schools, young people will start listening when they hear about the history of a person because they start identifying with certain parts, negatively or positively. However also when I read from my book about dialogue between Israelis and Palestinians, everybody will start listening when you give them a personal story, a life story about somebody. And every personal story as I said has very strong political connotations and therefore I feel it's a powerful tool to keep the memory alive.

DH: Do you try to personalize the story?

AS: Yes, you could say so. Because it's easier to explain certain developments when you use a certain character like in a novel because it becomes emotionally tangible and is not just rationally or cognitively approached. And if that tool is used well I think one can motivate people to start thinking or to reflect and to change their perspective maybe more than a history book sometimes can, because here we are confronted with facts and figures and they don't touch you emotionally. They don't make things really tangible, how . . . what really happened in those days and I think that is important to keep up the memory.

DH: Alex, do you have any positive sense of ancestry?

AS: I prefer they're not my ancestors.

DH: Oh, okay.

AS: I feel that having dealt with my ancestors, how negative it all was, it certainly helped me shape my identity and make it stronger. I don't have any positive role models of the past. When I was younger, I wasn't interested in ancestors in general. My father would even have his funny saying sometimes, just because you are related, you don't have to love your relatives and he would tease his children with that occasionally. You know although he loves us very much. And on the other hand growing up with a mother where the family was above everything, almost like a fetish. Where the family was the group in which you could keep your secrets hidden, yeah. So I had two role models in my parents where I would feel, well, you know ancestry is not particularly a good concept for me. It's not something I can draw something positive out of but I'm talking here of the process of me as a young woman; that has definitely changed. I absolutely feel that only when I work through the past [regarding my ancestors] that I was able to become a stronger individual in the present and as I said I feel much stronger to stand up for my political opinions, et cetera, since I went through the process of contrasting myself with my ancestors. Ancestry is in that sense indeed very important to me. But what I'm saying is I have no positive role models and so I certainly don't feel they—well of course they passed something down to me in terms of me trying to do the opposite of what they did. And here I'm only talking about my grandparents but . . . it's hard to define yourself either positively or negatively towards your ancestors and I certainly only had a negative role model in that.

DH: Do you have any sense of ongoing or living relationships that you have with ancestors today?

AS: Well, you know . . . the person I probably dialogue with the most often is my mother, my late mother, because she left so many gaps behind and so many things I didn't know about her early life that it was very painful for me to find out how her early life had looked and what burdens she carried and also to understand in what imprisonment she lived, being her parents' child—the child of a perpetrator and his by-standing wife. I feel that I have much more understanding of my mother and much more forgiveness for her after understanding this and also, as far as my grandparents are concerned, yes they are alive in the sense of being a very negative influence.

It was a nightmare in many ways because I really had to look at this so closely to understand what had happened and what had gone on that it was awful, yes, and I feel that many negative energies are certainly still in the family because somebody like me who would take a different perspective and stand up for this position, you are confronted with a lot of negative energy, yeah. In some of my relatives' eyes I have completely twisted history, and have outlined a completely different perspective of their parents, one aunt even said that I ruined their reputations, stained their honor. She said literally,

"You are the wolf who has eaten the grandmother." I mean, I've heard horrible things and I'll give you an example of a key experience once. I happened to come across a book just before finishing my book, written by a psychologist from Munich who has written about denial in families because he's worked intergenerationally with families and could see how things were passed down and I was very excited reading this because I thought, I recognized a lot of stuff in this book that explained some of the behavior of my mother and in my family. So I called him and I said, "So would you be ready to read my manuscript of my book *Silence Hurts: A German Family Story?*" And he said, "Yes I will." And he did, and he gave me some helpful advice here and there and then the book was published and a few months later this man calls me and says, "So, Alexandra, how are you doing?" And I talked to him and I told him about the really harsh reaction from my family and how hard it was to protect myself in this situation and how painful it was, et cetera, et cetera. And then at the end of the conversation he said, "Alexandra, you do drive carefully, don't you?" and I laughed because I said, "Hey come on, I mean that's exaggerating." I mean, I thought he was being a bit mystical or whatever. And then I hung up and the moment I hung up, I had such a shock because I remembered that two days ago before that conversation, I almost had a car crash.

8

RECIPROCAL
ARRANGEMENTS

Interviewees frequently speak of a natural reciprocity between people of the past, the present, and the future. Ancestors prepare the ways for descendants who honor and remember ancestors, and together they cultivate the fields of their futures.

When interviewees describe what interest or good it does for ancestors—who are now presumably in spiritual states—to have descendants "bless them" (variously phrased), they answer, "to be remembered," "to carry on their ways," or "the ancestors want their descendants to do well because it means they [ancestors] did well."

Many interviewees believe living descendants can perform actions that benefit their ancestors. Such practices as codified through Christian, Catholic, Muslim, Buddhist, Hindu, and Native American practices endorse various interpretations of how the living can benefit the dead, and many of these interpretations come through interviewees' descriptions of rituals and other remembrances. When the dead are thus blessed, the living also benefit, for the honored dead in return bless the living. Father Tran says, "We always pray for the dead, no matter what. And then one day they become a saint and they pray for us."

Reciprocity between previously living and presently living might be understood as the organization of the cosmos, with significance that must go beyond a simple, intimate connection between a single loving ancestor and his individual descendant. Interviewees offer a greater, cosmological picture of life and death circulating throughout a vast mystical system. Glenda Mattoon explains her perspective.

DH: A funeral might be held for the benefit of the dead, to help the dead along their way and so on. Do you share such a concept? The descendant, not as intercessor exactly, but as a help person?

GM: A helper because we—I—still have a physical body which my great-great-great-grandmother does not have because she's deceased. I can do for her work that she could have done herself on the Earth when she had a physical body if she had had that knowledge, which she didn't. Okay, so I can act as a surrogate if you will, and then she has the opportunity to decide whether or not she accepts or rejects what I did for her.

DH: Is she aware in the same time as you of the work that you do on her behalf?

GM: I can't really answer that. I really don't know. I really don't know.

Glenda Mattoon trusts in the symbiosis of the universe in a way similar to that of Chief Sleeper's interconnected, living, spiritual universe. Sleeper trusts that he and his ancestral spirits are like guardians one of the other. Those who fall from this spiritual responsibility suffer the consequences: isolation, psychological disintegration, and spiritual sickness. Not only what the dead can do for the living is important, but when the living and the dead cultivate healthy, living relationships, both the living and the dead are spiritually empowered.

INTERVIEW WITH JASON FELIHKATUBBE

"They Celebrate with Us"

DH: [After introductions, Mr. Felihkatubbe is asked what types of questions people commonly ask him relating to family histories and genealogy.]

JF: A lot of people have questions. I have gotten questions like historical type questions and if I don't know the answer I'm generally able to point them in the right direction where they need to go. I get genealogy questions. When I do have the time I have no problem researching either these questions or family information because take, for example, the Choctaw nation website. You get a lot of requests about were they on the [tribal] rolls. Because people don't understand exactly how the rolls work and so it's answering questions like that.

DH: Have you done this for very long?

JF: I started working with the Oklahoma Gen Web Project back in 2002.

DH: And can you tell me what you mean when you say *ancestors?* Who or what is it that you're referring to?

JF: Well [laughs], I guess in a sense we're talking about our grandparents, our great-grandparents, their parents, their grandparents, et cetera and so forth.

DH: So . . . those are all direct line people.

JF: Right.

DH: Would you limit ancestors and ancestry to direct-line ancestors?

JF: Yes and no. I would say yes because kind of anybody who does genealogy, their primary goal is to find their direct ancestors. But I say no because sometimes to get to that point you need to look at cousins or brothers or what not and trace their lines in order to find yours, if that makes sense.

DH: Sure, so you'll run across those people.

JF: Right, right.

DH: In a personal sense, do you think of your ancestry in terms of specific people?

JF: That's a good question [laughs]. I would say it is more direct-line.

DH: If uncles, cousins, great-aunts, and so on are not your ancestors, how would you describe your relationship to them?

JF: Well, I think of them as family. . . . I mean in a general sense to me family would be kind of like everybody. You know your aunts, your uncles, even the step-relatives that you do maintain relationships with. I would think of all of them as family but yeah, ancestry I would say I would think more of it as your direct line.

DH: You do a lot of work with ancestry and genealogy, and with important people in the tribal nations. What do you say is the significance of searching for people in the past and looking up their names and their dates?

JF: Well, for me it is about who we are. Our culture, our ethics, our thinking you know in the present because those are all ideas [and ways] that were passed down to who we are today.

DH: When you say "we," who are you referring to?

JF: You know, all people in general [laughs], everybody in the present.

DH: So in what way are we who our ancestors were?

JF: I think of that more like . . . let's see how can I say this? You have the cultural perspective, okay. You know the traditional stories.

DH: Isn't that also true of uncles and aunts?

JF: Right, right. Definitely because you know, it's the traditional stories, the history, the food, all that's passed down and you are right it's not just through direct-line, it's also through the aunts and uncles and cousins, yeah.

DH: You said they are all family. Would you identify the family as a cultural group?

JF: Right, and they definitely could have an impact because if you think about, like a woman who's divorced when a child is say one or two years old and she marries again when that child is say four or five and that man in a sense becomes that child's father and his culture and his beliefs definitely do have an impact on that child. . . . Now, if the child is older, you know, say eighteen or twenty, and is maybe out of the house already, then that's not necessarily the case.

DH: So the culture can come from a variety of people. Well, would that mean then that the family could include a variety of people?

JF: Right, right.

DH: But the ancestry would not? You would say ancestry is DNA or bloodline?

JF: Right.

DH: Do you think of yourself as having a relationship to those people today?

JF: I would like to think so, yeah.

DH: In what way? Can you say something about that?

JF: Well let's take example, language, I mean I'm not fluent in my family's native language.

DH: Your family's native language?

JF: Choctaw. . . . You know my father was raised by his grandparents and they didn't speak English, they refused. But for my father it was important that we learn English first. Well, it was my grandparents who taught me my first words in our language and I'm learning from a cousin and for me that's one of the ways that we do connect with our ancestors, with our past, because this language, you know it's older than we are and it goes all the way back to the very beginning so to speak. So for me, language is one of the ways we do connect with our ancestors and with the past.

DH: When you speak some of the language of your ancestors from generations ago, do you feel like you're speaking the same language they were speaking?

JF: Yes and no, I say yes because Choctaw has not changed as much as say English has. I mean the written language itself is fairly new, you know it's what, about one hundred and fifty years old, one hundred years old, somewhere in that range and they're still trying to define it, trying to update it so that it includes words that fit the modern times without borrowing from English directly. So in a sense, yes because it hasn't changed that much but I mean it is still evolving like English so on the other hand, no.

DH: How does this help you connect with those people? Are you really connecting with them or are you connecting with sort of an idea of them, maybe one that somebody has described to you?

JF: I think it would be both because if you take, for example, the stories that you mentioned, when you have stories of family, direct family, it's a way of understanding how they lived, what they went through, their times. But then there's also stories too like traditional stories you know, folk tales and stuff, like the Choctaw have the one about how the possum got its tail or something like that. You know that's a way of connecting culturally, I mean there's stories that are passed down between families over the generations that haven't changed but as far as stories of the individuals themselves, I mean it depends on what person you're talking to because everybody has a different perspective and it does give you insight as to their lives and what they went through at that time.

DH: Who has relayed stories to you, family stories, more than anyone else?

JF: Let's see, it would be both of the grandparents.

DH: I guess you knew your grandparents, right?

JF: Yes, yes.

DH: When you learn aspects of culture and when you connect to ancestors, particularly people you didn't know, is there any sense that you really are connecting with those real people in some respect? That they're aware of you, that you're aware of them? Or is it a reconstruction of the past so that you can simply understand them better?

JF: That's a good question. I would think it's a little bit of both. I mean, because you don't want to forget, forget about them or forget about where they came from or where you come from, you don't want to forget what they went through in order for you to be here at this point. So in that sense I guess it would be a reconstruction but you know I really can't think of anything like what you were describing.

DH: So in what way is it both? Are you saying it's likely both but you can't explain it?

JF: Yeah, exactly. Because I was entertaining all of these ideas; I'm like, hmm—I mean . . . my father has been dead for twenty years now and I had . . . dreams and for me that was really him. It wasn't an image, it wasn't a remembrance so to speak, it was happening now and in the present in this dream.

DH: Did you know your father?

JF: Yes I did.

DH: Is that only possible because you knew your father or would that also be possible for one of your ancestors whom you had never met?

JF: Hmmm, well . . . good question. I mean, yeah . . . you've got some good ones today! I think I would want to say that for most people those interactions are going to deal with the people that they knew in their lifetime but on the other hand I wouldn't see why an ancestor wouldn't be able to visit you in some form or another.

DH: So you wouldn't only allow that, you wouldn't doubt somebody who said that this had happened?

JF: Right.

DH: Do you think there is any sort of reciprocal arrangement—that's kind of a crude word because it's sort of mechanical, but an agreement or . . . what would the word be . . .

JF: I'm not sure if it's necessarily agreement . . . but it makes you, it's kind of motivation. It does make you want to work harder. You know, if I think about my father you know . . . we didn't see him that much when he was alive because he was always working constantly and that's one of my most vivid images of him, seeing him in the coffin, feeling his hands, how torn and rough you know, it was worse than sand paper. But it was so that we could have a good life, so that we could have a roof over our heads, food on our table, you know so that we could attend good schools and those are things that you remember. Because, like my mother, we laugh and joke they were poor hillbillies, but she'll tell you stories of how they couldn't afford toothbrushes, they had to use their finger and just put toothpaste on that and that's how they brushed their teeth. There were six of them and so the girls all shared one bed, the boys all shared another. They shared clothes, I mean they were poor and hearing those stories [about] how my parents grew up and they worked hard so that we didn't have to go through that same thing. And I definitely think that that is a motivation for you, something that pushes you because they did work so hard, you don't want to let them down. You don't want to end up in the same circumstances either because it's also like a warning so to speak, if you don't excel I mean this is where you could be and do you really want those circumstances? I know your parents don't want that for you because that's why they worked so hard.

DH: So, when you honor that are you honoring the memory of them or are you honoring [something more]?

JF: I think it's both. I mean, how . . . we were raised—just that death isn't the end. There is some sort of spirit world and for us, you know my father is still looking down upon us. And for our family, when I walked down the aisle and I was getting my bachelor's degree, he was there with us in spirit.

DH: And when you say "in spirit," you don't mean as a symbol, you mean he really was there?

JF: Right. He was there. So I don't think the time thing is an issue. Now I mean for me and for my family, when we do those things, those passed can see them and they are there to celebrate with us.

DH: Is there any sense of accountability alongside the responsibility?

JF: I want to say yes. I mean, certainly you don't want to forget the bad things. Because they're just as important as the good.

DH: In what way do you mean that they're just as important?

JF: Well, okay take for example the one grandfather. How do I describe . . . as a kid he was Grandpa. . . . But as I became a teenager, that's when I learned that he was not the man that we had thought he was. You know, he was an alcoholic; he was verbally abusive towards my grandmother. We don't think it was physical. He was just a miserable man. He constantly cheated; he did this. Anything you could, it was him. And I think it serves—it's important because it serves as an example. Especially with something like alcoholism. Because we have that experience, we know. Well I don't personally have that experience but my mother does. So I think that's what deterred her from drinking and why she doesn't drink. And I drink very little. You know I probably drink maybe one glass of wine but I mean, that is not who I want to become so I think that by remembering the bad, it also serves as an example for those in the present.

DH: And does this also help, if you're able to improve on that and to be aware of the things he did then could this also be in some sense atonement for him?

JF: Hmm, I think . . . I think in a way it definitely could be, yeah.

DH: Does that body of ancestors change over time? Or is there a sort of a constant family identity?

JF: I would like to think that it does apply to the future but at the same time I see cousins who know the same information and some went through worse and I could see the pattern repeating itself.

DH: You mean good and bad patterns?

JF: Right.

DH: If it repeats itself then it might suggest that the family doesn't change much.

JF: I think it has to do with each individual.

DH: Right, this [raises another] good question. What is the role of the individual in all of this?

JF: Because, let's. . . I mean if we're talking about my mother and her family you know like I say, her father drank and cheated and everything, he couldn't hold down a job, things of that nature. My mother grew up like that and did not want that; she did not want that for her children either and she made sure that didn't happen. She made sure that we weren't even exposed to that. Whereas there are some of her brothers and sisters who went down the same path and worse. I mean one's sitting in prison right now. . . . So I think it has to do—a lot of it does have to do with the individual because somebody, somewhere has to wake up and say, "This isn't how we're supposed to live." Especially when it comes to the bad, whereas the others, they just get caught up in that repetitive cycle that they just don't realize anything.

DH: How much of an influence would you say that your ancestors and your family are on your personal decisions? Because you said individuals make decisions and make choices about selecting the good and trying to do things well and right. Would you say that your ancestors, or your family—either one of those—are also an influence on you in your personal life and in your decisions?

JF: I think that they are . . . I think they are a direct influence. Or maybe I should say an example so to speak for you to decide what is best and what is not. Because obviously like with the one grandfather that was alcoholic, I don't want anything you know, I don't want to be like that. I don't want my children to be like that.

DH: Do you think that he would want you to not be like that? Do you think he would agree with you? "Please don't do what I did"?

JF: I'm going to say yes. In that particular instance because it got to the point where I did not see him for about twelve, fifteen years but he and I finally came to terms. I did see him, which I don't know why or what feeling I had but I knew it would be the last time I saw him and it ended up being that way before he was murdered. And I think you know, at that time when I did see him that last time he was different. And I think that if it were up to him, yes, he would be happy that we were not like that and that we were doing better.

CONCLUSION

For thousands of years, humans have sanctified ancestors in religious, political, and family traditions. In our modern agnostic and materialistic age, ancestral sanctifications of many types are still common. Ancestors continue to deserve special honors and celebrations and carry great personal and cultural meaning. Even among educated, humanistic, and cosmopolitan people, ancestral narratives and myths carry great and sacred significance to individuals and communities of descent.

There are many things in this world and the next that we do not understand, and there is so much for our humanity to learn. Darold Treffert says,

> I venture into areas I would least likely expect myself to look into. . . . The term *mystical* in that sense is probably too narrow. . . . I tell you at this point, I'm unlikely to exclude anything. And that's not my nature. My nature is German and precise but as I delve into this a little more, trying to explain things, I don't think I would exclude anything. . . . But the door is opening a little bit.

If we listen to them, our ancestors and our elders might help us open the door a little wider. Perhaps there is something magnificent waiting for us on the other side.

DIRECTORY OF
INTERVIEWEES

Stanley Arai, Ford Omori, Terri Omori, and June York are members of the Vista Buddhist Temple in Vista, California.

Leon Dixon is a mathematician and cofounder of the W. E. B. Du Bois Center, in Kansas City, Missouri.

David Dollahite is a family historian, scholar, author, and professor of family life at Brigham Young University.

Daniel Essim is a doctor of pharmacy and district director of health and wellness for Walmart in southern Texas.

Jason Felihkatubbe is Osage Nation coordinator and Choctaw Nation archivist in Oklahoma.

Stanley Fuke is director of school libraries for Clark County School District in Las Vegas, Nevada.

David Gelsanliter is a volunteer at the Buddhist Center library in Albuquerque, New Mexico.

Irene Goto is an ordained minister's assistant at the Seattle Buddhist Church and a longtime supporter of her local Bon Odori.

Peter Grant is a professor of biology and dean of arts and sciences at Southwestern Oklahoma State University in Weatherford, Oklahoma.

Thomas Benjamin Hertzel is a family historian and genealogist. He is the author of *The Royal Descents of Judith Ivye, Wife of Anthony Prater.*

Simon Jacobson is a lecturer, rabbi, and author of *Toward a Meaningful Life.*

Grandmother Kim (by request) is a mother and grandmother living in South Korea. Translators, Esther Oh and Jack Park.

Yaakov Kleiman is a scholar and author of *DNA and Tradition: The Genetic Link to the Ancient Hebrews.*

Jeff Livingston is cofounder of a family farming colony in southern Iowa.

Henrietta Mann is a scholar, Cheyenne tribal elder, author of numerous publications, and president of the Cheyenne Arapaho Tribal College in Weatherford, Oklahoma.

Glenda Mattoon has served thirty-five years as patron services librarian at the Church of Jesus Christ of Latter-day Saints library and archive in Norman, Oklahoma.

Kiyoko Messenger is a ninety-two-year-old calligrapher and Japanese American participant in Bon Odori. With the assistance of the Venerable Sozui Sensei, temple priest and expert on Buddhist studies.

Rama Swami Mohan is a public relations officer at the temple Sri Maha Vallabha Ganapati Devasthanam in Queens, New York. Rama Swami has performed or assisted many times in the practice of Pinda Daan, a rite conducted on behalf of a person's recently deceased ancestors.

Jean Neal is administrative coordinator at the John Hope Franklin Center for Reconciliation in Tulsa, Oklahoma.

Lee Guem Ok (grandmother), Mr. Park Sin Joo (father and husband), and Hwang Jeong Soon (mother, wife, and stepdaughter) are three elders of the Park family of Busan, South Korea.

Alexandra Senfft is an author, guest speaker, and scholar of Middle Eastern languages. She has published numerous essays and *Schweigen tut weh: eine deutsche Familiengeschichte (Silence Hurts: A German Family Story)*, analyzing her own family's legacy of a father and grandfather who was a convicted Nazi war criminal.

Sheryl Siddiqui is a member of the Islamic Council of Oklahoma in Tulsa, Oklahoma.

Charles Sleeper is Traditional Chief of the Arapaho and professor of Arapaho languages, retired, Cheyenne-Arapaho Tribal College in Weatherford, Oklahoma.

Janna Thompson is professor of philosophy at La Trobe University in Australia. She is the author of *Intergenerational Justice: Rights and Responsibilities in an Intergenerational Polity*.

Loubert Trahan is a family genealogist who has created a directory identifying more than 120,000 Acadian and Cajun (and other) relatives.

Father Christopher Tran is a Roman Catholic priest whose grandmother was martyred in Vietnam before Christopher was born.

Darold Treffert is a psychiatrist and researcher on savant syndrome and author of numerous books and articles, including *Savant Syndrome: An Extraordinary Condition. A Synopsis: Past, Present and Future*.

Dr. Muatasem Ubeidat is professor of genetics and molecular biology at Southwestern Oklahoma State University in Weatherford, Oklahoma.

Sri Acharya Srinivasa Vedala is a Sanskrit scholar and temple priest at the Hindu Temple of Oklahoma City.

The author with Christopher Tran. Courtesy of David Hertzel.

SELECTED
BIBLIOGRAPHY

Almond, Philip. "Adam, Pre-Adamites, and Extra-Terrestrial Beings in Early Modern Europe." *Journal of Religious History* 30, no. 2 (2006).

Anderson, Margaret L., and Patricia Hill Collins. *Race, Class, and Gender: An Anthology.* 7th edition. College Park: University of Maryland, 2010.

Bae, Choon Sup, and P. J. van der Merwe. "Ancestor Worship—Is It Biblical?" *HTS Teologiese Studies/Theological Studies* 64, no. 3 (2008): 1299–1325.

Combs, Jo Anne. *The Japanese O-Bon Festival and Bon Odori: Symbols in Flux.* Degree Dissertation, 1979.

Connolly, Angela. "Healing the Wounds of Our Fathers: Intergenerational Trauma, Memory, Symbolization and Narrative." *Journal of Analytical Psychology* 56 (2011): 607–26.

Dawkins, Richard. "The Descent of Edward Wilson," *Prospect.* May 24, 2012.

Durkheim, Émile. *The Elementary Forms of Religious Life.* London: George Allen & Unwin, 1915.

Hertzel, David. "Ancestry, History, and Meaning in the 21st Century Classroom," *World History Connected* 7, no. 3 (2010).

Jaenke, Karen. "Dreaming with the Ancestors," *Dreaming* 20, no. 4.

Janelli, Roger L., and Dawnhee Yim Janelli. *Ancestor Worship and Korean Society.* Stanford, CA: Stanford University Press, 1982.

Jang, Hung Chull. "Religious Cultural Hybridity in Chudoski (Ancestor Memorial Service/Ceremony in Korean Protestantism)." *Journal of Religious History* 31, no. 4 (December 2007).

Johnson, Allan G. *The Blackwell Dictionary of Sociology: A User's Guide to Sociological Language.* Oxford: Blackwell, 2000.

Jung, C. G. *Memories, Dreams, Reflections.* New York: Pantheon Books, 1963.

———. "The Structure and Dynamic of the Psyche," in *The Collected Works of Carl Jung*. Volume 8. Princeton, NJ: Princeton University Press, 1996.

Kahneman, Daniel. "Maps of Bounded Rationality: A Perspective on Intuitive Judgment and Choice." Prize Lecture. December 8, 2002. Princeton University.

Kenrick, Jenny, Caroline Lindsey, and Lorraine Tollemache. *Creating New Families: Therapeutic Approaches to Fostering, Adoption, and Kinship Care*. London: Karnac, 2006.

Krippner, Stanley, Fariba Bogzaran, and Andre Percia de Carvalho. *Extraordinary Dreams and How to Work with Them*. Albany: State University of New York Press, 2002.

Lambert, Ronald D. "Constructing Symbolic Ancestry: Befriending Time, Confronting Death." *Journal of Death and Dying* 46, no. 4 (2002/2003): 303–21.

Lee, Kidong. "The Indigenous Religions of Silla: Their Diversity and Durability." *Korean Studies* 28 (2004): 49–74.

Lenz, Claudia. "Genealogy and Archeology: Analyzing Generational Positioning in Historical Narratives." *Journal of Comparative Family Studies* (2011): 319–41.

Markus, Hazel Rose, and Paula M. L. Moya. *Doing Race: 21 Essays for the 21st Century*. New York: Norton, 2010.

Matthews, Donald Henry. *Honoring the Ancestors: An African Cultural Interpretation of Black Religion and Literature*. New York: Oxford University Press, 1998.

Park, Chang-Won. "Between God and Ancestors: Ancestral Practice in Korean Protestantism." *International Journal for the Study of the Christian Church* 10, no. 4 (2010): 257–73.

Pickering, Judith. "Bearing the Unbearable: Ancestral Transmission through Dreams and Moving Metaphors in the Analytic Field." *Journal of Analytical Psychology* 57 (2012): 576–96.

Radmonsky, Lynne. "White Skin, Black Soul: Initiation and Integration in African Traditional Healing." *Culture and Psyche* 3, no. 3 (2009): 33–43.

Rossano, Matt J. "The Religious Mind and the Evolution of Religion." *Review of General Psychology* 10, no. 4 (2006): 346–64.

Voss, Gustav S. J. "Missionary Accommodation and Ancestral Rites in the Far East." N.p., 1943.

Yanagita, Kunio. *About Our Ancestors: The Japanese Filial System*. Translated by Fanny Hajun Hayen and Ishiwara Yasuyo. Reprint. New York: Greenwood Press, 1988.

Zerubavel, Eviatar. *Ancestors and Relatives: Genealogy, Identity, and Community*. New York: Oxford University Press, 2012.

SELECTED WORKS BY INTERVIEWEES

Dollahite, David. *Strengthening Our Families: An In-depth Look at the Proclamation of the Family*. Salt Lake City: Bookcraft, 2000.

Gelsanliter, David. *Jump Start: Japan Comes to the Heartland*. New York: Farrar, Straus and Giroux, 1990.

Hertzel, Thomas Benjamin. *The Royal Descents of Judith Ivye, Wife of Anthony Prater*. Baltimore: Genealogical Publishing Company, 2015.

Jacobson, Simon, and Menachem Mendel Schneerson. *Toward a Meaningful Life: The Wisdom of the Rebbe*. New York: William Morrow, 1995.

Kleiman, Yaakov. *DNA and Tradition: The Genetic Link to the Ancient Hebrews*. New York: Devora, 2004.

Mann, Henrietta. *Cheyenne-Arapaho Education, 1871–1982*. Boulder: University of Colorado Press, 1997.

Senfft, Alexandra. *Schweigen tut weh: eine deutsche Familiengeschichte (Silence Hurts: A German Family Story)*. Berlin: Claassen, 2007.

Thompson, Janna. *Taking Responsibility for the Past: Reparation and Historical Injustice*. New York: Blackwell, 2002.

Treffert, Darold. *Islands of Genius: The Bountiful Mind of the Autistic, Acquired, and Sudden Savant*. London: Jessica Kingsley Publishers, 2010.

Ubeidat, Muatasem, and Charles Rutherford. "Purification and Renaturation of Dictyostelium Recombinant Alkaline Phosphatase by Continuous Elution Electrophoresis." *Protein Expression and Purification* 27, no. 2: 375–83.

INDEX

soul: Fuke on, 98; Jacobson on, 65,
70–71; Kleiman on, 77; Livingston
on, 115
Sozui, sensei, 38–49, 39*f*
spirituality: Arai on, 147; Dollahite on,
126; Essim on, 184; Jacobson on, 62,
64, 72; Kleiman on, 16; Mann on, 9,
11; Messenger on, 46–47, 49; Omori
(Ford) on, 148; Omori (Terri) on,
147–48; Sleeper on, 164–65
Stenen, Iver, 127–30
stories: Dixon on, 84–86; Dollahite on,
127–29; Felihkatubbe on, 160–61,
219, 221; Livingston on, 22, 114,
117–18. *See also* narrative: ancestral
suffering, 3; and ancestral narratives,
140–42; Tran on, 28
Sundance, 11–12, 163
support from ancestors, Kleiman on, 78

teachers as ancestors, 80–84. *See also*
mentors
technology, Jacobson on, 62
Tevlin, Catherine, 136
Thompson, Janna, 21–22, 92, 109
time, 159–61; Felihkatubbe on, 222;
Jacobson on, 64, 68; Lee Guem Ok
on, 34; love and, 190–91; Sleeper on,
164
traditional chief, term, 161
Trahan, Loubert, 16–17, 36–37, 121–22,
140, 158–59, 204–5
Tran, Christopher, 23–29, 24*f*, 141–42,
190, 217, 229*f*
transmission of beliefs: ancestral narrative
and, 103–10; Arai on, 147; Dixon on,
85–86; Dollahite on, 133; Fuke on,
101; Kleiman on, 79; Livingston on,
117–18; Messenger on, 41; Park Sin
Joo on, 195, 197; Senfft on, 206, 210,
212; Sleeper on, 166, 172

trauma, Senfft on, 206–8, 210–11
Treffert, Darold, 3, 35*f*, 83, 225
trust, 22–23
Tubman, Harriet, 85

Ubeidat, Muatasem, 73, 74*f*, 92, 108–9,
157
unknown ancestors, 72–74; Sleeper on,
173

values: Gelsenliter on, 119; Livingston
on, 22; Mann on, 6–8; Senfft on, 206;
time and, 159. *See also* transmission
of beliefs
Vedala, Acharya Srinivasa, 19, 157,
177–78
Vietnam, Tran on, 23–29
visits by ancestors, 21, 176–80; and
ancestral narrative, 107–8; Dollahite
on, 129–30, 132–34; Felihkatubbe
on, 221–22; Fuke on, 99–100;
Grandmother Kim on, 35–36;
Jacobson on, 66; Lee Guem Ok Park
on, 199, 201; Livingston on, 115–16,
192; Messenger on, 48–49; Omori
(Terri) on, 149–50; Park Sin Joo on,
196; Sleeper on, 167–68; Tran on,
28–29

Washita, battle of, 6–7
water: Arai on, 143–44; Sleeper on,
168–69
White Buffalo Woman, 5–8
Woods, Ella, 173
worship of ancestors, Fuke on, 101–2

Yiddish, 57
Yizkor, 67
York, June, 141–56, 179–80

Zechut avot, 78